6|7

Spices of Life

Spices of Life

SIMPLE AND DELICIOUS RECIPES FOR GREAT HEALTH

Nina Simonds

PHOTOGRAPHS BY
TINA RUPP

Alfred A. Knopf NEW YORK 2005

This Is a Borzoi Book Published by Alfred A. Knopf

Copyright © 2005 by Nina Simonds

Photographs by Tina Rupp. Additional photographs by Mark Alcarez (page 13), Tim Allen (pages 190,
191), Amy Haskell (page 72), Norma Miller (page 226), Alain Sexauer (page 122), and Holly Shull
Vogel (page 122).

Library of Congress Cataloging-in-Publication Data
Simonds, Nina
  Spices of life : simple and delicious recipes for great health / by Nina Simonds. — 1st ed.
      p.   cm.
  Includes bibliographical references and index.
   ISBN 0-375-41160-7
  1. Cookery (Herbs) 2. Spices. 3. Quick and easy cookery. I. Title.
TX819.H4S6 2005
641.6'383—dc22

                                                                                        2004021089

Manufactured in Singapore
Published February 2, 2005
Second Printing, June 2005

For Don,
my devoted and loving partner in this crazy and
wonderful dance of life

Live each season as it passes; breathe the air;
drink the drink; taste the fruit,
and resign yourself to the influences of each.
—*Henry David Thoreau*

Health food makes me sick.
—*Calvin Trillin*

acknowledgments

How to begin? This is always the most difficult part for me since *so many* people are involved in the making of all of my books and this one certainly is no exception, but I have only limited space. However, I must thank the following:

The many special friends and colleagues (in the United States, Europe, and Asia) and my family who have inspired and supported me throughout my career.

My inspirational teachers and authorities, who contributed to the content of this book and whose work I drew from: Dr. Jim Duke, Dr. U. K. Krishna, Dr. Andrew Weil, Dr. Walter Willett, Dr. David Heber, Dr. T. Colin Campbell, Dr. Lilian Cheung, Dr. Jeffrey Blumberg, Uby Munoz, Lucia Douglas, Darina and Myrtle Allen, and Chef Suresh Vaidyanathan. Thank you also to Norma Miller and Claudia Rodin for sharing great recipes.

My dear friends and recipe testers, who were indispensable in testing, tasting, and then helping with the food preparation for the wonderful photos: Debby Richards, Francoise Fetchko, and Julie Lutts. In London, special thanks to Shelagh Shipley, Lindsay Wilson, and Joy Adapon for helping me in my little Notting Hill kitchen. A special thank-you to Julie Lutts for her help with the cover design.

Dr. Tavalone Krishna, Vinita Rashinkar, and the staff at the Indus Valley Ayurvedic Centre in Mysore for their generous hospitality and rejuvenating therapies.

Special thanks to Roger Berkowitz (who conceived of the book's title), Rich Vellante, Carla Celona, Joan Giblin, Ann Flannery, and all the crew at Legal Sea Foods, plus Anne de Ravel and Karen Cathey, who worked so hard on the "Spices of Life" project and who made it a smashing success.

Thank you to our dear neighbors Jimmy Raye and Bill Healy, and to Jennifer Lynch at Crate & Barrel, who were so generous in lending props for the photographs, to Susan Babine and the Hawthorne Hotel for their gracious hospitality, and to Kate Hammond from the Grapevine Restaurant for her gorgeous olives.

Thanks to Tina Rupp, an amazingly talented and ever resourceful photographer, and her assistant, Teresa Horgan, who came to my house, reorganized my pantry, and created the magical photographs for this book.

Thanks to Ariel Apte, whose unique and innovative talents brought order to the numerous components in this book, creating a beautiful and cohesive design.

A special thank-you to Peter Andersen at Knopf for the time and energy he generously gave to the design, and to the tremendous team at Knopf, who have brilliantly supported my work and helped to produce this book, including Paul Bogaards, Tracy Cabanis, Carol Carson, Rita Madigal, Karen Mugler, Sheila O'Shea, and Ken Schneider.

A big kiss and thank-you to Abigail Gehring and Juliette Hobbs, who kept my family supplied with chocolate chip cookies and provided generous assistance in helping me with the sometimes overwhelming chores and details of my daily life.

Thanks also to Jane Dystel, my terrific agent and energetic cheerleader, for her continual support, advice, and friendship.

A special thank-you to my esteemed editor (and taskmaster), Judith Jones, who continually challenged and helped me to make this book better.

And last, but certainly not least, to Don and Jesse Rose, who have been steadfast in their support, especially during the writing of this book, and who have filled so many of my days with joy, love, and laughter. I am blessed.

Nina Simonds
May 2004

Spices of Life

this book was first inspired by a visit to an organic spice garden in the mountains of kerala, along the southwestern coast of India.

There Manu Abraham, a third-generation spice grower, showed me buds of clove growing alongside allspice, mace, nutmeg, cardamom, and cinnamon trees, and roots of ginger and turmeric. As he pointed out each spice, he told me about its therapeutic properties.

Later that evening, I ate a superb vegetarian meal. It started with a memorable curry fragrant with a "garam masala" (spice powder made up of star anise, coriander, cinnamon, cloves, black pepper, and mustard powder) and ended with a cardamom-flavored pudding studded with raisins and cashews. Each bite reminded me of how delicious and satisfying "healthy" food can be. It was a revelation.

As unlikely as it sounds, it is possible to enjoy the pleasures of food when eating for good health. It's hard for people to believe that food can really taste good when it's good for you. I think it's because too many people have forgotten about the satisfying flavors of basic food. Some haven't even experienced it. Our palates have become corrupted by sugar, fat, and the artificial flavors of processed foods, and the flavors are very seductive. This, combined with lack of exercise and oversized portions, has resulted in a dramatic rise in obesity, particularly among children.

Chronic diseases such as diabetes, cancer, and heart disease are increasing at an alarming rate. Low-carbohydrate and low-fat diets may achieve a temporary reprieve or weight loss, but they do not sustain good health or provide great pleasure.

With this book, I hope to seduce the reader with food that is prepared simply with fresh, seasonal ingredients enhanced by vibrant herbs and seasonings, and that provides satisfaction as well as sustenance. Most of the recipes are designed for convenience and simplicity, since we all lead such busy lives. The food also reflects my eclectic personal tastes, which extend beyond the realm of Asian cooking. The recipes are inspired by research as well as my recent travels through Asia and Europe. I also share a number of my family's favorites, the food I cook on an everyday basis.

Considering the growth of evidence confirming the importance of embracing a holistic approach to health, this book also suggests ways of altering your living patterns as a means of maintaining good health and preventing disease. Most of the strategies are easy: the idea of achieving a balance between work and relaxation; rediscovering the joys of sharing food with family and friends; living with mindfulness; and pausing to appreciate the good moments. Yet they all make a difference and can greatly enrich our lives.

For centuries, Eastern doctors and cooks have embraced a belief in the preventative and healing properties of food. This was the main focus of my last cookbook, *A Spoonful of Ginger.* Since then I have been exploring many different cultures where "food as health-giving" is a daily practice, as you'll see from this book's multicultural selection of recipes. This book also offers recipes and tips from selected people like Darina and Myrtle Allen, Lucia Douglas, and Chef Suresh Vaidyanathan, who have integrated many of these practices into "a way of life."

I've also spent quite a bit of time finding out about the latest nutritional information, and throughout the book you'll find interviews with people connected to such research. For instance, there's Dr. Jim Duke, one of the Western world's foremost authorities on herbs and spices. Dr. Duke was the leading botanist for the USDA, and he compiled an herbal database with the latest scientific studies. In the "Main-Dish Salads" chapter, Dr. Duke selects the most important culinary herbs and explains their health-giving and healing properties, drawing from his considerable knowledge of ancient lore and contemporary research.

For some time it has become apparent that not only food but lifestyle is integral to good health. Today Westerners are looking to the East, where people embrace a more balanced, holistic approach to health. For this reason I went to the Indus Valley Ayurvedic Centre in India to meet Dr. U. K. Krishna and learn about the practices of Ayurveda, the ancient art of Indian medicine. Some of what he taught me, particularly where the emphasis is on living, has been integrated into "My Daily Routine." As I have come to believe, and will demonstrate to you, these ideas and others can be effortlessly integrated into our daily lives.

I truly believe that by adopting a few changes, you can make a difference in the quality of your life and health. Hopefully this book, with its pleasurable "prescriptions," will demonstrate that *you can have it all*—the pleasures of the table as well as excellent, long-lasting health.

a note about recipes and symbols

The recipes in this book should be used as rough guidelines. Don't be afraid to be creative or spontaneous and substitute other ingredients that are more readily available or seasonal.

Herbs, foods, and other natural remedies are not substitutes for professional medical care. For a specific health problem, consult a qualified health-care giver for guidance.

These symbols are used throughout the book, signaling:

+ *current nutritional information*

❋ *Traditional Chinese Medicine*

§ *Ayurveda (Traditional Indian Medicine)*

my daily routine

You may be wondering what my daily regimen consists of. How do I plan meals for myself and my family, and how do I integrate what I've learned in my travels into my daily life?

To begin with, we eat very simply. A typical dinner consists of grilled fish or meat; stir-fried or steamed greens; roasted vegetables; and rice, couscous, quinoa, or roasted potatoes. Otherwise I might make a huge salad with leftovers and other ingredients from the refrigerator and pantry. I'm a big fan of eclectic soups and salads where you take different ingredients, including leftovers, and incorporate them into the dish(es) you are making.

I usually plan my meals in advance, but I am also open to spontaneous impulses depending on what is in the market and in season. Let me share with you some of my other daily habits:

EXERCISE The first thing I do when I get up in the morning is exercise. You may prefer to do this at another time. You have to work out your routine according to your own biological clock. I like to start the day on a positive note. I alternate running with working out on machines with weights, spinning on a stationary bicycle, or doing yoga—depending on my mood and the weather. The important thing about making exercise a daily ritual is to establish a routine and stick to it.

TEA A warm cup of herbal tea is the first thing I drink in the morning, since it is soothing for your stomach (aids digestion) and the body.

BREAKFAST My breakfast usually consists of seasonal fruits, and yogurt mixed with granola or cereal and sprinkled with some ground flaxseed. I like to add fresh blueberries, dried cranberries, or other dried or fresh fruit for variety. When I am traveling (especially in Asia), I often eat what the natives do. . . . In China, I have warm, slightly sweetened soy milk and flaky sesame breads. In Japan, I eat miso soup, steamed rice, and pickles. In Europe, I drink tea and indulge in a croissant with some fruit. Breakfast is an important meal and shouldn't be skipped, especially if you want your body and mind to perform at their optimum level. (I *insist* that at the very least my teenage son drink a glass of orange juice, eat a banana, and have a multiple vitamin every morning before leaving for school.)

VITAMINS Although I eat well, I usually take vitamins and a few herbal supplements. (See Dr. Andrew Weil's recommendations on page 72.)

WATER I drink lots of water and tea (herbal and decaf) throughout the day. Ideally, you should drink six to eight glasses of water a day (or drinks that are mostly water, including tea). Many people are addicted to coffee and drink it throughout the day, but you should try to restrict your intake to one cup in the morning and, if necessary, one cup in the afternoon, then drink water throughout the day.

LUNCH My lunch usually consists of soup, which may be homemade or a freshly prepared store-bought version. I often supplement the soup with cooked vegetables or tofu. (See the "Homey Soups" introduction for other suggestions.) In warm weather, I eat salads or roll-ups stuffed with fresh and cooked vegetables, hummus, or dressing. Since I usually don't have much time during the day, when I am preparing dinner I like to make a little extra food for leftovers for the next day's lunch.

AFTERNOON Midafternoon is a time when I often feel an energy lag, so I take a break. I meditate, do some stretches, or simply close my eyes and take some deep breaths. It's extraordinary what a difference it can make. I'm a great believer in teatime (perhaps it's because I recently spent two years in England). I usually have a snack of fruit, a little sweet, and a cup of tea or a latte (decaffeinated is recommended).

DINNER For specific dinner strategies, see "Planning Your Dinner Menus Through the Week," which follows.

EVENING About an hour after dinner, once or twice a week, I like to practice yoga, do some stretches, or take a walk, depending on the season and weather. Yoga, in particular, helps me to relax and keeps my body flexible. (Depending on your individual body clock, this might be your time for aerobic exercise.)

RELAX I try to wind down activities at least one to two hours before I go to sleep. For me, reading an upbeat book or magazine works well.

planning your dinner menus through the week

Considering the busy schedules that most families have (work, sports, and school activities), planning a nourishing dinner that everyone can enjoy together may be a challenge, but it is important to gather the family together for a meal once a day. Make dinner, or any meal, a celebration (even with the simplest dishes) and a daily ritual where the family gets together to talk, relax, and enjoy food as well as one another's company. Here are some other strategies I use when planning the menu through the week:

OVER THE WEEKEND Use the weekend to shop and to plan meals (or at least the entrées) for the week. Use the time to prepare dishes that can be eaten during the week or frozen for future meals.

STOCK UP Keep your pantry well stocked (see "Basic Staples" on page 14) so that you can grab major ingredients (rice, pasta, etc.), herbs, and condiments easily.

PLAN AHEAD Plan a substantial meal on weekends or at the beginning of the week so that you can use leftovers (grilled meat or seafood or cooked vegetables) for other dinners and lunches. Vary the menu for the leftover meals by serving different vegetables or side staple dishes to keep things interesting. For instance:

Sunday Dinner:
Jesse's Spicy Grilled Chicken Breasts (make extra for leftovers)
Warm Roasted Winter Vegetable Salad or Spicy Garlic Soba with
Mushrooms and Greens
Seasonal fruit, or see "Light and Sumptuous Sweets" chapter

Monday Lunch

Soothing Miso Soup with tofu and leftover stir-fried spinach

Monday Dinner (made with leftover grilled chicken)

Chicken Lo Mein with Garlic Chives and Bean Sprouts
or
Chicken and Black Bean Salad with a Spicy Tomato Salsa
Seasonal fruit, or see "Light and Sumptuous Desserts" chapter

Tuesday Dinner

Middle Eastern Herbal Rice stir-fried with chicken, roasted vegetables, and snap peas (made with leftover vegetables, grilled chicken)

FRUITS AND VEGETABLES Prepare different fruits and vegetables to make your dinner plate as colorful as possible. Fill two-thirds of your plate with fruits and vegetables and reduce the meat or seafood portion to 3 to 6 ounces. (See David Heber's suggestions on page 198.)

CHILDREN If your children won't eat vegetables, substitute different types of fruit. Encourage them to drink natural fruit juices such as orange juice, cider, etc. (For other suggestions on getting children to eat well, see the section on Lilian Cheung and "Eat Well and Keep Moving" on page 44.)

EXAMPLE Set a good example for your children by eating properly and enjoying food. Teach children about the importance of eating good food so that their bodies will operate at peak performance. (This is a persuasive line of reasoning that I use with my teenage son, who is an avid athlete.)

TOGETHER Involve your family in the process of planning meals, shopping (especially at farmers' markets), and cooking food.

basic staples
(with some substitutions)

The vast majority of ingredients for these recipes can be found in any well-stocked supermarket. Stores now carry an extensive selection of ethnic condiments and an ever-expanding supply of fresh fruits and vegetables, both familiar and exotic. (For mail-order and Web sources, see page 360.)

Some basic ingredients, with suggestions for substitutions, are listed here. Feel free to improvise if necessary. Most of the bottled ingredients will keep for a year, some indefinitely, stored in a cool, dry place.

CHICKEN BROTH I used to rely on reduced-sodium canned chicken broth, but these days I find the most flavorful is free-range or organic chicken broth in aseptic cartons. Unopened, they will keep for months (check the "sell by" date) in a cool, dry place.

CHILE PASTE I prefer the Vietnamese brands in jars, since the canned Chinese varieties tend to be salty. Chile paste will keep indefinitely in the refrigerator but tends to lose its bite over time.

substitution: Use a slightly smaller amount than called for of crushed dried red chile peppers or dried chile flakes.

CHINESE RICE VINEGAR Rice vinegars tend to be lighter and sweeter than wine and fruit vinegars. Asian cooks generally use two types of rice vinegar: clear and black. If possible, use Japanese clear vinegar, which is generally of better quality than the Chinese brands. The black vinegar I recommend is the Chinkiang brand, imported from China.

substitution: Cider vinegar has a slightly different flavor but can be used in place of clear vinegar. Reduce the quantity by one-third. For black vinegar, substitute a slightly smaller amount of Worcestershire sauce.

COCONUT MILK Coconut milk is made by soaking freshly grated coconut in water and then squeezing out the liquid. Regular coconut milk tends to separate, with the cream rising to the top, so shake before using. Buy unsweetened coconut milk. Thai brands are usually reliable. I often substitute light coconut milk for regular. It will keep in the refrigerator for one week.

DRIED CHILE PEPPERS Dried chile peppers are available in a range of sizes in some supermarkets and in all Asian markets. Usually, the smaller the pepper, the more intense the heat. Store tightly wrapped in plastic bags.

substitution: Use a smaller amount of dried chile flakes.

DRIED CHINESE BLACK MUSHROOMS Dried black shiitake mushrooms are available in a variety of grades, with prices to match. The best and most expensive are those with the thickest caps. I usually use a medium grade with large, thick caps. Dried mushrooms will keep indefinitely tightly wrapped in plastic bags in the freezer. They may attract moths when stored in a pantry.

substitution: Dried Italian porcini mushrooms have a very different flavor, but they make an adequate substitute. Fresh shiitake mushrooms have a much milder taste than the dried version, and are not really an appropriate alternative.

FISH SAUCE An essential flavoring in Vietnamese and Thai cooking, where it is known as *nuoc mam* and *nam pla,* respectively. Choose a pale-colored Thai version such as the Squid brand. It will keep indefinitely on a shelf.

substitution: In some recipes, soy sauce may be substituted, but the flavor is not the same.

FIVE-SPICE POWDER This fragrant spice mixture varies with the manufacturer. The usual seasonings are star anise, powdered licorice root, cinnamon, Sichuan peppercorns, cloves, and fennel.

substitution: You can make your own five-spice powder by combining ¼ teaspoon each ground aniseed, ground coriander, ground cinnamon, and ground ginger, and ⅛ teaspoon freshly ground black pepper. In some recipes, allspice is an acceptable substitute.

HOISIN SAUCE Ground bean sauces, such as hoisin, are found in various forms all over China. They come in cans and jars and will keep indefinitely stored in the refrigerator.

substitution: In many dishes, hoisin and sweet bean sauce (available in a can) can be used interchangeably.

LEMONGRASS Lemongrass is a root used primarily as a flavoring in Southeast Asian cooking. Remove the dry outer leaves, and use as directed. You can freeze what's left to preserve it.

substitution: Dried lemongrass that has been reconstituted in hot water can be used in some recipes. Otherwise, two or three strips of thin lemon peel, blanched to remove bitterness, is an acceptable alternative.

OILS These days I find myself using olive oil for almost all my cooking, except for Indian dishes, in which I use peanut oil or ghee. I like the flavor and health-giving properties of olive oil. (It helps to lower cholesterol and blood pressure, and prevent heart disease.) I usually use virgin olive oil for frying and extra-virgin olive oil for dressings, pasta, and cold dishes.

Armando Manni is the founder and owner of Manni Oils, a very small company in Tuscany that makes what he calls a "live" oil, since it has a higher antioxidant and polyphenolic level than any other oil. Manni has some helpful tips about buying high-quality olive oil, which is best used sparingly in dressings, on pasta, and so on.

- Buy only oil bottled in very dark glass. Light increases the oxidation process and shortens the life of the "vital" components of the oil.
- It's preferable to buy oil with the harvest year on the label.
- Buy only oils with a "best before" date notice. Ideally, oil should be consumed soon after opening.
- Smell your oil. Don't forget that olive oil is a fruit juice. If you are not able to detect any kind of aroma, chances are your oil is no longer live and no longer fresh.

OYSTER SAUCE Lustrous and rich, oyster sauce is a concentrated mixture made from fermented oysters, salt, and assorted seasonings. It is an especially appropriate seasoning for seafood and many vegetable dishes. Stored in the refrigerator, it will keep indefinitely.

RICE WINE OR SAKE Rice wine or yellow wine is the all-purpose Chinese wine that is used in cooking or consumed as a beverage. "Cooking" rice wine, which contains salt, is now widely available. For both cooking and drinking, I recommend Shaohsing, which can be purchased at Asian markets, or sake, which is commonly available where wine and spirits are sold.

substitution: A very good-quality dry sherry, Scotch, a dry white wine, or vermouth is appropriate.

SOY SAUCE Soy sauce is available in three grades: light, or low-sodium;

medium, or all-purpose; and heavy, or dark. Light is generally reserved for cold sauces and dressings; medium is used for all types of cooking; and heavy is reserved for barbecuing or roasting. Japanese soy sauce, found in most supermarkets, is appropriate for all dishes.

TAMARIND Tamarind is available in different forms, but the most common is the dried pulp, which gives curries and other dishes a tart, sour flavor. Store dried tamarind pulp wrapped tightly in plastic in the refrigerator and it will keep for many months.

substitution: Although the flavor is not exactly the same, in some recipes several tablespoons of freshly squeezed lemon juice may be substituted.

TOASTED SESAME OIL Asian sesame oil is made from roasted sesame seeds, and it is not interchangeable with the pressed sesame oil found in health food stores. Chinese and Japanese brands are preferable.

other basic items to have on hand (besides the obvious)

CANNED GOODS A can or two of whole, peeled plum tomatoes.

GRAINS A good selection of grains: I usually have both brown and white basmati (or jasmine) rice and some rice mixes, quick-cooking couscous, and quinoa on hand.

OLIVES Good-quality black olives.

PASTA Dried or fresh/frozen pasta (linguine or spaghettini) and a selection of Asian noodles such as soba (or buckwheat) noodles and Chinese or Thai rice stick noodles, sometimes labeled as rice vermicelli.

PEPPER Whole black peppercorns (so that I can grind my own pepper).

SALT Sea salt.

SPICES A good selection of herbs and spices: See "Dr. Jim Duke's Herbal Farmacy" (page 158) and "Key to Primary Indian Spices" (page 288) for some suggestions.

VINEGAR Balsamic vinegar and red wine vinegar: I like to buy a fairly good, high-quality balsamic vinegar, and the same goes for red wine vinegar.

tips on storing herbs and spices

REFRIGERATE FRESH HERBS; they are best used the day they are bought, but you can store them upright with stems or roots in water in the fridge for several days. Or chop fresh herbs into a paste, adding a very small amount of olive oil, and store in a tightly sealed container in the freezer, where it will keep up to 6 months.

BURY GINGER (and galangal and other root herbs) in a pot of sand, and they will keep on your counter indefinitely.

WRAP SEASONINGS like curry leaves, fresh chile peppers, and lemongrass tightly in plastic wrap and store them in the refrigerator for up to 2 weeks.

CHOP LEMONGRASS and store in the freezer. It will keep up to 6 months.

STORE WHOLE AND GROUND SPICES in airtight containers in a cool, dry cupboard or pantry away from heat, light, and moisture, which will lessen their quality. Whole spices will keep for 6 months or longer. Ground spices usually lose their pungency after 6 to 8 months. If unsure, smell the spice. Label spices with the date of purchase when you buy them.

Once opened, pastes, sauces, and other perishable items should be transferred to tightly sealed containers and stored in the refrigerator.

a word about organic and free-range

I highly recommend organic meats, fruits, and vegetables. They usually cost more, but they taste better. Organic farmers use natural methods for replenishing the nutrients in the soil. Better soil quality allows micronutrients to enrich fruits and vegetables, enhancing their flavor and nutritional value. Since farmers tend to leave fruits and vegetables longer on the vine to ripen naturally, their flavor is greatly increased. Recent preliminary evidence suggests that the levels of certain nutrients, especially vitamin C, some minerals, and some polyphenols (naturally occurring antioxidants that may help bolster the immune system) are higher in organically grown crops.

I also usually recommend buying free-range meats (ideally fed on grass), since they are raised free from hormones, antibiotics, and artificial growth enhancers. Because the animals also usually grow at their own rate, the flavor matures and increases.

a note about seafood

We have been bombarded recently with advisories against certain types of seafood, and it's become very confusing. Some warnings have to do with unhealthy levels of toxins, others with scarcity and over-fishing. Seafood advisories vary depending on the source, and most authorities, including the FDA and EPA, advise pregnant or nursing women and young children to avoid shark, swordfish, tilefish, and king mackerel due to unhealthy levels of methylmercury. Cautious consumers may want to include canned and fresh tuna in that category. Conditions change and there are a number of Web sites you can consult, including the Monterey Bay Aquarium (www.mbayaq.org), SeaWeb (www.seaweb.org), and www.thefishlist.org. For a very accessible and practical guide I recommend "The Essential Eating Well Seafood Guide" (www.eatingwell.com).

something to graze on

I've always loved to nibble at several small dishes of food, rather than eat large, multicourse meals, even as a little girl. Western nutritionists, by tradition, tend to frown on this habit, but once you're hooked, it's hard to give up.

I was thrilled to discover, when I went to Asia to live, that snacking is a way of life there. All Asians, especially the Chinese, love to snack, but perhaps the most notorious are the Cantonese, who have elevated the practice to a fine art. They sit in dim sum parlors at *least* once a day sipping tea and nibbling on nuts, pickled vegetables, dumplings, and all kinds of savory and sweet pastries. It's my idea of snack heaven. Most of these foods are not only delicious but quite healthful—a far cry from the processed potato chip–and–cheese curl fare many Westerners gorge on.

These days it's encouraging to see that grazing, or the idea of creating a meal from small dishes, is becoming more widely accepted in the United States. Tapas from Spain and *mezze* from the Middle East are featured now in restaurants and are part of the repertoire of many home cooks.

I've incorporated this eating style into our meals at home mainly because there's a simplicity and an informality about these dishes that is in keeping with the way I live. I've also tried to encourage my family, especially my teenage son, to snack on more wholesome foods (not an easy task).

As you'll see, many of the recipes in this chapter are quite simple and basic, using fresh, top-quality, seasonal ingredients. Many can be prepared conveniently in advance, reheated briefly, or just served at room temperature or chilled. And quite a few don't even require silverware or chopsticks: Your hands, along with a generous supply of napkins, will do.

Chapter opener:
Grazing dishes, front
to back: Herbal Pesto
on Grilled Flatbread;
Hoisin-Glazed
Spareribs; Edamame;
Mom's Barbecued
Chicken Wings

grazing menus

The following recipes can be served by themselves as nibbles or snacks. I often group some of them together to make satisfying meals. For instance:

Spicy Shrimp Cocktail
Roasted Asparagus with a Garlic Dressing
Herbal Pestos on Grilled Flatbreads (or steamed rice or crusty bread)
Mango Lassi

Edamame
Mom's Barbecued Chicken Wings
Sweet and Sour Baby Carrots
Crisp Scallion Pancakes
Gingery Peach-a-Berry Cobbler

Gingery Scallops with a Maple Syrup Glaze or Hoisin-Glazed Spareribs
Bite-Size Vegetables with Two Dips
Steamed rice or crusty bread
Roasted Winter Fruit with Ginger and Port Wine

Teriyaki Beef
Glazed Baby Onions
Jesse's Favorite Crispy-Baked Potato Pancakes
Spiced Pears in Red Wine

For dessert, I might serve fresh fruit in season, such as sliced oranges, or indulge in one of the desserts from the "Light and Sumptuous Sweets" chapter.

Edamame (Fresh Green Soybeans)

Edamame are a wonderful snack. I also like to serve them as hors d'oeuvres with drinks. I keep a bag in my fridge to nibble on in the late afternoon when I get hungry. They are available frozen in Asian markets and many health food stores. I prefer those still in the pod, but you may also buy the beans without pods.

+ *Research has shown that **soy foods** reduce the risk of heart disease by lowering cholesterol. The FDA recommends 25 grams of soy protein a day, but recent research suggests that consuming just 20 grams (or two to three servings) produces benefits. Soy also contains phytoestrogens that help to reduce symptoms of PMS and perimenopause and may reduce the risk of certain forms of cancer.*

INGREDIENTS

1-pound bag frozen edamame or soybeans in pods

2 teaspoons salt (sea salt preferred)

FIRST Bring 6 cups of water to a boil in a large pot. Drop the edamame into the boiling water, stir, and return to a boil over high heat. Reduce the heat to medium-high. Cook for 1 to 1½ minutes, then taste. The edamame should be slightly crisp but tender; if not, cook another ½ minute, then drain in a large colander. Refresh the beans under cold running water, tossing by hand so that they cool evenly. Drain thoroughly.

SECOND Transfer the cool soybean pods to a large bowl and add the salt. Toss lightly to coat evenly, and serve. To eat, simply suck the soybeans out of their pods.

Spiced Almonds

NIBBLES FOR SIX (ABOUT 4 CUPS)

Both adults and children love crisp spiced almonds. The nuts freeze beautifully, so I prepare them in large batches and freeze them in plastic bags to have on hand. We sneak handfuls in late afternoon when we need a little snack and don't want to spoil dinner. To serve, just defrost them at room temperature or reheat briefly in the oven.*

INGREDIENTS

- 1 teaspoon virgin olive oil
- 1 pound raw, skinned almonds (or walnuts or peanuts)
- 2 egg whites, lightly beaten
- ½ cup sugar
- 1½ tablespoons five-spice powder, *or* a mixture of 1½ to 2 teaspoons ground allspice and 1½ teaspoons ground ginger
- 1 teaspoon salt

FIRST Preheat the oven to 300 degrees. Lightly grease a cookie sheet with the oil.

SECOND Put the almonds in a bowl. Mix the egg whites with the almonds and stir to coat. In a paper or plastic bag, mix the sugar with the spices and salt. Drain the almonds in a strainer and drop them into the bag. Holding the bag shut, shake it to coat the almonds with the spices and salt.

THIRD Spread the coated nuts in a single layer on the greased cookie sheet and roast, stirring occasionally, for 40 to 45 minutes, until golden and crisp. To test for doneness, cut an almond in half and make certain the inside is opaque and crisp. Let cool, then transfer to a serving dish. (These will keep for up to 1 week in a tightly covered container and indefinitely in the freezer.)

+ Although **almonds** are high in fat, it is monounsaturated, so they help to reduce cholesterol. Almonds also contain impressive amounts of vitamin E, which can prevent heart disease, and they're a rich source of calcium.

❋ § Cinnamon and star anise, which are included in five-spice powder, are prescribed by Asian physicians to improve digestion and soothe the stomach.

*To recrisp the nuts, bake them in a 350-degree oven until crisp (about 10 to 15 minutes, tossing occasionally) before serving.

Bite-Size Vegetables with Two Dips

Here are two of my most widely requested recipes: a pungent toasted sesame dip and a spicy peanut dip. You can prepare one or the other. Both can be served with a selection of vegetables and are especially appealing to children. Cucumbers, celery, snow peas, or zucchini spears, cut into bite-size pieces, are also delicious. To transform either of these dips into a sauce, add about 3 to 4 tablespoons of water or chicken broth until you have the consistency of heavy cream. Serve as a dressing with assorted shredded vegetables arranged over cold cooked noodles.

+ *Red peppers contain one of the highest concentrations of key antioxidants, which prevent many forms of cancer, heart disease, stroke, and cataracts. For more information, see David Heber's "Seven Colors of Health" chart on page 199.*

INGREDIENTS

2 or 3 red, yellow, or orange peppers, rinsed and cored

1   pound peeled baby carrots

Toasted Sesame Dip or Spicy Peanut Dip (recipes follow)

FIRST Cut each pepper in half lengthwise and remove the seeds and any white membrane inside. Cut each piece diagonally across so you have bite-size "scoops" for dipping.

SECOND Arrange the baby carrots and peppers in separate mounds in a basket lined with a colorful linen napkin or on a platter, leaving a space in the middle for the dip.

Toasted Sesame Dip

MAKES 1½ CUPS

INGREDIENTS

6 or 7 cloves garlic

2 ½-inch-square pieces fresh ginger, peeled

¼ cup Chinese toasted sesame paste*

7 tablespoons smooth peanut butter

3 tablespoons toasted sesame oil

5 tablespoons soy sauce

4½ tablespoons Chinese black vinegar or Worcestershire sauce

2 tablespoons sugar

2 tablespoons water, or more if needed

1 teaspoon toasted sesame seeds for garnish (optional)

FIRST With the machine running, drop the garlic and ginger down the feed tube of a food processor fitted with a steel blade, and mince finely. Add the remaining ingredients (except the sesame seeds) one at a time, processing until smooth after each addition. The mixture should be somewhat sticky and firm, but thinner than the texture of peanut butter.

SECOND Spoon into a serving bowl and sprinkle with the sesame seeds (if using). Place the dip in the center of the vegetables, and serve.

*Toasted sesame paste is sold in Asian markets. It is made with toasted sesame seeds and is stronger than the Middle Eastern variety (tahini), which is not an acceptable substitute. If unavailable, use all smooth peanut butter.

Spicy Peanut Dip

MAKES ABOUT 2 CUPS

INGREDIENTS

5 cloves garlic

3 1-inch-square pieces fresh ginger, peeled

1 cup smooth peanut butter

2½ tablespoons toasted sesame oil

¼ cup soy sauce

3½ tablespoons Chinese black vinegar or Worcestershire sauce

3 tablespoons sugar

1 teaspoon dried chile flakes, or to taste*

3 tablespoons water, or more if needed

1 tablespoon minced scallion greens for garnish (optional)

FIRST With the machine running, drop the garlic and ginger down the feed tube of a food processor fitted with a steel blade, and mince finely. Add the remaining ingredients (except the scallions) one at a time, processing until smooth after each addition. If the dip seems too thick, add a little water. If it seems too thin, add more peanut butter.

SECOND Spoon into a small bowl and sprinkle the top with the scallions (if using). Place the bowl with the dip in the center of a round platter or a round, shallow basket. Arrange the vegetables in separate piles around the dip, and serve.

*If you don't like it hot, omit or reduce the chile flakes.

+ *Recent studies have provided evidence that **sesame seeds** lower blood sugar levels. Sesame seed oil is used in various remedies and has health-giving benefits similar to those of olive oil.*

❊ § *Garlic has always been considered antibacterial and has been used as an antibiotic in treating infections. It is helpful in treating bronchial, digestive, and circulatory ailments. See "Dr. Jim Duke's Herbal Farmacy" on page 158 for more information.*

Sweet and Sour Baby Carrots

Cantonese cooks have devised this master marinade for "quick-pickling" vegetables such as carrots, cucumbers, or radishes. I like to prepare large batches, since the crisp, tart pickles are great for munching at mealtimes or between meals as snacks.

+ *Carrots contain considerable amounts of beta-carotene, which helps to prevent certain types of cancer and strengthen the immune system. Refer to the "Seven Colors of Health" chart on page 199 for more information.*

INGREDIENTS

8   slices fresh ginger, about the size of a quarter, smashed with the flat side of a knife

1   cup Japanese clear rice vinegar

1   cup sugar

1½ pounds peeled baby carrots

Mix together the ginger, rice vinegar, and sugar in a large bowl, stirring until the sugar dissolves. Add the carrots and toss lightly to coat. (If you are using other vegetables, peel and cut into bite-size sticks or pieces before adding to the marinade.) Cover with plastic wrap and refrigerate overnight, stirring occasionally. Serve chilled. (These will keep for at least 1 week in the refrigerator.)

Glazed Baby Onions

NIBBLES FOR SIX

Italians like to slow-cook pearl onions in balsamic vinegar until the vinegar reduces to a rich glaze and they are meltingly tender. I substitute Chinese black vinegar, adding a little fresh ginger for extra flavor.

INGREDIENTS

1½ pounds small or pearl onions, peeled

2 cups water

½ cup Chinese black vinegar or balsamic vinegar

2 tablespoons minced fresh ginger

FIRST With a sharp knife, trim the ends of the onions, leaving a small part of the stem. Put in a heavy saucepan or a casserole and add the water, vinegar, and ginger. Mix with a wooden spoon and bring the liquid to a boil over high heat. Reduce the heat to medium-low and simmer uncovered, stirring occasionally, for about 40 to 45 minutes, or until the liquid has reduced considerably.

SECOND Continue cooking until the liquid has reduced to a glaze, about 5 more minutes, tossing the onions to coat. Serve warm, at room temperature, or chilled.

*+ Studies suggest that the sulfur compounds in **onions**, which irritate the eyes and cause tears, lessen swelling and reduce allergic reactions. Raw onions may prevent blood clots. Freshly cut raw onions, while a bit harder to digest, are better for you, but cooked onions are beneficial as well.*

⁘ § Black vinegar, similar to clear rice vinegar, invigorates blood circulation, is an antiseptic, and refreshes the brain when the fumes are inhaled.

Spicy Shrimp Cocktail

SATISFYING SNACKS FOR SIX

Since I am a New Englander by birth, I prefer to eat seafood simply. Crisp-cooked shrimp with a horseradish-flavored sauce is the essence of simplicity. I add extra flavor by first poaching the shrimp with a little rice wine and some ginger and scallions, which imparts its own subtle and unique seasoning. You can also use the cooked shrimp in other dishes, such as Vietnamese Shrimp and Fennel Salad (page 142).

+ *Tomatoes and tomato-based products like ketchup contain lycopene, a protective substance that reduces the risk of certain forms of cancer. See the "Seven Colors of Health" chart on page 199 for more information.*

❉ § *Hot chiles are traditionally used by Asian doctors to increase the appetite and to aid digestion.*

INGREDIENTS

2 tablespoons rice wine, sake, or very dry sherry

6 slices fresh ginger, smashed with the flat side of a knife

6 whole scallions, ends trimmed, smashed with the flat side of a knife

1½ pounds medium to large shrimp in shells

SPICY COCKTAIL SAUCE (MIXED TOGETHER)

1 cup ketchup

1½ tablespoons horseradish, or to taste

1½ teaspoons hot chile paste, or to taste

2 tablespoons freshly squeezed lemon juice, or to taste

FIRST Bring 6 cups of water plus the rice wine, ginger slices, and scallions to a boil, then add the shrimp. Once the water reaches a boil again, cook the shrimp for 1½ minutes, or until cooked through. Drain in a colander and let cool slightly, then remove the shells and any black veins. Put the shrimp in a bowl and chill.

SECOND Spoon the Spicy Cocktail Sauce into a bowl and place in the middle of a platter. Mound the chilled shrimp around the sauce and serve.

Roasted Asparagus with a Garlic Dressing

Roasting asparagus spears in a very hot oven or grilling them gives them a unique and delicious flavor and texture. I serve them plain or add them to main-dish salads the next day or later. Serve them hot or at room temperature.

INGREDIENTS

2   pounds fresh asparagus
1½ tablespoons virgin olive oil

GARLIC DRESSING

3   tablespoons light or sodium-reduced soy sauce (if using regular soy sauce, add 2 to 3 more tablespoons water)
1   tablespoon minced garlic
1   teaspoon sugar
2   tablespoons water

FIRST Preheat the oven to 475 degrees.

SECOND Snap off the tough woody ends of the asparagus and rinse the spears. Drain on paper towels. Spread the asparagus out on a cookie sheet and brush or toss with the olive oil.

THIRD Roast the asparagus 10 to 12 minutes, or until tender when pierced with the tip of a knife. Alternatively, you may grill or steam the asparagus for 4 to 5 minutes, until tender. Arrange the asparagus on a serving plate.

FOURTH Stir together the ingredients of the Garlic Dressing until the sugar has dissolved. Pour over the asparagus or serve as a dipping sauce. Serve the asparagus warm or at room temperature.

+ *Asparagus spears have been shown to relieve indigestion in the form of heartburn and nausea as effectively as some drugs. They are also a proven diuretic.*

❋ § *Garlic has been praised by Asian doctors for thousands of years for its antibacterial and anti-inflammatory properties. Ayurvedic doctors also believe that it may lower cholesterol and blood pressure. See "Key to Primary Indian Spices" on page 288 for more information.*

Crisp Scallion Pancakes

MAKES 8 LARGE PANCAKES

Scallion pancakes are a classic snack that can be found all over Asia. I usually make bigger pancakes and cut them into sections. It saves time and requires less oil this way. The cooked pancakes can be frozen, defrosted, and reheated to be served later.

✳ The **scallion** has been valued for thousands of years. The white section or bulb is mainly used, but the green stalk also has medicinal properties. It promotes perspiration, detoxifies poisons in the body, and is often prescribed to treat colds.

INGREDIENTS

3   cups cake flour*

1½ cups all-purpose flour, or more as needed

1   teaspoon baking powder

1   teaspoon salt

2   tablespoons virgin olive oil (for dough)

1¾ cups boiling water

1½ cups finely chopped scallion greens

About ½ cup all-purpose flour (for kneading)

¼   cup toasted sesame oil

¾   cup olive oil

*If cake flour is unavailable in your supermarket, you may order it from King Arthur Flour online at www.bakerscatalogue.com or through its catalogue (see "Mail-Order and Web Sources").

FIRST Stir together the flours, baking powder, and salt with a wooden spoon in a mixing bowl. Add the 2 tablespoons olive oil and the boiling water, and stir until a rough dough forms. Add the finely chopped scallions and mix together evenly. If the dough is too soft and sticky, knead in about ¼ to ½ cup more all-purpose flour. Turn the dough out onto a lightly floured surface and knead for 5 minutes, or until smooth, kneading in more all-purpose flour if the dough is sticky. Cover with a cloth and let rest for 20 minutes, or longer if possible.

SECOND On a lightly floured work surface, roll the dough into a snake about 2 inches thick. Cut into eight sections and cover with a towel to prevent drying out.

THIRD Place one piece of dough cut side down on the work surface and, using a rolling pin, roll out to a 6-inch circle. Brush the top with sesame oil. Roll up into a cylinder and pinch the ends to seal. Flatten the roll slightly with your hands and, with the seam inside, coil it into a snail shape. Set aside on a lightly floured surface. Cover with a towel and prepare the remaining dough pieces the same way. Let rest for 15 minutes.

FOURTH Lightly flour the work surface and roll each coiled pancake out to a 6-inch circle about ¼ inch thick. Place on a lightly floured tray. Preheat the oven to 200 degrees.

FIFTH Heat a heavy skillet, pour in the ¾ cup olive oil, and heat to 350 degrees. Slip a pancake into the pan, and fry over medium heat, turning once, until golden brown and crisp on both sides, about 5 to 7 minutes total. Remove with a spatula or slotted spoon and drain briefly in a colander, then transfer to absorbent paper. Arrange the cooked pancake on a cookie sheet and keep warm in the oven while you fry the remaining pancakes, reheating the oil between batches. Cut each pancake into four wedges. Serve immediately or place in the oven to keep warm.

§ *All parts of the scallion or green onion are believed to have health-giving benefits. Ayurvedic doctors believe the onion is a blood purifier, benefits the nervous system, and enhances libido.*

Herbal Pestos on Grilled Flatbread

SNACKS FOR SIX

Since I often have guests, but like everyone else have a limited amount of free time, I make large batches of fresh herbal pastes, cover them with a bit of olive oil so they don't darken, and store them covered in my fridge. They keep indefinitely and are wonderful as a base for sauces and salad dressings, or as a topping for uncooked and grilled vegetables or seafood. (See "Main-Dish Salads" chapter.) They're also delicious as a spread on toasted or grilled bread, or as a garnish for some of the vegetable dishes in the "Pleasures from the Garden" chapter.

+ **Basil** *acts on the digestive and nervous system, easing indigestion, flatulence, nausea, and stomach cramps. It also has a sedative effect and is used in the treatment of insomnia, anxiety, and irritability. See "Dr. Jim Duke's Herbal Farmacy" on page 158 for more information.*

§ *The leaves of the basil plant are often rubbed on insect bites to relieve itchiness and discomfort.*

INGREDIENTS

6   rounds good-quality pita bread, brushed lightly with virgin olive oil and grilled over a low fire until golden brown

FRESH BASIL PESTO

4   cloves garlic, peeled

4   cups fresh sweet basil leaves, rinsed, drained, and blotted dry

4   tablespoons virgin olive oil

1   cup raw pine nuts

2   tablespoons balsamic vinegar

1   teaspoon salt

FIRST While the machine is running, drop the garlic down the feed tube of a food processor fitted with a steel blade, or into a blender, and mince finely. Add the basil leaves and pulse, scraping the sides with a spatula. Process until smooth, adding a little of the olive oil.

SECOND Add the pine nuts and pulse to mince them evenly. While the machine is running, pour the vinegar into the mixture and slowly add the remaining oil, pouring in a thin stream. Once the oil has been incorporated, add the salt. Pulse several times to mix evenly. Spoon the pesto into a bowl and chill. Spread liberally over the grilled pita rounds and serve.

FRESH MINT PESTO

- **5** cloves garlic, peeled
- **1** small hot red chile, ends trimmed and seeds removed, or 1 teaspoon dried chile flakes
- **1** cup fresh mint leaves, rinsed, drained, and blotted dry
- **½** cup fresh basil leaves, rinsed, drained, and blotted dry
- **¼** cup toasted sesame oil
- **2** tablespoons Japanese clear rice vinegar
- **¼** pound extra-firm tofu, pressed in paper towels or a cotton towel under a weight for 20 minutes to remove excess water
- **1** teaspoon salt
- **½** teaspoon freshly ground black pepper
- **3** tablespoons freshly squeezed lemon juice

FIRST While the machine is running, drop the garlic and hot red chile down the feed tube of a food processor fitted with a steel blade, or into a blender, and mince finely. Add the mint and basil leaves and pulse, scraping the sides with a spatula. Process until smooth, adding a little of the toasted sesame oil.

SECOND While the machine is running, pour in the vinegar, then slowly add the remaining oil, pouring in a thin stream. Once the oil has been incorporated and the pesto has thickened, cut the tofu into ½-inch cubes and put in the food processor, along with the salt, pepper, and lemon juice. Pulse several times, until the ingredients are evenly mixed. Spoon the pesto into a bowl and chill. Spread liberally over the grilled pita rounds and serve.

+ *Recent research has shown that the volatile oil contained in fresh mint is antibacterial. The diluted oil is often rubbed on the chest for respiratory infections. The whole plant has an antispasmodic effect and is used to aid digestion, reduce cramps and gas, and in the treatment of irritable bowel syndrome.*

§ *Mint is considered a cooling herb and is recommended to counteract body heat.*

Jesse's Favorite Crispy-Baked Potato Pancakes

MAKES ABOUT 28 PANCAKES

My son Jesse has always adored potato latkes and scallion pancakes. One Chanukah, inspired by his love of these two dishes, I revised the latke recipe, adding scallions instead of onions. I also developed an easy crispy-bake method that eliminates deep-frying.

INGREDIENTS

- ¼ cup virgin olive oil
- 2 pounds Idaho or other baking potatoes (about 4 or 5), peeled
- 5 whole scallions, ends trimmed and minced (about 1 cup)
- 5 tablespoons all-purpose flour
- 1 teaspoon salt
- ½ teaspoon freshly ground black pepper
- 1 large egg, lightly beaten
- 1 large egg white, lightly beaten
- 1 cup sour cream and/or applesauce for serving

FIRST Preheat the oven to 450 degrees. Brush two baking sheets liberally with the olive oil, reserving a tablespoon. Using a hand grater, or the shredding disk of a food processor, grate the potatoes and transfer them to a large mixing bowl. Add the minced scallions, flour, salt, and pepper. Mix and add the egg and egg white, and the reserved tablespoon of oil, and stir to mix.

SECOND Drop the batter by tablespoons onto the oiled cookie sheets. Press lightly to flatten and form circular pancakes, about 3 inches in diameter. Bake for 10 to 12 minutes, until golden brown on the bottom. Using a spatula or tongs, flip the pancakes over and flatten them. Bake another 5 to 6 minutes, or until golden brown. Let the pancakes cool slightly on a cooling rack, arrange on a serving platter, and serve with sour cream and/or applesauce on the side. To reheat, bake for 10 minutes in a preheated 350-degree oven.

Gingery Scallops with a Maple Syrup Glaze

SATISFYING SNACKS FOR SIX

I love to accentuate the sweetness of fresh scallops by drizzling a little maple syrup over them and wrapping a paper-thin slice of prosciutto around the outside. For vegetarians and those who prefer a simpler recipe, the prosciutto may be omitted. Leftovers can be reheated and added to a main-dish salad the next day.

✳ § *See page 43 for the beneficial properties of ginger.*

INGREDIENTS

½ **pound prosciutto, very thinly sliced and trimmed of fat (optional)**

1½ **pounds sea scallops, rinsed and drained**

8 **10-inch bamboo or metal skewers (bamboo soaked in water to cover for 1 hour)**

MAPLE SYRUP GLAZE (MIXED TOGETHER)

1¼ **cups maple syrup**

5 **tablespoons rice wine, sake, or very dry sherry**

1½ **tablespoons minced fresh ginger**

1 **tablespoon extra-virgin olive oil**

FIRST If using the prosciutto, cut each slice lengthwise into thirds or pieces that are 4 inches long and 1 inch wide. Wrap a piece of prosciutto around each scallop and thread onto the skewers.

SECOND Divide the Maple Syrup Glaze in half. Add the olive oil to half and pour over the scallops. Make certain they are well coated. Put the other half in a saucepan and keep warm.

THIRD Prepare a fire for grilling or heat the broiler. Arrange the scallops about 3 inches from the source of heat. Grill or broil about 3 to 4 minutes on each side, turning once and brushing with the glaze. Remove and arrange the cooked scallops on a serving platter. Pour the heated glaze over the scallops and serve hot or warm.

Mom's Barbecued Chicken Wings

SIX SERVINGS

My mother was not particularly fond of cooking, yet whatever she made was delicious. She always looked for shortcuts, and this barbecued chicken was a weekly ritual. Use this marinade for different grilled or broiled vegetable and meat kebabs. I usually serve this with a tossed salad or steamed vegetable for a meal that always draws rave reviews.

INGREDIENTS

BARBECUE SAUCE

1½ cups bottled Italian salad dressing *or* Homemade Dressing (mixed together):

- ¾ tablespoon dried oregano
- ½ tablespoon dried basil
- ½ cup wine vinegar
- ⅔ cup virgin olive oil

2 tablespoons minced garlic

½ cup ketchup

2½ tablespoons soy sauce

2½ tablespoons light brown sugar (optional)

4 pounds chicken wings, rinsed and drained*

FIRST To make the Barbecue Sauce, mix the bottled or homemade dressing with the garlic, ketchup, soy sauce, and brown sugar (if using). Add the chicken wings and stir to coat, then cover with plastic wrap, and let the wings marinate for several hours or overnight, if possible, in the refrigerator.

SECOND Preheat the oven to 375 degrees. Line two cookie sheets with aluminum foil and arrange the wings on the pans in one layer, pouring the barbecue sauce on top. Roast the wings for about 50 to 60 minutes, turning once, until they are a deep golden brown. Remove and serve hot, at room temperature, or chilled.

*You can substitute chicken breasts or legs for the wings. If using legs, increase the cooking time to 1 hour and 20 minutes, turning several times.

Hoisin-Glazed Spareribs

SIX SERVINGS

Everyone loves barbecued spareribs, and this recipe has to be one of my favorites. Have these garlicky glazed ribs as an appetizer or an entrée with vegetables and steamed rice. Serve with hot mustard for extra spice.

+ **Garlic** has always been praised for its healing powers, and before the development of antibiotics, it was used routinely to fight infections. Some experts suggest that it should be taken with antibiotics to increase their effectiveness. See "Key to Primary Indian Spices" on page 288 for more information.

INGREDIENTS

3   **pounds baby back, country-style, or Chinese spareribs (if they are long, you may ask the butcher to cut them across the length)**

MARINADE (MIXED TOGETHER)

1   **cup hoisin sauce**
¼   **cup soy sauce**
6   **tablespoons rice wine or sake**
¼   **cup ketchup**
3   **tablespoons sugar**
2   **tablespoons minced garlic**
3   **tablespoons water**

FIRST In a large pot bring 3 quarts of water to a boil. Add the spareribs and return to the boil, then reduce the heat to medium and cook for about 20 minutes. Drain the spareribs and let cool.

SECOND Using a sharp knife, separate the ribs, cutting between the bones. Place in a bowl. Pour the mixed Marinade ingredients onto the ribs and toss to coat. Cover with plastic wrap, and let marinate for at least 4 hours, or overnight, in the refrigerator.

THIRD Preheat the oven to 350 degrees. Arrange the spareribs on a baking sheet that has been lined with aluminum foil, spooning the marinade on top. Bake for 35 to 45 minutes, until golden brown and crisp. Transfer to a serving platter and serve warm or at room temperature.

Alternatively, you can grill the blanched spareribs over a medium-hot fire, turning several times, for 20 minutes, or until cooked through.

Teriyaki Beef

This is one of those dishes that everyone loves, especially children. I usually let the meat marinate in the teriyaki sauce overnight to absorb the ginger-garlic dressing. Instead of beef, try chicken breasts or turkey cutlets, which are also delicious.

INGREDIENTS

TERIYAKI SAUCE

- ½ cup soy sauce
- ⅓ cup rice wine or sake
- 3 tablespoons water
- 2 tablespoons sugar
- 1 tablespoon toasted sesame oil
- 2 tablespoons minced fresh ginger
- 1½ tablespoons minced garlic

1½ pounds beef sirloin or London broil, trimmed of fat and gristle

10 scallions, trimmed and cut into 1½-inch lengths

About 15 10-inch bamboo or metal skewers (bamboo soaked in water to cover for 1 hour)

FIRST Prepare the Teriyaki Sauce: Put the ingredients in a saucepan and bring them to a boil, stirring to dissolve the sugar. Let cool slightly.

SECOND Cut the beef across the grain into thin strips that are 3 inches long and ¼ inch thick. Thread the meat through the skewers so that the pieces lie flat, alternating with the scallion sections, starting and ending with the scallion sections. Arrange the skewers on a pan that has been lined with aluminum foil.

THIRD Liberally brush the beef with the teriyaki sauce and let marinate for 1 hour or overnight, in the refrigerator, covered with plastic wrap.

FOURTH Prepare a medium-hot fire for grilling or heat the broiler. Arrange the skewered beef and scallions on the grill or broil about 3 to 4 inches from the source of heat and cook, turning once, for about 4 to 5 minutes for medium-rare, or longer as desired. Remove and arrange on a serving platter, and serve.

+ ✳ § *Ginger has been revered by Asian doctors for centuries, and recently, due to considerable research, it has gained the respect of Western doctors. Ginger aids digestion, and prevents and cures nausea. See "Key to Primary Indian Spices" on page 288 for more information. To make a cup of ginger tea, put 6 slices of smashed fresh ginger about the size of a quarter in a mug. Add boiling water, cover with a saucer, and let steep 5 to 10 minutes.*

Lilian Cheung
"Eat Well and Keep Moving"

Dr. Lilian Cheung's nutritional mission has always been to educate children about eating well. Like many others in her field, she has watched with growing concern as the diet and lifestyle of American children have deteriorated. We originally met at meetings of the Nutrition Roundtable at the Harvard School of Public Health, where she often shared the details of her work. Lilian is director of health promotion and communication for the Department of Nutrition at the Harvard School of Public Health. Her book, coauthored with Mavis Jukes, *Be Healthy! It's a Girl Thing: Food, Fitness, and Feeling Great,* was published in 2003.

From my own experience, I knew that the average child doesn't eat nearly enough fruits and vegetables. And according to scientific studies:

- 15 percent of children and adolescents are overweight.

- Children are eating too much fat—especially saturated fat.

- Children spend far too much time watching television and sitting at computers.

In response, she and several colleagues at the Harvard School of Public Health, with the Baltimore city public schools, developed a program, "Eat Well and Keep Moving," with a multifaceted approach that helps upper-elementary children adopt healthy nutritional habits and physical activities. By linking classroom education, food services, physical education, and parental as well as community involvement, the program has been shown to significantly improve children's diets and lifestyle habits. The program (hard copy and CD-ROM) is available through Human Kinetics, Inc., the publisher (www.humankinetics.com). In addition to the Baltimore schools, at least twelve elementary schools in the Boston area are using the program, and the software has been purchased by educators all over the United States.

Adults, Dr. Cheung feels, are role models that children emulate. Opposite, she offers a number of important suggestions for parents and children to follow.

LILIAN CHEUNG'S TIPS TO EAT WELL AND KEEP MOVING

■ Eat REGULAR AND BALANCED meals, with plenty of fruits and vegetables.

■ Eat BREAKFAST every day.

■ Limit refined starches and sugars and have more WHOLE-GRAIN foods.

■ SET A RULE banning eating in front of the television.

■ Tell children that eating is a real ADVENTURE.

■ LIMIT SWEET BEVERAGES such as soda.

■ Use healthy, UNSATURATED FATS such as olive, corn, safflower, canola, and soy bean oil.

■ Keep only HEALTHY SNACKS of unprocessed foods on hand, like fresh and dried fruit, crunchy vegetables with assorted dips, yogurt with appealing toppings, fruit smoothies made with milk or yogurt and sweetened with fresh fruit combinations, homemade hot chocolate, and banana and zucchini bread or carrot cake with a dusting of powdered sugar.

NINA'S TIPS FOR MAKING GOOD FOOD MORE APPEALING TO CHILDREN

■ When you're planning your meals and cooking them, ENCOURAGE CHILDREN TO TAKE PART in the process. Give them individual jobs that make them feel important.

■ Make dinner or any meal a CELEBRATION (even with the simplest dishes) and a DAILY RITUAL where the family gets together to talk and enjoy one another's company.

■ When introducing new foods, encourage children to try a "taste" first. PRAISE THEM FOR TRYING.

■ Cut or fashion food into ATTRACTIVE SHAPES to make it look appealing. For example, crinkle-cut vegetables and fruits and make attractive pinwheel sandwiches with different breads and fillings.

■ BUILD ON WHAT YOU KNOW your children like: If they are fans of tomato sauce or ketchup, experiment with other tomato-based dishes.

■ ADD FRUITS AND VEGETABLES to dishes you know they already like, such as pancakes, omelets, smoothies, or noodles.

■ If all else fails, RELAX. Most pediatricians say that children will naturally expand their palates as they mature. Don't give up, but continue to introduce them to new, tasty, and healthy foods and to set a good example.

appetizers that make a meal

Traditionally appetizers are considered the first course of a meal, but more and more I find myself planning meals at home with an appetizer playing center stage as the meal. In restaurants, invariably my attention focuses immediately on the appetizer section, and more often than not, I am delighted and intrigued by the variety of offerings.

Perhaps it's because I find appetizers extremely satisfying. I love the feeling of getting up from a meal feeling comfortably full rather than stuffed. And with obesity increasing at such an alarming rate, perhaps more Westerners should be thinking along these lines.

I also love the diversity that appetizers offer. From the many, many times I've traveled in Asia, I have cultivated a passion for crispy panfried pot stickers from China and flaky vegetarian turnovers (samosas) from India. Since I lived in Europe for two years recently, my palate has been whetted by the superb and health-giving dishes of the Mediterranean. I've been inspired to expand my appetizer repertoire and cook Flaky Spinach Pie from the Middle East (substituting olive oil for the butter) and sumptuous frittatas from Italy.

Dumplings, sushi, wraps, and blini can be served on their own as a meal. Other dishes, like the warm Spinach Salad or Thai-Style Mussels, should be paired with a staple like country bread or steamed rice for a filling lunch or dinner. Hopefully the recipes in this chapter will inspire you to consider the appetizer in a new context, as I do—not as just a first course, but as a complete and totally satisfying meal by itself.

Chapter opener:
Turkey Saté with
Spicy Peanut Sauce

Grilled Shrimp Rolls with Spicy Vietnamese Dressing

SIX SERVINGS

I adapted and lightened this classic, using grilled shrimp with fresh basil, which are served wrapped in lettuce leaves and dipped in a tantalizing dressing. It's easier, healthier, and just as delicious.

+ **Basil** has long been respected for its healing properties: It possesses antiviral properties that may account for its use as a folk remedy for warts. It also soothes itching from insect bites. See "Dr. Jim Duke's Herbal Farmacy" on page 158 for more information.

§ In Ayurvedic medicine, basil juice is recommended for coughs and earaches.

INGREDIENTS

1½ pounds medium shrimp, shelled

1   tablespoon minced fresh ginger

⅓   cup rice wine or sake

1½ teaspoons toasted sesame oil

2   heads Boston lettuce, core trimmed, leaves separated, rinsed, and drained

6   10-inch bamboo or metal skewers (bamboo soaked in water to cover for 1 hour)

2   cups fresh sweet basil or Thai holy basil leaves, cleaned, stems removed, and placed in a bowl

SPICY VIETNAMESE DRESSING
(MIXED TOGETHER)

Juice of 5 limes (about 1 cup)

1   teaspoon dried red chile flakes

1¼ tablespoons minced garlic

¼   cup sugar

⅓   cup fish sauce

FIRST Score along the backsides of the shrimp with a sharp knife so that they will butterfly when cooked. Remove any black vein and put the shrimp in a bowl.

SECOND Add the ginger, rice wine or sake, and sesame oil to the shrimp, toss lightly, cover with plastic wrap, and let marinate for 30 minutes to an hour in the refrigerator.

THIRD Prepare the Spicy Vietnamese Dressing and pour into a serving bowl. Blot the lettuce in paper towels and arrange in a basket or a bowl. Thread the shrimp loosely through the skewers so that they lie flat.

FOURTH Prepare a medium-hot fire for grilling, and place the grill about 3 inches above the coals. Arrange the shrimp on the grill and cook for about 5 to 7 minutes on each side, or until cooked through. Remove the cooked shrimp from the skewers and arrange on a serving platter. To serve, place one or two shrimp in a lettuce leaf, put a basil leaf on top, and roll up in the lettuce leaf. Spoon some of the dressing on top or dip the shrimp roll in the dressing and eat with your fingers.

Turkey Saté with Spicy Peanut Sauce

SIX SERVINGS

Although saté (or satay) originated in Indonesia, it has become exceedingly popular all over the world. I like to use turkey, as well as pork and chicken. It's a great light meal for lunch or dinner. Leftovers can be tossed into main-dish salads.

INGREDIENTS

1¼ pounds turkey cutlets, trimmed of any fat or gristle

MARINADE (MIXED TOGETHER)

⅓ cup fish sauce

¼ cup dry white wine

1 tablespoon minced lemon zest

3½ tablespoons minced garlic

2 to 3 heads Boston lettuce, stems trimmed, leaves separated, rinsed and drained

3 carrots, peeled, ends trimmed, and finely grated (about 2 cups)

SATÉ SAUCE

1 cup smooth peanut butter

1 cup coconut milk (mix before adding)

3 tablespoons fish sauce

3 tablespoons peeled and minced fresh ginger

3 tablespoons light brown sugar

1 tablespoon soy sauce

1 teaspoon dried chile flakes

2 tablespoons virgin olive oil

3 tablespoons chopped fresh cilantro leaves (optional)

FIRST Put the turkey cutlets in a bowl, add the Marinade, toss lightly to coat, and let sit 30 minutes or longer in the refrigerator.

SECOND Slightly flatten the lettuce leaves with a chef's knife. Arrange the leaves in overlapping rows on a platter and sprinkle little bunches of shredded carrots on top.

THIRD In a blender, or a food processor fitted with a steel blade, puree the Saté Sauce ingredients until smooth. Pour into a serving container and set aside.

FOURTH Prepare a medium-hot fire for grilling or preheat the broiler. Place the grill 3 inches above the heat source. Brush the grill with the olive oil. Grill or broil the turkey slices about 4 to 6 minutes per side, depending on the thickness. Remove from the heat, let cool slightly, and cut on the diagonal into thin slices. Arrange several pieces of meat on each lettuce leaf and sprinkle with shredded carrots and chopped cilantro, if using. To serve, spoon some of the Saté Sauce on top of each portion.

+ *Since **peanuts** (as well as other nuts) are high in zinc, iron, and magnesium, they strengthen the immune system. Peanuts are high in fat, but it is mono-unsaturated fat.*

✻ *Peanuts are believed to lubricate the intestines and harmonize the stomach.*

Fragrant Vegetarian Dumplings

With their pungent seasonings of black mushroom, ginger, and sesame oil, these dumplings could never be described as bland. I like to gather friends together and make a huge batch, then freeze them in plastic bags. All I have to do is remove from the freezer as many as I need, and when they are at room temperature, drop the dumplings into boiling water for a delicious and satisfying one-dish meal. Serve them alone or with a stir-fried, roasted, or steamed vegetable.

INGREDIENTS

¾ pound firm tofu, cut through the thickness into ½-inch slabs

10 dried Chinese black mushrooms, softened in hot water for 20 minutes, drained, and stems removed

½ cup whole canned water chestnuts (about 10), blanched for 10 seconds in boiling water, refreshed in cold water, and drained

1 cup grated carrots

SEASONINGS

3½ tablespoons peeled and minced fresh ginger

3½ tablespoons minced scallions, white part only

2 tablespoons soy sauce

1½ teaspoons salt, or to taste

2 teaspoons toasted sesame oil

2 egg yolks, lightly beaten

2 or 3 tablespoons cornstarch, as needed

45 to 50 thin round dumpling or gyoza skins

SPICY DIPPING SAUCE (MIXED TOGETHER)

½ cup soy sauce

¼ cup water

1 tablespoon minced fresh ginger

1 tablespoon minced garlic

¾ teaspoon hot chile paste, or to taste

FIRST Wrap the tofu slabs in paper towels or a cotton towel, and place a heavy weight such as a cast-iron skillet on top. Let stand for 30 minutes to press out the excess water, then, using a fork, mash the tofu until smooth in a large bowl.

SECOND Shred the black mushroom caps by hand or mince them in a food processor fitted with a steel blade. Blot the water chestnuts dry with paper towels and chop finely by hand or in the food processor.

THIRD Put the tofu, black mushrooms, water chestnuts, carrots, and Seasonings in a bowl. Stir vigorously with a spoon or your hands to mix well. Add the egg yolks and 2 tablespoons cornstarch, and stir until smooth and sticky. Sprinkle in another tablespoon of cornstarch if the filling is too loose.

FOURTH Place ½ tablespoon of the filling in the center of each dumpling skin and moisten the edge with a finger dipped in water or a beaten egg. Fold over to form a half-moon shape. Press the edges together to enclose the filling and seal. Place the finished dumplings on a baking sheet that has been lightly dusted with cornstarch.

FIFTH Bring 3 quarts water to a boil in a large pot and add a third of the dumplings. Once the water returns to a boil, cook for 3 to 4 minutes over medium-high heat. Remove from the water with a strainer and place the cooked dumplings on a serving platter. Cook the remaining dumplings in two more batches as directed. Serve with the Spicy Dipping Sauce.

+ Serve these dumplings for their wonderful flavor and anytime you feel a cold or the flu coming on. They are chock-full of foods (tofu, black mushrooms, and ginger) that strengthen the immune system, and garlic, which protects against bacterial and viral infections.

Flaky Spinach Pie

I adore spinach turnovers (spanakopitas), but this flaky pie is a faster and easier alternative. It's full of fresh spinach, dill, scallions, and feta cheese, and it's wonderful as an appetizer, side dish, or light meal. I like to make a large batch and eat leftover cold slices for lunch or reheat for another dinner.

+ *Most of us think of* **spinach** *as a great source of iron, but in fact it is far richer in antioxidants, which lower the risk of cancer, heart disease, and cataracts. See the "Seven Colors of Health" chart on page 199 for more information.*

INGREDIENTS

12 strudel or phyllo sheets (or 1 14-ounce package frozen Greek phyllo sheets)

1½ tablespoons olive oil

18 to 20 whole scallions, ends trimmed and chopped finely (about 4 cups)

2 10-ounce bags (or 1¼ pounds) spinach, cleaned and stems removed

4 cups fresh dill sprigs, cleaned, stems removed, and chopped

6 large eggs, lightly beaten

¾ pound feta cheese (preferably Greek), crumbled into small pieces

½ teaspoon salt, or to taste (optional, depending on the saltiness of the cheese)

¾ teaspoon freshly ground black pepper

⅓ cup virgin olive oil for brushing the phyllo sheets

FIRST Let the phyllo sheets sit in the package at room temperature for an hour so that they will be easier to handle. Heat a wok or a deep skillet, add the 1½ tablespoons oil, and heat until very hot but not smoking. Add the scallions and stir-fry about 1 minute over medium-high heat, until fragrant and golden at the edges. Add the spinach and stir-fry until the spinach leaves are just cooked and limp. Using a slotted spoon or a spatula, spoon the spinach and scallions into a colander and let cool slightly, then squeeze between your hands to remove as much liquid as possible. Chop the mixture coarsely.

SECOND Put the cooled spinach and scallions in a mixing bowl and add the chopped dill, eggs, feta cheese, salt (if necessary), and pepper. Mix together.

THIRD Preheat the oven to 350 degrees. Brush a 14 × 9½ × 2½-inch lasagna pan lightly with olive oil. Cut the phyllo sheets to conform roughly to the size of the pan, leaving an extra inch on each side. Work with one phyllo sheet at a time, and cover the rest with a towel so that they don't dry out. Spread one sheet flat on the bottom in the middle of the pan. Brush lightly with olive oil and place another sheet on top. Brush again lightly with more olive oil and continue, adding about 4 more phyllo layers and brushing each with olive oil. Spoon the spinach mixture on top of the sheets and spread to a smooth, even layer with a rubber spatula. Place another phyllo sheet on top of the spinach filling, brush with olive oil, and continue stacking the phyllo and brushing with the oil, until you have another 6 layers. Brush olive oil on the top layer.

FOURTH Place the pan on the middle shelf of the preheated oven and bake 45 to 50 minutes, until the phyllo is a deep golden brown and the pie has puffed up. Using a sharp knife, cut into 3-inch squares. Serve warm or at room temperature.

❋ § Dill, particularly the seeds, has always been prescribed in Asia as a remedy for relieving gas and improving digestion. Its essential oil relieves cramps and helps to settle colic.

Crusty Pot Stickers

As a student in Taiwan many years ago, I made pot stickers, or panfried dumplings, a staple in my diet. Thirty years later, I still adore the contrast of the crisp fried dumpling skin and the tender meat-and-vegetable filling seasoned with garlic chives. Try cooking them in a nonstick pan to prevent the pot stickers from living up to their name.

INGREDIENTS

4½ cups finely chopped Chinese (Napa) cabbage

1 teaspoon salt

¾ pound lean ground pork, such as butt or shoulder

3½ cups finely minced Chinese garlic chives (if unavailable, substitute 1 cup minced leeks plus 1 tablespoon minced garlic)

SEASONINGS (MIXED TOGETHER)

2½ tablespoons soy sauce

1 tablespoon rice wine

2½ teaspoons toasted sesame oil

2 tablespoons peeled and minced fresh ginger

1 teaspoon salt

1½ tablespoons cornstarch, or more as needed

50 to 55 thin round dumpling or gyoza skins

2½ to 3 tablespoons olive oil

1 recipe Spicy Dipping Sauce (page 52)

FIRST Stir the cabbage and salt together in a large bowl and let sit for 30 minutes. (This will draw water out of the cabbage.) Using your hands, squeeze as much water as possible out of the cabbage, then combine with the ground pork, garlic chives, and Seasonings. Stir vigorously. If the mixture seems loose, add another ½ tablespoon of cornstarch.

SECOND Place ½ tablespoon of filling in the center of each dumpling skin and fold the skin over to make a half-moon shape. Spread a little water or beaten egg along the edge of the skin and press down to seal the edges. Place the sealed dumplings on a baking sheet lightly dusted with cornstarch.

THIRD Heat a 10-inch nonstick or cast-iron frying pan, pour in 2½ tablespoons of oil, and heat until very hot but not smoking. Swirl the pan to make certain the bottom is completely covered. Arrange rows of dumplings in the pan to make the first batch, placing them snugly against one another, with the joined edges up, to cover the bottom of the pan. Fry over medium-high heat until golden brown on the bottom. Add ¾ cup hot water, cover, and cook the dumplings about 3 to 4 minutes. Lift off the lid and cook until the water has evaporated. If the dumplings are sticking, drizzle ½ teaspoon of oil around the diameter of the pan and roll the pan to spread the oil. Continue frying for another 1 to 2 minutes, until the bottoms are golden brown and crisp. Using a spatula, carefully scrape under the dumplings and around the sides to dislodge them from the pan. Invert a dinner plate or a platter over the pan and flip the pan over to unmold the dumplings, fried side up, on the plate. Keep warm while preparing the next batch or serve immediately. Serve the dumplings with the Spicy Dipping Sauce.

§ *Chinese doctors credit garlic chives with toning the kidneys and improving sexual functions. The vegetable also energizes and removes dampness and stagnation from the body.*

Man-Size Vegetarian Samosas

MAKES 12 TURNOVERS

Traditionally, samosas are small, triangular-shaped pastries fried in oil. But, they are often baked, as in this recipe, and can be substantial enough for a light meal. I've also altered the shape slightly to make the preparation easier. Serve these warm from the oven or at room temperature, plain or with Fresh Cilantro Chutney (page 284).

INGREDIENTS

DOUGH

- 4 cups all-purpose flour
- 1½ teaspoons salt
- 1⅓ cups chilled unsalted butter, cut into tablespoon-size pieces
- 2 large eggs, slightly beaten
- 10 to 11 tablespoons cold water

VEGETARIAN FILLING

- 3 carrots (about ¾ pound), peeled, ends trimmed, and cut into ¼-inch dice
- 4 potatoes (about 1 pound), peeled and cut into ⅓-inch dice
- 2½ tablespoons virgin olive oil
- 2½ cups finely chopped onions (about 2 small)
- 2½ tablespoons minced fresh ginger
- 1½ tablespoons minced garlic
- 1½ fresh hot green chile peppers, ends and seeds removed, and chopped *or* 1 teaspoon dried chile flakes

SPICE MIXTURE (MIXED TOGETHER)

- 2½ tablespoons ground cumin
- 1½ tablespoons ground coriander
- 1½ teaspoons ground cinnamon
- 1 teaspoon salt
- ½ teaspoon ground black pepper
- ½ teaspoon ground turmeric

- 1½ cups frozen peas, defrosted to room temperature
- 1 tablespoon freshly squeezed lemon juice
- ¾ cup chopped fresh cilantro leaves

- 1 egg, lightly beaten and mixed with 1 tablespoon water and ¼ teaspoon salt

YOGURT-MINT SAUCE (MIXED TOGETHER)

- ½ cup low-fat plain yogurt
- 3 tablespoons chopped fresh mint leaves

FIRST Put the flour and salt in the work bowl of a food processor fitted with a steel blade. Drop the butter pieces into the bowl and pulse until the mixture resembles coarse cornmeal. While the machine is running, pour the eggs down the feed tube, then add the cold water, pouring in slowly, until the dough forms a ball. If the dough is very dry, add a bit more water. Scoop the dough out onto a lightly floured work surface and knead lightly with the heel of your hand, until the dough comes together but is still a little rough. Separate the dough into two pieces. Wrap each in plastic wrap and refrigerate for at least 30 minutes.

SECOND Cook the carrots in boiling water in a saucepan until tender, about 2 minutes. Add the potatoes and continue cooking for 8 to 9 minutes more, until both vegetables are tender. Remove from the heat, drain, and refresh in cold water. Drain again.

THIRD Heat a wok or a large skillet, add the oil, and heat until very hot. Add the onions, and stir-fry over medium heat until the onions become soft and lightly golden, then add the ginger, garlic, and chile peppers and stir-fry until fragrant. Add the Spice Mixture and continue stirring for 15 seconds more. Add the carrots, potatoes, and peas and toss lightly to coat with the spice mixture. Add the lemon juice and fresh cilantro and mix evenly. Scoop the mixture onto a platter and refrigerate until cool.

FOURTH Preheat the oven to 400 degrees. Cut each section of dough into 6 pieces and put half of them back in the refrigerator. Roll out the pieces on a lightly floured work surface to 8-inch circles that are about ⅛ inch thick. Spoon a heaping ½ cup of the filling onto the center of each circle and brush the edges lightly with some of the beaten egg mixture. Fold over to a half-moon shape and seal. Press the edge with the tines of a fork to create a decorative finish. Place on a nonstick cookie sheet or one that has been brushed with melted butter.

FIFTH Prepare the remaining samosas. Chill for 10 minutes. (Or you can freeze them at this point and bake them at a later date.)

SIXTH Brush the surface of each samosa with the beaten egg mixture.

SEVENTH Bake the samosas about 25 to 30 minutes, or until golden brown. Let cool slightly and remove with a spatula to a cooling rack. Serve warm or at room temperature with the Yogurt-Mint Sauce or Fresh Cilantro Chutney.

Spinach Salad with Sun-Dried Tomatoes

SIX SERVINGS

I often use tender baby spinach for this colorful and appealing salad. I first arrange the ingredients in a bowl. Just before serving, I pour a warm, tart sun-dried tomato and garlic dressing on top. Serve the salad with crusty bread for a light yet satisfying meal.

INGREDIENTS

- 1 pound (or 1½ 10-ounce packages) fresh spinach or baby spinach leaves
- 1 cup roasted red peppers (roasted as directed on page 124, or a 12-ounce jar, roughly 4 red peppers), drained, and blotted dry with paper towels
- 1 15-ounce can chickpeas, blanched briefly in boiling water, refreshed, and drained

4 to 5 ounces feta cheese, crumbled between your fingers into small bits

WARM TOMATO-GARLIC VINAIGRETTE

3 to 4 tablespoons virgin olive oil

10 to 12 sun-dried tomatoes packed in oil, drained, and cut into julienne strips

2½ tablespoons minced garlic

⅔ cup balsamic vinegar

1 teaspoon salt, or to taste

⅓ teaspoon freshly ground black pepper

FIRST If using large spinach leaves, tear the stems from the leaves and discard the stems. Toss the large leaves or baby spinach into a sink and add cold water to cover. Swish the leaves with your hands to remove the dirt and lift out the leaves. Place in a colander or a salad spinner to remove the excess water. Arrange the spinach leaves in a salad bowl.

SECOND Cut the roasted peppers into thin julienne strips. Arrange on the spinach leaves, along with the blanched chickpeas. Sprinkle the feta cheese bits all over the salad.

THIRD Heat a heavy sauté pan or a wok, add several tablespoons of the oil, and heat until very hot but not smoking. Toss in the sun-dried tomatoes and garlic, and stir-fry for 10 seconds, until very fragrant. Add the vinegar, and heat until very hot. Slowly pour in the remaining oil and continue heating. Once the dressing is very hot, add the salt and pepper and taste for seasoning. Carefully drizzle over the spinach salad and serve immediately.

+ *Spinach is particularly high in antioxidants, which, according to studies, lower the risk of heart disease, cancer, cataracts, and stroke. For more information, see the "Seven Colors of Health" chart on page 199.*

✳ *According to traditional Chinese medicine, spinach moistens dryness in the body and is effective in the treatment of constipation.*

§ *Chickpeas are astringent, cool, light, and pungent after digestion, but they tend to dry the body, so they are not good for people with a Vata constitution (see page 294).*

Roasted Onion and Mushroom Frittata

SIX SERVINGS

Frittatas (Italian omelets) are extremely versatile, since they can be served plain or filled with different cooked vegetables, all types of herbs, and even cooked meats such as ham or sausage. I particularly like roasting onions in the oven to bring out their sweetness and combining them with meaty sautéed wild mushrooms. I often top the frittata with some lightly dressed grilled chicory or radicchio (see page 240) tossed with fresh herbs for a delightful, satisfying meal.

INGREDIENTS

- 2 teaspoons olive oil
- 2 medium white onions, peeled
- 8 large eggs, lightly beaten
- 1 teaspoon salt
- ¼ teaspoon freshly ground black pepper
- 2½ tablespoons unsalted butter
- ¾ pound shiitake, porcini, or portobello mushrooms
- 1½ teaspoons minced garlic
- 1½ tablespoons good-quality balsamic vinegar
- 2 tablespoons chopped fresh herbs such as chives, parsley, or chervil

FIRST Preheat the oven to 400 degrees. Lightly brush a cookie sheet with the olive oil. Cut the onions into ½-inch slices and separate into rings.

SECOND Arrange the onion rings on the cookie sheet and bake, turning once, about 12 to 15 minutes, until golden at the edges. To make the edges crisp and golden brown, broil for an additional 3 to 4 minutes on each side. Remove from the oven and let cool. Mix the eggs with the salt and pepper.

THIRD Heat a large heavy skillet until hot, add the butter, and heat until melted and sizzling. Add the mushrooms and garlic and sauté, stirring from time to time, over medium heat, until the mushrooms are cooked and dry. Add the balsamic vinegar and stir to coat. Sprinkle the roasted onion rings evenly over the mushrooms and slowly pour the eggs into the pan. Turn the heat to medium-low and cook for about 10 to 12 minutes, until the eggs are set and the bottom is golden. While the eggs are cooking, preheat the broiler.

FOURTH Place the frying pan under the broiler and cook for another 3 to 5 minutes, until the top is golden and set. (Alternatively, you may flip the eggs over in the pan and continue cooking for another 5 minutes on the stove, until the bottom is golden.) Remove from the pan and cool slightly. Cut into wedges, arrange on a plate, and sprinkle with the chopped fresh herbs.

+ *Ideally, buy **eggs** that are from free-range, organically fed chickens. Eggs should be eaten in moderation, but they contain a surprising number of essential vitamins and nutrients, especially for young children to help build strong bones.*

Simple Smoked Salmon Sushi

This free-form sushi is simply made by overlapping slices of smoked salmon to form a wrapper for the rice and onion, lemon zest, and capers. The rolls can be made on aluminum foil, then left to chill, and sliced just before serving. This dish is ideal for entertaining, and leftovers can be served as a light lunch or dinner.

INGREDIENTS

- 2 cups Arborio or Japanese short-grain rice
- 2¼ cups water

RICE SEASONINGS (MIXED TOGETHER)

- 4 tablespoons Japanese clear rice vinegar
- 2 tablespoons sugar
- ¾ teaspoon salt

- 1 lemon
- 1 pound thinly sliced smoked salmon
- ½ small red onion, ends trimmed, and chopped finely
- 4 heaping tablespoons capers, drained, and squeezed lightly

DIPPING SAUCE (MIXED TOGETHER IN A SERVING DISH) (OPTIONAL)

- ⅓ cup soy sauce
- 5 tablespoons freshly squeezed lemon juice, or to taste
- ⅓ cup water

FIRST Place the rice in a medium-size bowl and, using your fingers as a rake, rinse it under cold running water to remove some of the talc. Drain in a colander.

SECOND Put the rice and water in a heavy 2-quart saucepan with a lid. Bring to a boil uncovered. Once the water boils, reduce the heat to low, cover tightly, and simmer for about 15 minutes. Remove the pan from the heat and let sit until all the water has evaporated and craters appear on the surface, about 5 minutes. Fluff the rice lightly with a fork to separate the grains, then add the Rice Seasonings and mix evenly with a wooden spatula. Spread the hot rice out on a tray and let it cool, then lightly cover with plastic wrap.

THIRD Using a vegetable peeler, remove the yellow skin from the lemon. Drop into boiling water and blanch for about a minute. Refresh in cold water, dry in paper towels, and cut into very thin julienne shreds.

FOURTH Spread out a bamboo rolling mat (*sudare*) or a 10-inch square of heavy-duty aluminum foil on a counter. Using one-quarter of the salmon, arrange overlapping slices on the foil to form a 6-inch square.

FIFTH Prepare a bowl of water with some rice vinegar on the side for rinsing your hands so that the rice doesn't stick to them. Spread 1 cup of the vinegared rice evenly over the salmon, leaving a ½- to ¾-inch strip uncovered at the far edge of the square. Sprinkle a line of onions, capers, and lemon peel one-third from the edge closest to you.

SIXTH Picking up the corners of the edge of the rolling mat or the aluminum foil closest to you, roll the salmon and rice away from you, jelly roll–style, to form a roll. Press in the ends and lightly squeeze with the mat or foil so that it is a firm roll. Place in the refrigerator and chill for about 30 minutes. Repeat the process to make three more rolls. (You may also keep the rolls in the refrigerator until about 30 minutes before serving.) Trim the ends and cut the rolls into ½-inch-thick sections, using a sharp knife that has been dipped into water between slices. Arrange the slices on a serving plate and serve plain or with the Dipping Sauce, if desired.

+ *Salmon* and other oily fish, such as tuna, mackerel, bluefish, and sardines, are rich in omega-3 fatty acids, which lower blood pressure, cholesterol, and the risk of heart disease. They also reduce the risk of stroke by reducing the risk of blood clotting.

Fresh Herbal Blini with Smoked Salmon and Other Fixings

MAKES ABOUT 24 PANCAKES

Blini are delectable pancakes made with buckwheat flour that are served with caviar or smoked salmon. I developed a passion for them at French cooking school in Paris. I often substitute white flour for the buckwheat flour, if it is unavailable. Blini are ideal for parties since they can be made ahead and freeze beautifully. Simply defrost them and reheat in a moderate oven.

INGREDIENTS

1½ cups buckwheat or white flour

¾ teaspoon salt

1   envelope active dry yeast (or 1 table-
    spoon)

1½ cups milk, heated until warm

2   large eggs, at room temperature, and
    separated

¼   teaspoon cream of tartar

¼   cup cream or milk

¾   cup chopped fresh dill or chives

1½ tablespoons virgin olive oil

½   pound smoked salmon, smoked trout,
    or smoked mussels

1   cup yogurt or sour cream (optional)

FIRST Put the flour and salt in a large mixing bowl. Dissolve the yeast in the warm milk. Lightly beat the egg yolks and stir them into the milk, then slowly pour into the bowl with the flour. Beat lightly with a whisk until you have a smooth batter. Cover with a damp towel and let rest for about 2 hours, until double in bulk.

SECOND In another bowl, beat the egg whites with the cream of tartar until stiff. Fold the egg whites into the batter along with the cream and the herbs until the batter is evenly mixed.

THIRD Wipe the inside of a well-seasoned or nonstick frying or crepe pan with a paper towel soaked in the oil. Heat the pan until hot and spoon ¼ cup of the batter into the pan and flatten slightly to a round pancake about 3 inches wide. Cook over medium heat for about 3 to 4 minutes, until bubbles appear on the surface (the cooked surface should be golden brown). Flip over, cook for a minute, and remove to a platter. (You may keep the cooked blini warm in a preheated 200-degree oven.) Continue cooking the remaining batter and arrange the cooked blini on the platter. Cut the salmon slices into bite-size pieces and arrange on a serving plate. Eat the blini with a slice of smoked salmon and a dollop of yogurt or sour cream, if desired. Or try one of the alternate fillings below.

You also may prepare the blini with different fresh herbs and serve other fillings.

- **SCALLION BLINI** *Substitute ¾ cup chopped scallion greens for dill and serve with coarsely shredded spinach sprinkled with feta cheese.*

- **BASIL BLINI** *Use ½ cup chopped basil for dill and serve with sun-dried tomatoes or fresh tomatoes and thin slices of fresh mozzarella.*

- **CHIVE BLINI** *Use chopped fresh chives or cilantro for dill and serve with assorted wild mushrooms that have been sautéed with olive oil and garlic.*

- **CILANTRO-CUMIN BLINI** *Substitute chopped fresh cilantro for dill, add 1 teaspoon ground cumin or to taste and serve with Cucumber Raita (page 174) or herbal chutneys (see page 284).*

+ *Dill has long been credited as a remedy for relieving gas and stomach pain. It aids digestion and helps to settle and prevent colic. Dill also increases milk production in nursing mothers. Dill seeds are chewed to freshen bad breath.*

Thai-Style Mussels with Coconut and Basil

For years, mussels and clams have been farmed off the coast of Malaysia. In Asia, gorgeous green-lipped mussels are cooked in soups, steamed, or braised. I think their fresh, briny juice is a perfect complement to the aromatic seasonings and rich coconut milk in this dish.

INGREDIENTS

4 pounds mussels

SEASONINGS

3 dried red chile peppers or 1½ teaspoons dried chile flakes

2 stalks lemongrass, ends trimmed, tough outer stalks removed, and cut into thin sections*

1 1½-inch piece fresh ginger, peeled and cut into small pieces

1½ teaspoons ground cumin

1½ teaspoons ground coriander

1 teaspoon salt

½ teaspoon freshly ground black pepper

½ cup good-quality rice wine or sake

½ cup water

1 cup coconut milk

2½ tablespoons fish sauce

1½ teaspoons sugar, or to taste

2 tablespoons olive oil

5 shallots, ends trimmed, peeled, smashed, and cut into thin slices

2½ cups fresh sweet basil or Thai holy basil leaves, rinsed, drained, and cut into thin julienne shreds

*Fresh lemongrass is available at most Asian markets. You may substitute dried, but first reconstitute by softening in boiling water to cover for 20 minutes.

FIRST Tap each mussel on a hard surface to make certain it closes, discarding any mussels that do not. Pull off the beards and rinse the mussels well under cold running water to remove any sand or seaweed.

SECOND In a food processor fitted with a steel blade, or in a blender, chop the chile peppers, lemongrass, and ginger to a coarse mixture. Add the remaining Seasonings and continue blending. Empty into a small bowl. Mix together the rice wine, water, coconut milk, fish sauce, and sugar.

THIRD Heat a large, heavy pot with a tight-fitting lid, add the oil, and heat until hot. Add the shallots and sauté over medium-low heat until soft, about 3 to 4 minutes. Add the chopped seasonings and continue frying until fragrant, about 15 to 20 seconds. Add the coconut milk mixture and bring to a boil. Cook for several minutes, then add the mussels, cover, and cook, shaking the pan occasionally, for about 8 to 10 minutes, or until the mussels open. Sprinkle in the basil and carefully fold the herb into the mussels and their liquid. Serve immediately.

Spicy Pork in Lettuce Packages

SIX SERVINGS

I love informal "wrapped" dishes like this where a spicy stir-fried meat and vegetable mixture is scooped into fresh lettuce leaves and eaten by hand. You may substitute ground chicken, turkey, or beef for the pork.

INGREDIENTS

1½ pounds lean ground pork, preferably butt or shoulder

PORK SEASONINGS (MIXED TOGETHER)

- 2 tablespoons soy sauce
- 1½ tablespoons rice wine or sake
- 1½ teaspoons toasted sesame oil

3 heads Boston or leafy lettuce, stems trimmed, rinsed, and drained

2½ tablespoons virgin olive oil

SPICY SEASONINGS (MIXED TOGETHER)

- 3 tablespoons minced fresh ginger
- 4 tablespoons minced garlic
- 1¾ teaspoons hot chile paste, or to taste

3 cups scallion greens, cut into ½-inch lengths

2¼ cups water chestnuts, blanched in boiling water for 10 seconds, drained, and chopped coarsely in a food processor or by hand

FRAGRANT SAUCE (MIXED TOGETHER)

- 5 tablespoons soy sauce
- 3½ tablespoons rice wine or sake
- 2 tablespoons Chinese black vinegar or Worcestershire sauce
- 1 tablespoon sugar
- 1 teaspoon salt, or to taste
- ¼ teaspoon freshly ground black pepper
- ½ cup good-quality reduced-sodium chicken broth or water
- 1 teaspoon cornstarch

1½ cups pine nuts, toasted until golden brown (optional)

FIRST Put the ground pork in a bowl, add the Pork Seasonings, and mix together with your hands.

SECOND Lightly flatten the lettuce leaves with the flat side of a knife or cleaver and arrange around the outside of a large platter or in a separate basket for serving.

THIRD Heat a wok or a heavy skillet, add 1½ teaspoons of the oil, and when hot but not smoking, add the ground pork and stir-fry over medium-high heat, mashing and breaking it up. Cook until it changes color and separates. Drain in a colander to remove the fat, and wipe out the pan.

FOURTH Reheat the pan, add the remaining oil, and when very hot, add the Spicy Seasonings. Stir-fry until fragrant, about 10 seconds, and add the scallion greens and water chestnuts, tossing the mixture over high heat for about 1 minute. Add the premixed Fragrant Sauce and stir, letting it thicken. Return the cooked meat to the pan and toss to coat with the sauce. Add the toasted pine nuts, if using. Scoop the mixture onto the serving platter. Each diner spoons some of the cooked meat mixture onto a lettuce leaf, rolls it up, and eats it.

+ *Chinese doctors credit **water chest-nuts** with clearing heat from the body and nourishing the kidneys. A tea made with fresh water chestnuts and honeysuckle flowers is recommended for coughs and bronchitis.*

Dr. Andrew Weil and His Latest Advice on Supplements

Dr. Andrew Weil is an internationally recognized expert on medicinal herbs, mind-body interactions, and integrative medicine. He is also the author of eight books, including the best sellers *Eight Weeks to Optimum Health* and *Eating Well for Optimum Health.* Dr. Weil is the founder and director of the Program in Integrative Medicine at the University of Arizona's Health Sciences Center, where he is training a new generation of physicians.

Dr. Weil asserts that when it comes to obtaining the vital vitamins and minerals the body needs to maintain good health, the best possible source is food. "A varied diet with plenty of fruits and vegetables, whole grains, and legumes is the most natural and enjoyable way to meet nutritional needs," he says. "There are times, however, when a good diet may not be good enough. Researchers are finding that some important vitamins and minerals (vitamin E, for instance) are hard to get in amounts considered protective against disease through diet alone, no matter how conscientious an eater you are."

It's important to remember that supplements are by no means substitutes for eating well, Dr. Weil cautions. "Supplements are part of an overall health strategy to optimize the body's own natural healing potential, including eating well, exercising regularly, managing stress, not smoking, and limiting alcohol consumption."

Dr. Weil emphasizes the importance of taking antioxidants such as vitamin C, vitamin E, selenium, and mixed carotenoids. Although some doctors may recommend antioxidant supplements, Weil suggests that whole foods such as "lots of fruits and veggies, green tea, and dark chocolate" are more effective.

Opposite are Dr. Weil's recommendations for supplements and appropriate dosages, with a brief explanation of their therapeutic effect.

SUPPLEMENT	DAILY DOSAGE	BENEFITS	SPECIAL RECOMMENDATIONS
MIXED CAROTENOIDS	25,000 IU	Mixed carotenoids may have a greater cancer-protective value than beta-carotene alone.	Look for a product that contains a wide range of carotenoids, including beta-carotene, alpha-carotene, lutein, lycopene, and others.
VITAMIN C	200 mg	Unlike most animals, humans lack the ability to make vitamin C in their bodies, which prevents disease.	Buy nonchewable forms to protect tooth enamel. Take 100 mg twice a day with meals to avoid upset stomach.
VITAMIN E	400 IU for under age 40; 800 IU for age 40 and older	Vitamin E is made up of eight different compounds, four tocopherols and four tocotrienols. Scientists believe these compounds lower cholesterol and prevent cancer.	The optimum dose combines mixed tocopherols and mixed tocotrienols. The label should say "d [not "dl"] alpha-tocopherol with other tocopherols" or "mixed tocopherols." Take with a meal containing some fat.
SELENIUM	200 mcg If you have had cancer or are at increased risk for it, take 300 mcg a day.	Selenium is a trace mineral found in some foods. It plays a role in converting fats and proteins into energy and may help to prevent cancer and heart disease.	Take organic, yeast-bound forms with vitamin E to enhance absorption. ("Yeast-bound" will be indicated on the label and is generally more effective.)
B COMPLEX	1 capsule	B vitamins have been shown to reduce the risk of stroke, protect against depression, and prevent birth defects.	Buy a B-100 B-complex supplement that contains 400 mcg of folic acid (also called folate), 100 mcg of B_{12}, and other B vitamins. Take with a meal.
CALCIUM	1,000 to 1,500 mg for women; no more than 1,000 mg for men	Calcium builds strong bones, promotes healthy teeth, helps to regulate nerve and muscle function, and prevents high blood pressure. Most American adults get only half of the Recommended Dietary Allowance (1,000 to 1,300) from food.	Take calcium citrate in divided doses of 500 mg each. Take with half as much magnesium, because calcium is constipating and magnesium has a mild laxative effect.
VITAMIN D	400 IU for adults and 800 IU for seniors	Vitamin D aids calcium absorption, promotes bone health, and may play a role in the prevention of breast and prostate cancers.	Some calcium products contain vitamin D. Supplementation is especially important during the winter months for those who live in northern latitudes. Take with a meal.

homey soups

I've always loved soups, now perhaps more than ever before. They're soothing, nurturing, and homey, and at the same time they can be refined and delicate. Soups also offer an enterprising way to pack numerous health-giving nutrients into a bowl. It's the dish I most crave when I am feeling the need to strengthen my defenses.

Traditionally, in the West, soups are served as a first course to stimulate the palate; in China, they are often served toward the end of the meal to aid digestion. In my house, I like to serve soups as *the* meal, and we eat them almost every day for lunch and very often for dinner—except during the warmer months. But even then I probably wouldn't turn down a bowl of good soup.

With almost all soups, light or hearty, the key factor is the quality of the broth. I used to be a purist and insist on homemade broth *from scratch,* and with some soups it's still important. But these days many markets offer very good-quality canned or ready-prepared broth, which can be doctored or used as a base. *If you are using a store-bought broth, make certain that it's top-quality and reduced-sodium (and if at all possible organic or from free-range chickens, for the best flavor).* When I'm particularly busy, I often create meal-in-one soups by starting with a ready-prepared soup from a good market and adding green vegetables such as fresh spinach or partially cooked broccoli or green beans, tofu slices, and little bits and leftovers from previous dinners. It's a great way to clean out your refrigerator and create a unique dish.

My soup tastes vary widely, as you can see from the selection in this chapter. There are some special Asian recipes, such as my favorite miso soup, the delicate Cantonese Sweet Corn Chowder, and a spicy *rasam* (Indian Hot and Sour Seafood Chowder). My Great-Aunt Sophie's Chicken Soup is one of my family's most treasured recipes.

The seasons often influence my soup cravings: In cooler weather, I adore soups like the gutsy Roasted Onion and Garlic Soup or the Wild Mushroom Bisque; Sun-Dried Tomato Soup epitomizes the taste of summer. Perhaps soup is regarded by some as humble fare, but to my mind no dish could give greater pleasure or offer better sustenance.

Quick Chinese Chicken Broth

MAKES 6 CUPS

Making this simple soup is second nature to me since it's so easy, yet it is the base for many Asian soups, sauces, and casseroles. Conveniently, it can be made in advance and frozen or reheated. I also serve the cooked chicken with a drizzle of soy sauce and a vegetable for a light meal.

INGREDIENTS

2½ pounds (preferably free-range or organic) chicken wings, legs, and/or thighs

10 cups water

¾ cup rice wine or sake

6 slices fresh ginger, about the size of a quarter, smashed with the flat side of a knife

FIRST Rinse the chicken parts under cold running water. Drain and put in a large pot with the water, rice wine, and smashed ginger. Bring to a boil, reduce the heat to low so that the liquid is at a low boil, and simmer uncovered for 1½ hours, skimming to remove any impurities.

SECOND Strain the broth through a fine-mesh strainer, removing the chicken pieces, and skim to remove any fat. Use the broth as directed in recipes. (The broth will keep up to 1 week in the refrigerator or frozen for up to several months.)

The Easiest Chicken Broth

MAKES 6 CUPS

This easy recipe is for those who don't have time to make chicken broth from scratch, but want a flavorful base for a soup or stew. Use a good-quality reduced-sodium chicken broth or bouillon for the best results.

INGREDIENTS

4½ cups store-bought (preferably reduced-sodium) chicken broth*

1½ cups water

½ cup rice wine or sake

6 slices fresh ginger, about the size of a quarter, smashed lightly with the flat side of a knife

Put the chicken broth, water, rice wine or sake, and ginger in a pot, bring to a boil, and cook at a low boil for 15 minutes. Strain out and discard the ginger, and use the broth as directed in recipes.

+ *See "Key to Primary Indian Spices" on page 288 for the health-giving properties of fresh ginger.*

*You also may substitute the equivalent amount of a good-quality chicken bouillon cube dissolved in water.

Soothing Miso Soup with Shiitake Mushrooms

SIX TO EIGHT SERVINGS

This is the soup I crave when I am fighting a cold or the flu—or when I need nurturing. With the shiitake mushrooms, tofu, and miso, it's chock-full of immune enhancers. It's also deliciously mellow and easy to prepare.

+ **Miso,** *a concentrated paste made from fermented soybeans and grains, provides the body with protein. Consuming ample amounts of soy can also reduce perimenopausal symptoms, improve cholesterol, and lower blood pressure.*

INGREDIENTS

- ½ **pound fresh shiitake mushrooms, rinsed lightly**
- 6 **cups Easiest Chicken Broth (page 79), or 2 cubes good-quality chicken bouillon dissolved in 6 cups water**
- ½ **pound soft tofu, cut into slices about ¼ inch thick and 1½ inches long**
- ½ **cup plus 1 tablespoon light-colored or mustard-colored ("white") miso paste, or to taste**
- ¼ **cup rice wine or sake (optional)**
- 6 **ounces or half of a 10-ounce bag baby spinach or regular spinach, stems removed, rinsed and drained**
- 2 **tablespoons minced scallion greens**

FIRST Cut the stems off the mushrooms, discard, and cut the caps into thin slices.

SECOND Pour the chicken broth into a soup pot or stockpot and bring to a low boil. Add the mushroom and tofu slices and return to a boil. Reduce the heat to low and simmer for 10 minutes.

THIRD Put the miso paste in a small bowl, slowly pour in the rice wine (if using) and ¼ cup of the chicken broth, stirring until smooth. Add a little more chicken broth if it seems too thick.

FOURTH Add most of the miso mixture to the chicken broth and stir to blend. Taste for seasoning, adding more miso if needed. Stir in the cleaned spinach leaves and heat the soup to a boil, skimming the surface to remove any impurities. Ladle the soup into serving bowls and sprinkle with the minced scallion greens for garnish. Serve.

Great-Aunt Sophie's Chicken Soup

SIX TO EIGHT SERVINGS

My Great-Aunt Sophie was the matriarch of my mother's family. She and my grand-mother promoted the health-giving properties of foods as early as the 1930s, when my mother was growing up. Here is one of her delicious tried-and-true panaceas. I've increased the garlic to suit my tastes.

INGREDIENTS

1   whole chicken (preferably free-range or organic), weighing about 3½ to 4 pounds

1½   heads garlic (about 21 cloves), smashed with the flat side of a knife, and peeled

6   medium onions, peeled, and cut into sixths

12   carrots, peeled, ends trimmed, cut lengthwise in half, and cut into 1½-inch lengths

6   parsnips, peeled, ends trimmed, cut lengthwise in half, and cut into 1½-inch lengths

1   bunch celery (about 1 pound), ends trimmed, and stalks cut into 1½-inch lengths

14   cups water

1   teaspoon whole peppercorns

1½   teaspoons salt, or to taste

FIRST Remove any fat from around the cavity opening and neck of the chicken. Rinse the chicken lightly and drain; then, using a heavy knife or cleaver, cut it through the bones into 10 to 12 pieces.

SECOND Put the chicken pieces and remaining ingredients, except for the salt, in a large, heavy stockpot or soup pot and bring to a boil over medium-high heat. Lower the heat so that the liquid is still at a simmer and cook about 1¾ hours, uncovered, skimming the broth to remove any impurities. Skim off any fat (you may chill overnight and remove the fat that has solidified). Add the salt, taste, and adjust the seasoning if necessary. Ladle chunks of chicken, vegetables, and soup into serving bowls and serve immediately.

+ Almost every ethnic culture has its version of chicken soup, which is considered a curative for many illnesses. Research has shown that it is effective in breaking up congestion from a cold. Asian doctors believe that it is a yang tonic and restores the body's energy.

+ See "Dr. Jim Duke's Herbal Farmacy" on page 158 for the health-giving properties of garlic.

Cantonese Sweet Corn Chowder

SIX TO EIGHT SERVINGS

This soup captures the sweetness of summer and corn. For the best flavor, use freshly picked ears of corn, but the taste is surprisingly satisfying even with frozen corn.

+ ***Corn** kernels are a good source of fiber, and recent research suggests that fiber may prevent certain types of cancer, especially that of the colon.*

⁂ *Asian doctors credit corn with improving appetite, regulating digestion, and strengthening the kidneys.*

INGREDIENTS

SOUP BASE

- **5 ears sweet corn, husked, or 2½ cups thawed frozen corn**
- **¼ cup rice wine or sake**
- **6 cups Easiest Chicken Broth (page 79)**

- **¼ pound boneless, skinless chicken meat**
- **3 tablespoons water**
- **¾ teaspoon toasted sesame oil**
- **1 cake silken tofu (about ½ pound), carefully cut into small dice**
- **1¼ teaspoons salt, or to taste**
- **2 tablespoons minced scallion greens for garnish**

FIRST Bring the Soup Base to a boil in a nonaluminum pot. Reduce the heat to low, cover, and let simmer for 30 minutes. Scoop out the corn or strain the broth, let cool, and cut the kernels from the ears, saving the kernels.

SECOND Chop the chicken meat, using a food processor fitted with a steel blade, to a coarse paste. With the machine still running, pour the water and toasted sesame oil through the feed tube and blend together. Scoop the minced chicken into a bowl.

THIRD If you are using ears of corn, puree the kernels in the food processor, adding a little of the soup liquid. Scrape the corn paste back into the pot with the soup. Heat until hot over medium heat and then slowly add the chicken bits, mixing with a whisk to cook evenly. Heat until boiling, lower the heat, cook for about 1½ minutes, then carefully add the tofu pieces. When they are hot, add the salt and mix. Taste for seasoning and adjust as needed. Ladle into soup bowls, sprinkling a little of the minced scallion greens on top of each bowl. Serve immediately.

Roasted Onion and Garlic Soup

SIX TO EIGHT SERVINGS

This fragrant onion soup is hearty in the true French manner, with a generous dose of garlic. Roasting the onions and garlic brings out their inherent sweetness and deep flavor. It is especially warming on a chilly day. If you like a lighter soup, use chicken broth instead of beef.

INGREDIENTS

- 1½ **pounds yellow or sweet white onions, peeled**
- 1½ **heads garlic (about 21 cloves)**
- 2 **tablespoons unsalted butter**
- 1 **tablespoon flour**
- 6 **cups beef or chicken broth, or bouillon**
- 1 **cup dry white wine**
- ¼ **teaspoon freshly ground black pepper**
- ½ **cup freshly grated Gruyère or Swiss cheese**

FIRST Preheat the oven to 400 degrees. Lightly brush a cookie sheet with olive oil. Cut the onions into ½-inch-thick slices and arrange on the cookie sheet. Separate the unpeeled cloves of garlic, smash with the flat side of a knife, and arrange around the onions on the cookie sheet. Bake about 20 minutes, then flip over the onion slices and continue baking another 20 to 25 minutes. If any of the outer rings of the onions get too dark, remove and set aside. Bake until the onions are lightly golden, then remove from the oven and let cool slightly. Squeeze the cooked garlic cloves from their skin into a bowl. Mash the pulp with a fork into a smooth paste.

SECOND Heat a heavy saucepan or stockpot, add the butter, and melt. When the foam begins to subside, add the onion rings and sauté over medium-low heat for about 5 minutes, stirring with a wooden spoon. Add the flour and stir with a wooden spoon or a whisk, cooking for about 1½ minutes. Add the mashed garlic and continue cooking for 5 to 6 minutes more over low heat. Pour in the beef or chicken broth and wine. Bring to a boil, lower the heat, and let simmer uncovered for 25 to 30 minutes, stirring occasionally, until the onions are very tender. Add the pepper and taste for seasoning. Ladle into serving bowls and serve with the grated cheese.

+ *Garlic, from a health perspective, is the most powerful member of the onion family, but both garlic and onions have been shown to prevent colds and improve nasal congestion, prevent stomach cancer, and lower blood pressure and prevent heart disease.*

❉ § *Asian doctors also recognize that garlic is antibacterial, lowers cholesterol and blood pressure, and aids digestion.*

Sun-Dried Tomato Soup with Fresh Basil

SIX TO EIGHT SERVINGS

This soup is best during tomato season, but with the flavor of top-quality sun-dried tomatoes and decent vine-ripened tomatoes, you can enjoy the taste of summer any time of the year. Add penne or elbow macaroni to the soup during the last 10 to 12 minutes and transform it into a meal-in-one dish for lunch or a light dinner.

+ **Tomatoes** contain lycopene, a phytonutrient that gives tomatoes their red color and has been shown to prevent prostate and digestive-tract cancers. See the "Seven Colors of Health" chart on page 199 for other properties.

INGREDIENTS

2   ounces good-quality sun-dried tomatoes

3   cups boiling water

3   cloves garlic, peeled

1½ tablespoons virgin olive oil

1½ pounds vine-ripened or other ripe tomatoes, stems removed, peeled, and cut into quarters

1½ teaspoons sugar, or to taste

¼   cup chopped basil leaves, rinsed and blotted dry*

1   teaspoon salt

¼   teaspoon freshly ground black pepper

¼   cup freshly grated Parmigiano-Reggiano cheese (optional)

*You may vary the flavor by substituting cilantro for the basil and adding a teaspoon of dried chile flakes.

FIRST Put the sun-dried tomatoes in a bowl and pour the boiling water on top. Let sit for 15 minutes, until they get very soft. Strain, separating the sun-dried tomatoes from the water and reserving both.

SECOND Drop the garlic cloves down the feed tube of a food processor fitted with a steel blade while the machine is running, or into a blender, and chop until fine. Put the softened sun-dried tomatoes into the food processor bowl or blender, and pulse to chop finely.

THIRD Heat a heavy 3-quart saucepan or pot, pour in the olive oil, and heat until hot, about 10 seconds. Add the sun-dried tomatoes and garlic and sauté over low heat for about 5 minutes, until fragrant.

FOURTH While the mixture is cooking, put about half of the tomatoes in the food processor fitted with a steel blade or the blender and puree until smooth. Repeat for the remaining tomatoes and add both batches to the soup pot. Sauté until fragrant, about 5 minutes, then add the sun-dried tomato water and the sugar. Bring to a boil and simmer uncovered over medium-low heat for 15 to 20 minutes, until very fragrant. Add the basil and cook for another 5 minutes. Add the salt and pepper. Taste and adjust the seasoning if necessary, but don't make too salty. Ladle the soup into serving bowls and sprinkle with the cheese, if desired. Serve immediately.

✳ Asian doctors credit tomatoes with purifying the blood, cleaning the liver, and detoxifying the body.

§ An Ayurvedic remedy for aiding digestion is to drink a cup of tomato juice with a pinch of cumin one hour after eating.

Norma's Pumpkin and Cannellini Bean Soup

SIX TO EIGHT SERVINGS

This wonderful Tuscan soup is a favorite of my friend Norma Miller, who wrote *Soups of Italy*. If cannellini beans are not available, substitute navy, Great Northern, or butter beans.

INGREDIENTS

1   tablespoon virgin olive oil

1½   ounces pancetta, rind removed, and cut into small dice (about ¼ cup)

3   cloves garlic, smashed with the flat side of a knife, and peeled

SEASONINGS (MIXED TOGETHER)

1   medium red onion, peeled, and minced

3   stalks celery, ends trimmed, and minced

¾   teaspoon dried chile flakes

5½   cups chicken broth (or 1½ chicken bouillon cubes dissolved in water)

1½   pounds pumpkin or butternut squash, peeled and cut into fine dice (about 4½ cups)

1   15-ounce can cannellini beans, blanched in boiling water, refreshed in cold water, and drained, *or* ¾ cup dried beans, soaked and cooked

1   teaspoon salt

¼   teaspoon freshly ground black pepper

2   tablespoons chopped fresh basil leaves, rinsed and blotted dry

6   tablespoons freshly grated Parmigiano-Reggiano cheese

FIRST Sauté the pancetta and garlic cloves in the olive oil, in a heavy, nonaluminum pot over low heat until the garlic turns golden. Remove the pancetta and garlic, and discard, leaving the fragrant oil. Add the Seasonings and sauté over medium-low heat until soft, about 10 minutes.

SECOND Add the chicken broth with the pumpkin, and bring to a boil. Lower the heat and simmer, covered, until the pumpkin or squash is very soft, about 40 minutes. Add the cannellini beans and continue cooking, covered, for about 15 minutes. Season with salt and pepper. (Remember that you will be adding basil and cheese.) Ladle the soup into serving bowls and sprinkle the tops with the chopped basil and grated cheese. Serve immediately.

+ *Cannellini beans and other beans (legumes), dried and fresh, are an excellent source of potassium and folic acid. They are also rich in soluble fiber; they help lower cholesterol levels, thereby preventing heart disease; and they stabilize blood sugar levels.*

❋ *Asian doctors believe that the protein from beans can help regulate the metabolism to keep the body in balance. Beans also aid the proper growth and development of the body and brain.*

+ *Since pumpkin and squash are rich in vitamins C and E and carotenes, they lower the risk of cancer, heart disease, stroke, and cataracts.*

Vietnamese Hot and Sour Scallop Soup

SIX TO EIGHT SERVINGS

I love the sweet, briny flavor of scallops with the hot and sour seasonings. You can prepare the base of this soup in advance, reheat it, and add the scallops, bean sprouts, and cilantro just before serving.

INGREDIENTS

- 3 stalks lemongrass, ends trimmed and outer stalks removed*
- 2 medium vine-ripened or other ripe tomatoes, cored and seeded
- 1 teaspoon virgin olive oil
- 2½ tablespoons minced shallots
- 1 17-ounce can straw mushrooms, blanched briefly in boiling water, refreshed in cold water, drained, and cut in half lengthwise
- 1 tablespoon sugar
- 5 cups water
- 1 pound sea scallops, rinsed and drained
- 5½ tablespoons fish sauce, or to taste
- 3½ tablespoons freshly squeezed lime juice
- 1 teaspoon dried chile flakes, or to taste
- 1½ cups bean sprouts, rinsed and drained
- 3 tablespoons minced fresh cilantro leaves

*Fresh lemongrass is available at most Asian markets. You may substitute dried, but first reconstitute by softening in boiling water to cover for 20 minutes.

FIRST Split the lemongrass lengthwise in half, cut into 3-inch lengths, and smash with the flat side of a knife or cleaver. Cut the tomatoes into ¼-inch dice.

SECOND Heat a heavy pot or casserole over medium-high heat until hot. Add the oil and heat until hot, about 20 seconds. Add the shallots and lemongrass and stir until fragrant, about 15 seconds. Add the tomatoes, straw mushrooms, and sugar and stir-fry for about 1 minute. Add the water and bring to a boil. Reduce the heat to medium-low and simmer uncovered for about 10 minutes.

THIRD While the soup is cooking, holding the knife on the diagonal, cut the scallops through the thickness into three slices. Add the fish sauce, lime juice, and chile flakes to the soup and simmer for about 2 minutes, then add the scallops and cook for another 2 minutes, until they turn opaque. Using tongs, lift out the lemongrass and discard. Carefully stir in the bean sprouts and cilantro and cook for a minute, until heated through. Ladle into a soup tureen or bowls and serve.

Hearty Cabbage Casserole

This soup is a simplified version of a Chinese classic, Lion's Head Stew. Four outer cabbage leaves are reserved and placed over the top of the soup. Once cooked, the browned leaves are said to resemble a lion's mane. If Napa cabbage is not available, use bok choy and lengthen the cooking time to 1 hour, or until the cabbage is very tender.

+ *While **raw cabbage** is considered more beneficial than cooked, it is rich in antioxidants and other nutrients that strengthen the immune system and improve resistance to disease. See the "Seven Colors of Health" chart on page 199 for other benefits.*

INGREDIENTS

1   medium head Chinese (Napa) cabbage (about 1 to 1½pounds)

4   teaspoons virgin olive oil

3   cloves garlic, smashed with the flat side of a knife and peeled

½   cup rice wine or sake

4   slices fresh ginger, smashed with the flat side of a knife

6   cups chicken broth (if canned, use reduced-sodium)

1   pound lean ground pork

SEASONINGS (MIXED TOGETHER)

1½ cups minced scallion greens

2   tablespoons minced fresh ginger

1   tablespoon minced garlic

2½ tablespoons soy sauce

1   tablespoon rice wine or sake

1½ teaspoons toasted sesame oil

½   teaspoon freshly ground black pepper

1   tablespoon cornstarch

1½ tablespoons soy sauce

¾   teaspoon salt, or to taste

FIRST Cut away the tough stem of the cabbage and discard. Remove and reserve four of the outermost leaves. Cut the remaining cabbage in half and cut the leaves into 2-inch squares, separating the leafy sections from the stem sections.

SECOND Heat a Dutch oven or a covered casserole, add 1 teaspoon of oil, and heat until very hot, about 30 seconds. Add the garlic cloves and the cabbage stem sections and stir-fry for 30 seconds over medium-high heat. Add the rice wine and smashed ginger slices and toss lightly; cover and cook for 1½ minutes. Uncover, and add the leafy cabbage sections and the chicken broth. Partially cover, and once the soup reaches a boil, uncover, reduce the heat slightly, and simmer for 30 minutes.

THIRD While the soup is cooking, put the ground pork and Seasonings in a bowl. Mix with your hands to combine the ingredients evenly, then shape into 6 plump oval shapes.

FOURTH Preheat the oven to 350 degrees. Heat a wok or a skillet, add the remaining tablespoon of oil, and heat until very hot but not smoking. Place the meatballs in the pan and sear until golden brown over high heat, then turn them over and sear on the other side. Remove with a slotted spoon and place the meatballs in the center of the cabbage soup. Cover with the four reserved leaves to create an attractive presentation. Replace the lid and put the casserole in the middle shelf of the oven. Bake for 45 minutes. Gently stir in the soy sauce and salt to taste and ladle into soup bowls. Serve immediately, taking a little cabbage and broth with each serving.

❉ *Cabbage lubricates the intestines and improves digestion. Cabbage soup is a Chinese folk remedy for constipation.*

Wild Mushroom Bisque

The smoky flavor of dried Chinese black (shiitake) mushrooms is blended with fresh shiitake and cremini mushrooms to create a rich and satisfying bisque. Vary the mushrooms depending on the season and what is available. I often prepare this soup up to the last step, then reheat and add the remaining ingredients at the last minute.

INGREDIENTS

- 8 dried Chinese black mushrooms (about ½ ounce)
- 1 cup hot water
- 1½ slices white bread, crusts removed
- 4 cups good-quality reduced-sodium chicken broth
- 2½ tablespoons unsalted butter
- 6 cloves garlic, peeled, and sliced finely
- 6 finely chopped shallots (about ½ cup)
- ½ pound fresh shiitake mushrooms, rinsed lightly, drained, stems removed, and caps sliced finely
- ½ pound cremini or portobello mushrooms, rinsed lightly, drained, stems removed, and caps sliced finely
- ½ cup good-quality dry sherry or rice wine
- ½ cup milk
- ½ cup heavy cream
- 1 teaspoon salt
- ¼ teaspoon freshly ground black pepper
- 2 tablespoons minced parsley, stems removed, rinsed, and blotted dry (optional)

FIRST Soak the dried black mushrooms in the water for 20 minutes. Pour through a strainer, reserving the water, and squeeze the black mushrooms to remove the excess water. Remove the stems, discard, and cut the caps into thin slices.

SECOND Put the bread in a bowl and add enough chicken broth to cover. Let stand about 10 minutes, until the bread is soaked through. Squeeze out the chicken broth and mash the softened bread lightly with a fork.

THIRD Heat the butter in a heavy saucepan or Dutch oven. Once the foam begins to subside, add the garlic and shallots. Sauté over medium heat, stirring constantly, for about 3 minutes, then add the dried and fresh sliced mushrooms. Cover and continue cooking the mushrooms for about 5 minutes, stirring occasionally, then add the bread and stir with a wooden spoon to incorporate evenly into the mushroom mixture.

FOURTH Either use a hand-held blender to puree in the pan or carefully pour the soup base into the bowl of a food processor fitted with a steel blade or into a blender and puree until smooth, adding a little chicken broth if it is too thick. Scrape the puree back into the pan and add the remaining chicken broth, reserved mushroom liquid, and dry sherry, and cook uncovered over medium heat for about 10 minutes. Add the milk, cream, salt, and pepper, and slowly heat until piping hot. Remove from the heat and taste for seasoning, adding more salt if necessary. Ladle into serving bowls, sprinkle with a little parsley, if desired, and serve immediately.

+ *Shiitake or black **mushrooms** contain lentinan, a component that strengthens the immune system and helps the body to fight disease.*

Indian Hot and Sour Seafood Chowder

SIX TO EIGHT SERVINGS

Every cook in southern India has his or her own recipe for this soup, which is known as *rasam*. It is often vegetarian, with a legume (lentil) base, and while it is traditionally spooned over rice, it may be drunk throughout the meal almost as a beverage. I like to add seafood to the broth and create a spicy meal-in-one dish, served with cooked basmati or jasmine rice.

INGREDIENTS

2 ounces dried tamarind pulp (available at most Asian markets)

3½ cups hot water

1 1½-inch piece fresh ginger, peeled and cut into little pieces

6 cloves garlic, peeled

1 fresh jalapeño chile, ends trimmed and seeds removed

1 14½-ounce can peeled tomatoes

¼ cup fresh cilantro leaves, rinsed and finely chopped

1 teaspoon ground turmeric

½ teaspoon freshly ground black pepper

SPICE SEASONINGS

1 teaspoon mustard seeds

3 or 4 curry leaves, shredded finely

1 teaspoon dried chile flakes

1 teaspoon ground cumin

1 teaspoon ground coriander

1½ pounds cod fillets, cut into 1½-inch squares

¾ pound raw shrimp, peeled and deveined

1½ teaspoons salt, or to taste

½ cup fresh cilantro leaves, rinsed, blotted dry, and chopped, for garnish

FIRST Roughly break up the tamarind pulp with your fingers and place in a bowl. Pour the hot water over to cover and leave to soak for 10 minutes. Strain through a sieve, pushing the pulp through with the back of a spoon. Discard the stones and fibers and pour the tamarind water into a casserole or soup pot. Bring to a boil, lower the heat, and simmer for 5 minutes.

SECOND Chop the ginger, garlic, and jalapeño in a blender to a paste. Add the tomatoes and blend until smooth, then scrape into the tamarind water and mix with the ¼ cup chopped cilantro, turmeric, and black pepper. Bring the soup to a boil, reduce the heat, and simmer about 15 minutes, stirring occasionally.

THIRD In another pan, dry toast the mustard seeds until they pop. Add the curry leaves and the remaining Spice Seasonings and toast for a minute until fragrant. Add these spices to the soup and cook for 1 minute to blend.

FOURTH Add the fish to the soup and cook, partially covered, over medium-low heat about 10 minutes, or until the fish is almost cooked. Add the shrimp, partially cover, and cook for about 3½ minutes, until the shrimp are cooked. Season with salt to taste. Sprinkle with the ½ cup chopped cilantro, ladle into soup bowls, and serve.

§ The tamarind and tomato base of this soup gives the dish a lovely and refreshing sour flavor. Ayurvedic cooks serve sour foods, in moderation, to stimulate appetite, improve digestion, and energize the body.

§ See "Key to Primary Indian Spices" on page 288 for the health-giving properties of many of the seasonings.

Walter Willett and Redesigning the Food Pyramid

Although Dr. Walter Willett, chairman of the Department of Nutrition at the Harvard School of Public Health, is one of the most widely quoted nutritional authorities in the United States, he is no stranger to confrontation. As a world-renowned researcher and one of the principal authors of Harvard's famous Nurses' Health Studies, an investigation of diet and health that began in 1976 and has followed more than 230,000 women, Willett has been involved in groundbreaking studies of diet, lifestyle, and health that have included:

- targeting obesity as a major cause of heart disease, diabetes, gallstones, and shortened life

- linking hydrogenated vegetable oil, red meat, some birth control pills, and hormone replacement therapy to various cancers

- associating exercise with a lowered risk of diabetes, and eating whole grains with reduced incidence of heart disease

- crediting the increased consumption of monosaturated fats such as olive oil, canola oil, and most nuts with a reduced risk of heart disease

Willett loves food, especially the Mediterranean diet, which embraces olive oil as a primary cooking oil and accentuates fresh seasonal ingredients—vegetables, fruits, whole grains, and legumes—with moderate amounts of seafood, poultry, and eggs and limited amounts of meat.

Willett was one of the first to warn Americans of the danger of partially hydrogenated vegetable fat (fat that has been transformed from liquid to solid) in margarine and numerous processed foods, which he says clogs arteries and contributes to the risk of diabetes. He also has promoted the health benefits of monosaturated and polyunsaturated fats, which he feels have been overlooked in the current antifat climate. Americans need to know, says Willett, that there are good fats and bad fats. He recommends limiting calories from bad fats as well as refined carbohydrates to avoid obesity.

Willett's latest crusade, which he outlines in his book *Eat, Drink, and Be Healthy: The Harvard Medical School Guide to Healthy Eating,* is redesigning the

WALTER WILLETT'S EATING STRATEGIES

- Replace white bread, rice, pasta, and other refined carbohydrates with **WHOLE GRAIN FOODS** at most meals. (In recipes calling for white rice, brown rice may be substituted.)

- Increase the consumption of **PLANT OILS**, such as olive, canola, soy, corn, sunflower, and peanut oil.

- Emphasize the importance of **VEGETABLES** (5 servings per day or "eating in abundance") and **FRUITS** (2 to 3 servings per day).

- Recognize the health benefits of **NUTS AND LEGUMES**, which lower the risk of heart disease and diabetes.

- **REDUCE** the intake of red meat, butter, and potatoes.

USDA Food Pyramid, which he says is seriously flawed. Above are the key strategies in his revised eating plan.

Willett also recommends daily exercise and weight control as crucial to maintaining good health. "Weight control is not impossible, nor does it mean deprivation," Willett contends. "Focus on the quality of your diet and make sure you feel satisfied at the end of the day. Most people can successfully control their weight with a reasonable diet and daily exercise."

Willett has shown that by adopting these habits we all can reduce the risk of major chronic diseases and live a longer, healthier life.

hearty stews and braises

My family has always had a passion for stews and braised dishes. It probably started with my Great-Aunt Sophie and her legendary brisket. I still dream about the tender meat and sweet carrots. Later, my mother, who was preoccupied with raising four small children, embraced stews as the perfect solution for dinner. She realized that since they are one-pot meals that can be prepared easily, require little tending, and can be cooked in advance and reheated with even better results, they were ideal for her busy schedule. So pot roast, brisket, and chicken cacciatore became staples in our weekly menus.

Now, as a working mother, I too appreciate the convenience of stews. And as a cook, I have come to love their versatility, since various meats and seafood can be paired with numerous vegetables and assorted seasonings to become a fragrant, satisfying, and comforting main dish that merely needs the addition of rice, noodles, couscous, or crusty bread to become a complete and wonderful meal. For the sake of good health, though, I tend to favor seafood over meat and I increase the ratio and variety of vegetables and seasonings in most recipes.

Traditionally stews are associated with slow cooking, and I've included a number of dishes in this chapter, like Star Anise Beef Stew, Saucy Italian Chicken, and Fragrant Cinnamon Pork with Sweet Potatoes, that fit this bill. Equally represented are a number of quick-braised dishes that require less time. There's Chile-Flavored Braised Halibut, Coconut Shrimp with Basil and Lime Leaves, and Lemongrass Chicken with Green Beans. With these dishes, there's the advantage of preparing the sauce base and precooking some ingredients in advance, then just reheating and mixing everything together to be simmered quickly before serving. The concept of stews is simple and may seem mundane, but as these recipes illustrate, with good ingredients and an adventurous use of seasonings, they are equally suited to feeding a family on an everyday basis or dazzling a table of guests for a festive dinner party.

Saucy Italian Chicken

SIX SERVINGS

This dish, with its garlicky tomato sauce, reminds me of the chicken cacciatore that my mother made when I was a child. It's hearty and warming to the body, so I often prepare it when the weather is raw. Serve it with country bread or rice and an additional vegetable if desired. I like to add artichoke hearts, but you can add other vegetables depending on the season.

+ *Tomatoes contain a phytonutrient, lycopene, that has been shown to lower the risk of prostate and other types of cancer, and to prevent heart disease. See the "Seven Colors of Health" chart on page 199 for other benefits.*

✳ *Asians believe chicken acts as an energy tonic and warms the body. Using organic or free-range chicken is highly recommended..*

INGREDIENTS

3   pounds chicken thighs and drumsticks (about 5 or 6)

1½ tablespoons virgin olive oil

2   medium onions, peeled and diced

10 cloves garlic, peeled and minced

1   14½-ounce can Italian tomatoes with basil, mashed with a fork to break up into small pieces

1   teaspoon dried oregano

½ cup dry white wine

1   teaspoon salt

½ teaspoon freshly ground black pepper

1   10-ounce package frozen artichokes, defrosted to room temperature

2   tablespoons fresh basil leaves, rinsed, blotted dry, and cut into thin shreds

FIRST Separate the chicken legs and thighs at the joint with a sharp knife. Heat a 4-quart heavy casserole with a lid, add the oil, and heat until very hot but not smoking. Arrange a batch of the chicken pieces in one layer, skin side down, in the pan and fry over high heat until golden brown, turning once. Remove from the pan with tongs, set aside, and fry the remaining chicken. Remove and set aside the second batch.

SECOND Lower the heat to medium, add the onions, and fry over medium-low heat until soft, stirring occasionally. Add the garlic, stir until fragrant, and add the tomatoes and oregano and cook for several minutes. Add the chicken pieces, wine, salt, and pepper, and stir. Cover and bring to a boil. Reduce the heat to medium-low, and let simmer, covered, for about 30 minutes, or until the chicken is just tender. Add the defrosted artichokes and stir with a wooden spoon to mix. Sprinkle the basil on top and continue cooking for another 10 minutes, uncovered. Serve immediately.

Portuguese Clam Stew

In the fall, you can buy lacinato kale (also known as Tuscan kale, cavolo nero, or black kale) in Italian markets and farmers' markets. It is tougher than ordinary kale, so it should be shredded and cooked for an additional 10 to 15 minutes. Serve this stew with warm crusty bread.

INGREDIENTS

- ½ pound Spanish chorizo (spicy cured pork sausage), cut into ¼-inch pieces
- 1 tablespoon virgin olive oil
- 1 medium onion, peeled and chopped finely
- 4 cloves garlic, peeled, smashed with the flat side of a knife, and sliced thinly
- ½ cup rice wine or dry white wine
- 4½ cups chicken broth
- 1 pound lacinato kale or regular kale, center ribs cut out and discarded, and leaves cut crosswise into thin slices
- 3 pounds littleneck clams (preferably small), scrubbed, soaked in cold water to cover for 1 hour, and drained
- ½ teaspoon salt, or to taste
- ¼ teaspoon freshly ground black pepper

FIRST Cook the chorizo over medium heat in a large nonstick skillet, stirring occasionally, until the fat is rendered and the sausage pieces are lightly browned, about 5 minutes. Transfer to paper towels to drain. Discard the fat.

SECOND Heat a large casserole or soup pot, add the oil, and heat until hot. Add the onion and cook over medium heat until almost golden, about 3 minutes. Add the garlic and cook for 1 minute, until very fragrant. Pour in the wine and chicken broth and bring to just under a boil. Add the chorizo and kale and let simmer uncovered for about 5 minutes.

THIRD Add the clams, cover, and once the liquid reaches a boil, reduce the heat to medium and cook, shaking the pot from time to time or stirring to allow the clams to cook evenly. Cook about 5 to 7 minutes, until the clams have just opened. Add salt and pepper, taste, and adjust the seasoning if necessary. Serve hot.

+ *Kale, black kale, and its cousins are all cruciferous vegetables. They contain generous amounts of beta-carotene, and help stimulate and strengthen the immune system, thereby preventing disease.*

Oyster Sauce Chicken with Bok Choy

Deliciously rich and fragrant, this is one of those dishes whose flavor improves with reheating. You may substitute any cooked green vegetable, such as snap peas or broccoli, or leafy greens, such as spinach, for the bok choy.

+ See the "green" group of the "Seven Colors of Health" chart on page 199 for the beneficial qualities of bok choy.

INGREDIENTS

MARINADE

4   whole cloves garlic, smashed with the flat side of a knife and peeled

6   whole scallions, ends trimmed, cut into 1½-inch lengths

10 slices fresh ginger, about the size of a quarter, smashed with the flat side of a knife

6   tablespoons rice wine or sake

2½ tablespoons soy sauce

3   pounds chicken legs and thighs, rinsed, drained, and separated at the joint (about 5 or 6 pieces)

BRAISING MIXTURE

2½ cups good-quality reduced-sodium chicken broth

¼   cup rice wine or sake

4   tablespoons oyster sauce

2   teaspoons sugar

1½ pounds bok choy or baby bok choy, stem ends and leaf tips trimmed

THICKENER (MIXED TOGETHER)

3   tablespoons water

1   tablespoon cornstarch

FIRST Mix the Marinade ingredients in a heavy casserole or Dutch oven with a lid. Add the chicken pieces and turn to coat them with the marinade. Cover with the lid and let marinate for 15 to 20 minutes.

SECOND Add the ingredients for the Braising Mixture to the casserole and stir. Bring to a boil, reduce the heat to medium-low, and cook for about 40 minutes, partially covered, until the chicken is tender.

THIRD While the chicken is cooking, trim the tough outer leaves from the bok choy and discard. Rinse the stalks and leaves and drain. Cut the wide stalk lengthwise in half, then cut diagonally into 2-inch lengths.

FOURTH Bring 2 quarts of water to a boil in a large pot. Add the bok choy sections and cook for about 3½ to 4 minutes, until just tender. Remove from the heat, drain, refresh under cold running water, and drain again. Arrange on a deep platter or in a bowl with a slight indentation in the middle.

FIFTH Using tongs or a slotted spoon, remove the chicken pieces and arrange over the bok choy. Skim off any fat from the braising liquid and bring to a boil. Slowly add some of the Thickener, stirring to prevent lumps, then continue, using enough to thicken the liquid so that it coats the back of a spoon. Pour the thickened sauce over the chicken and cooked bok choy, and serve with steamed rice.

✤ This "warming" dish of chicken, with its rich, vibrant sauce, is a perfect Yang tonic suitable for the cold weather or when you are feeling chilled.

Lemongrass Chicken with Green Beans

SIX SERVINGS

This vibrantly colored and flavored dish is a quick stew. You may prepare the sauce base and precook the green beans in advance, then simmer all the ingredients together just before serving. The dish also reheats beautifully.

+ For the health-giving benefits of **green beans**, see the "yellow/green" group in the "Seven Colors of Health" chart on page 199.

INGREDIENTS

SEASONINGS

2	dried red chiles, seeds removed, or 1½ teaspoons dried chile flakes
4	stalks lemongrass, ends trimmed, tough outer stalks removed, and cut into ½-inch lengths*
6	cloves garlic

1½ pounds skinless chicken breasts

1½ pounds green beans, ends snapped, cut on the diagonal in two

3½ tablespoons virgin olive oil

1½ medium red onions, peeled and cut into thin slices

1½ medium red bell peppers, cored, seeded, and cut into thin slices

2 tablespoons rice wine or sake

COCONUT SAUCE (MIXED TOGETHER)

1½ cups light coconut milk

2½ tablespoons fish sauce

1 tablespoon sugar

1½ teaspoons salt, or to taste

1 cup chopped fresh Thai holy basil or sweet basil leaves

*Fresh lemongrass is available at most Asian markets. You may substitute dried, but first reconstitute by softening in boiling water to cover for 20 minutes.

FIRST Drop the Seasonings in descending order into a blender or the feed tube of a food processor while the machine is running and process to a paste. Pulse several times to get a smooth mixture.

SECOND Arrange the chicken breast meat flat on a cutting board. Holding the blade of your knife parallel with the cutting board, cut the chicken into thin slices. Set aside.

THIRD Bring 2 cups water to a boil in a 3-quart casserole or a large skillet with a lid. Add the green beans and partially cook for about 4 minutes, then drain and refresh in cold water. Drain again and set aside.

FOURTH Reheat the pan, pour in 1½ tablespoons of the oil, and heat until very hot but not smoking. Add the chicken and stir-fry over high heat until the slices become opaque and are cooked, about 3 minutes. Remove from the pan and drain. Reheat the pan, add the remaining oil, and heat until hot. Add the seasonings, and cook over medium-low heat, stirring with a wooden spoon, for about 1½ to 2 minutes, until fragrant.

FIFTH Add the red onions and toss over medium heat for a minute, then add the red peppers and rice wine, and toss lightly for a minute. Cover and cook for 2 to 3 minutes, until tender. Turn the heat up to medium-high, add the green beans and the Coconut Sauce, and heat until boiling. Add the chicken pieces, cover, and simmer, covered, for about 5 minutes, or until the green beans are tender.

SIXTH Add the basil, toss, and taste for seasoning, adding more salt if necessary. Scoop the chicken and vegetables into a bowl and serve with steamed rice.

Saucy Black Bean Spareribs

Cantonese restaurants are renowned for their spareribs bathed in a pungent black bean sauce. I usually use country-style ribs or baby back ribs so that each bone is heavy with tender meat. Instead of frying the ribs, I sear them in a hot oven to render off the excess fat and transform them to a deep golden brown before braising.

INGREDIENTS

3 pounds country-style spareribs

MARINADE

2 tablespoons soy sauce

1½ tablespoons rice wine or sake

1 tablespoon virgin olive oil

MINCED SEASONINGS

2½ tablespoons fermented or salted black beans, rinsed, drained, and chopped finely

2½ tablespoons minced garlic

1 tablespoon minced fresh ginger

12 whole scallions, ends trimmed, cut into 2-inch lengths, and smashed lightly with the flat side of a knife

SAUCE (MIXED TOGETHER)

2½ cups good-quality reduced-sodium chicken broth or water

2½ tablespoons soy sauce

2 teaspoons sugar

THICKENER (MIXED TOGETHER)

4 teaspoons cornstarch

2 tablespoons water

1 teaspoon dried chile flakes for garnish (optional)

FIRST Trim any excess fat or gristle from the ribs and, using a heavy knife or cleaver, cut them into 2-inch lengths, cutting through the bones (or ask the butcher to do this). Put the ribs in a bowl, add the Marinade ingredients, and toss lightly to coat. Cover with plastic wrap and let marinate for 30 minutes at room temperature.

SECOND Preheat the oven to 450 degrees. Arrange the ribs on a baking sheet that has been lined with aluminum foil. Bake for 7 to 8 minutes on each side, or until golden brown.

THIRD While the ribs are baking, heat a 4-quart casserole or Dutch oven until hot, then add the oil and heat until hot. Toss in the Minced Seasonings, along with the scallions, and stir-fry over high heat until fragrant, about 10 seconds. Add the Sauce mixture and bring to a boil. Put the browned spareribs in the sauce, stir to coat, cover, and bring the sauce again to a boil. Reduce the heat to low, cover, and let simmer for 50 minutes to an hour, stirring occasionally, until the ribs are very tender.

FOURTH Uncover and, using a strainer or a slotted spoon, remove the spareribs to a bowl. Skim the surface of the sauce with a spoon to remove any fat or impurities. Bring the sauce to a boil and slowly add the Thickener, stirring continuously to prevent lumps, until thickened. Put the ribs back into the thickened sauce and carefully stir to coat. Sprinkle the top with the dried chile flakes, if desired, and serve from the pot with steamed rice and a stir-fried or steamed green vegetable.

: *Fermented or salted black beans have been used in Traditional Chinese Medicine since the sixth century. They are used in the treatment of ailments that affect the lungs and digestive system.*

Hoisin Turkey Thighs with Squash

SIX TO EIGHT SERVINGS

Turkey, with its rich, meaty flavor, is excellent in Asian dishes. It is especially good coated with the garlicky hoisin marinade and then paired with the sweet squash. You can replace the turkey with pieces of country-style spareribs or chicken and reduce the baking time to 45 minutes.

INGREDIENTS

3 pounds turkey thighs, trimmed of fat,* cut through bones into 2-inch pieces

MARINADE (MIXED TOGETHER)

1 cup hoisin or sweet bean sauce
¼ cup soy sauce
3½ tablespoons rice wine or sake
2 tablespoons minced garlic
2 tablespoons minced fresh ginger
1 teaspoon hot chile paste or dried chile flakes

2 cups 1-inch lengths scallion greens
3½ to 4 pounds butternut or acorn squash, peeled, cut in half, with seeds removed
1½ teaspoons toasted sesame oil

FIRST Put the turkey pieces in a bowl and add the Marinade, toss to coat, cover tightly with plastic wrap. Let marinate for 1 hour or longer in the refrigerator.

SECOND Preheat the oven to 400 degrees. Toss the scallions with the marinated turkey. Pour into a large casserole with a lid, cover, and place in the oven. Bake the turkey for 30 minutes, stirring once or twice.

THIRD While the turkey is cooking, cut the squash into 2-inch pieces. Toss with the toasted sesame oil. Arrange on a baking sheet lined with aluminum foil and cover with foil.

FOURTH Place the squash in the oven next to the turkey casserole. Bake both for 20 minutes. Stir the turkey, cover, and remove the aluminum foil from the squash. Continue baking for another 25 minutes, or until both are tender. A knife pierced through the center should come out easily. Arrange the squash in a deep bowl or on a platter with a lip, and spoon the turkey with its sauce on top. Serve with steamed rice.

*If the thighs are boneless, cook for 20 minutes less than specified in the recipe, or until they are tender.

Fragrant Cinnamon Pork with Sweet Potatoes

Redolent of cinnamon, star anise, garlic, and soy sauce, the tender pork and sweet potatoes are superb. If the pork is too lean it will dry out while cooking, so I use a cut like butt or shoulder.

INGREDIENTS

2 pounds boneless pork butt or shoulder, trimmed of excess fat and gristle

2½ teaspoons olive or canola oil

SEASONINGS

6 whole scallions, ends trimmed, cut into 1½-inch lengths, and smashed lightly with the flat side of a knife

6 cloves garlic, smashed lightly with the flat side of a knife, peeled, and sliced thin

6 slices fresh ginger, about the size of a quarter, smashed lightly with the flat side of a knife

1 teaspoon hot chile paste

2 to 3 sticks cinnamon

1 whole star anise, smashed, or 1 teaspoon aniseeds

BRAISING MIXTURE

4 cups water

⅓ cup soy sauce

¼ cup rice wine or sake

2 tablespoons sugar

4 sweet potatoes or yams (about 2 pounds), peeled and cut into 1½-inch cubes

2 tablespoons minced scallion greens for garnish

FIRST Cut the pork into 1½-inch cubes.

SECOND Heat the oil until very hot in a 4-quart casserole or a Dutch oven with a lid. Add half the pork pieces. Sear the outside of half the pork over high heat until brown, turning once. Remove and sear the remaining meat. Set aside.

THIRD Reheat the pan and oil, add the Seasonings. Stir-fry until fragrant, about 15 seconds, then add the Braising Mixture. Reduce the heat to low, cover, and let simmer for 20 minutes. Add the pork, bring the liquid to a boil, and reduce the heat to low. Let simmer, covered, for 35 to 40 minutes. Add the sweet potatoes, stir, cover, and continue cooking for about 25 minutes, or until the potatoes are tender. Serve the pork and potatoes atop a bed of blanched or steamed greens (see page 207), with some of the braising mixture spooned on top and accompanied by steamed rice.

✢ Chinese cinnamon, or cassia, has been used by Asian doctors for thousands of years. It is considered to be especially soothing to the stomach.

§ Ayurvedic doctors believe cinnamon harmonizes the flow of circulation in the body, aids digestion, and reduces nausea. See "Key to Primary Indian Spices" on page 288 for other benefits.

Star Anise Beef Stew

SIX TO EIGHT SERVINGS

Star anise, with its pungent licorice flavor, is a wonderful complement to beef and red wine, and adds another dimension to this dish. Use it carefully, as it can easily overpower. You may serve this dish over a crisp-cooked green vegetable or slices of fennel with steamed rice.

INGREDIENTS

2 pounds beef stewing meat, such as chuck or bottom round, trimmed of fat and gristle
½ cup all-purpose flour
1 teaspoon salt
½ teaspoon freshly ground black pepper
3 tablespoons virgin olive oil
8 cloves garlic, peeled and smashed lightly with the flat side of a knife
6 small onions (about 1 pound), peeled and cut into 6 wedges
1½ whole star anise, smashed lightly with the flat side of a knife
1 cup rice wine or sake
1 cup red wine
½ cup reduced-sodium chicken broth
1 pound baby carrots, or large carrots peeled and cut in half lengthwise, then into 1½-inch lengths
Salt and freshly ground black pepper to taste

FIRST Preheat the oven to 350 degrees. Cut the meat into 1½-inch cubes. On a plate or in a paper bag, mix together the flour, salt, and pepper. Coat the meat with the seasoned flour, either by rolling the pieces on a plate or dropping into the bag and shaking. Lightly squeeze the meat pieces to make the flour adhere to the surface. Discard the excess flour.

SECOND Heat a 4-quart casserole or a Dutch oven, add 1½ tablespoons of the oil, and heat until very hot. Add a batch of the beef and brown on all sides over medium-high heat. Remove from the pan with a slotted spoon and set aside. Heat the remaining oil, fry the remaining beef, and remove and set aside. Remove all but 1 tablespoon of the oil and add the garlic, onions, and star anise. Fry briefly over medium-high heat until fragrant, about 30 seconds. Add the rice wine, red wine, and chicken broth and stir to mix together. Add the beef cubes and carrots, and bring the liquid to a boil. Cover tightly and place on the middle shelf of the preheated oven. Bake about 1½ hours, stirring occasionally, or until the beef and vegetables are very tender. Taste for seasoning, adding more salt and pepper to taste, and skim any impurities from the surface. Serve with steamed rice or crusty bread.

Tender Brisket and Vegetables with Smoky Paprika

SIX TO EIGHT SERVINGS

My Great-Aunt Sophie's legendary brisket and my mother's delicious recipe were both inspirations for this dish. I like to call it an open-oven stew. I add smoked Spanish sweet paprika for a unique and memorable flavor.

INGREDIENTS

- 4 large cloves garlic, minced
- ¾ teaspoon freshly ground black pepper
- 1½ teaspoons smoked Spanish sweet paprika (also known as *pimentón*)*
- 1 teaspoon salt
- 1 4- to 5-pound flat-cut brisket, trimmed of excess fat
- 3 medium onions, peeled and sliced thinly
- 1 8-ounce can tomato sauce
- 2 cups water
- 4 medium carrots, peeled, ends trimmed, and cut crosswise into 1-inch lengths
- 1½ pounds large baking potatoes, peeled and cut into quarters or sixths

*Smoked Spanish sweet paprika (*pimentón*) comes from La Vera, Spain, and lends a distinctive flavor to chorizo, sauces, and stews. There are three varieties: sweet, bittersweet, and hot. It is sold in specialty food shops, or can be ordered online at www.thespicehouse.com.

FIRST Mix the garlic in a bowl with the pepper, smoked paprika, and salt. Rub by hand into the meat and let stand at room temperature about 30 minutes. Preheat the oven to 400 degrees.

SECOND Put the brisket in a medium-size roasting pan, fat side up. Arrange the onions around and on top. Roast about 30 minutes so that the onions are golden.

THIRD Reduce the oven temperature to 325 degrees. Pour the tomato sauce over the brisket and spread lightly. Slowly pour the water around the brisket and a little over the meat. Bake 2 hours, basting the meat two or three times with the liquid.

FOURTH Arrange the carrots and potatoes around the meat. Baste the meat and vegetables with the pan juices and sprinkle the carrots and potatoes lightly with salt. Roast 1 hour, then turn the heat up to 400 degrees. Roast another 45 minutes, or until the vegetables are very tender and golden. The brisket should also be tender when pierced with a knife. Let the brisket cool slightly before serving.

FIFTH Remove the meat to a cutting board, with the fat side up, and let cool slightly. Remove the carrots, onions, and potatoes with a slotted spoon and arrange around the edges of a serving platter or in a separate bowl. Skim the liquid, removing any fat. If the liquid is too thin, pour into a saucepan and cook uncovered over medium heat to thicken. Taste the sauce for seasoning, adding salt if necessary. With a sharp knife, carve the meat in thin slices across the grain. Arrange the slices in the center of the platter with the carrots and potatoes. Pour the sauce over the meat and vegetables, or serve on the side if preferred. (This dish can be prepared up to 2 days ahead. Cover and refrigerate. To reheat, arrange in a pan, adding a little water to the sauce if necessary. Cover with aluminum foil and heat in a 325-degree oven for 30 minutes before serving.)

§ Paprika consists of the dried, ground fruits of the mild capsicum, also known as pimento. In its mild form, it is believed to aid digestion.

Moroccan Spiced Lamb Stew

SIX TO EIGHT SERVINGS

This stew, which is traditionally served with couscous, may be made with lamb, chicken, or a combination of the two, and you can add all kinds of different vegetables, including cabbage, turnips, zucchini, eggplant, and peppers. Quick-cooking couscous, with a little broth from the stew and fresh herbs, is very good and saves an immeasurable amount of time.

INGREDIENTS

- 2 pounds lamb shoulder or breast, trimmed of fat and gristle and cut into 1½-inch cubes
- 6 medium onions, peeled and cut into quarters
- 8 cloves garlic, peeled and smashed with the flat side of a knife
- 2½ tablespoons chopped fresh ginger
- ¾ teaspoon crushed saffron threads
- 2 sticks cinnamon
- 5 cups good-quality reduced-sodium chicken broth
- 1½ pounds fennel bulbs with stalks, rinsed and trimmed, leaving ⅛ inch of the root base to hold the fennel together
- 5 carrots, peeled, cut lengthwise in half and into 2-inch lengths
- 1 14½-ounce can tomatoes, or 6 fresh tomatoes, peeled
- 1 bunch fresh cilantro, rinsed, drained, and tied together with string
- 1 15-ounce can chickpeas, blanched briefly in boiling water, refreshed in cold water, and drained thoroughly
- 1½ teaspoons salt
- ¾ teaspoon freshly ground black pepper
- 3 cups quick-cooking couscous
- ¾ cup chopped fresh cilantro leaves

FIRST Put the lamb pieces, onions, garlic, ginger, saffron, cinnamon, and chicken broth in a 5-quart casserole with a lid. Bring to a boil, reduce the heat to medium-low, and let simmer, covered, for 1 hour.

SECOND Cut each fennel bulb lengthwise in half, then cut the fennel into slices about ½ inch thick and 2 inches long. Cut the tomatoes in half, remove the seeds, and chop coarsely.

THIRD Add the carrots, fennel, tomatoes, and cilantro bundle to the lamb, stir, cover, and bring the stew again to a boil. Continue to cook over medium-low heat for 40 to 45 minutes, skimming the surface with a spoon to remove any impurities. Add the chickpeas, stir, cover, and continue cooking for about 10 minutes. Remove the cilantro bundle and discard.

FOURTH After the chickpeas have been added, prepare the couscous according to the package directions, substituting 1 cup of the lamb broth for 1 cup of the water. Fluff the cooked couscous with a fork to separate the grains, mix in the fresh cilantro, and spoon onto a platter. Ladle spoonfuls of lamb stew on top or serve separately. You may serve with bottled harissa sauce or some chile paste mixed with chopped garlic for extra flavor. If you would like to prepare your own harissa, see the recipe that follows.

Homemade Harissa

MAKES ABOUT 1 CUP

INGREDIENTS

1½ tablespoons minced garlic

1½ teaspoons hot chile paste or sambal oelek (found in Asian markets)

½   teaspoon ground cumin

¾   cup lamb broth from the stew or good-quality reduced-sodium chicken broth

¼   cup minced fresh cilantro leaves

Mix together the garlic, hot chile paste, and ground cumin in a small saucepan. Add the lamb broth and minced cilantro. Bring the mixture to a gentle boil and let simmer uncovered for about 15 minutes. Serve warm with the lamb stew. Spoon some of the sauce over the lamb stew and couscous for extra flavor.

+ *Fennel bulbs have been used as a vegetable and medicine since ancient times. Both the seeds and the bulbs aid digestion.*

Chile-Flavored Braised Halibut

SIX SERVINGS

Sichuanese chefs are justly renowned for their spicy sauces, which bombard the palate with contrasting elements of hot, sweet, salty, and sour flavors. This sauce is a perfect example, and it is excellent served with a stir-fried or steamed vegetable and rice dish.

✳ In Chinese medicine, hot chiles are used to aid digestion and to treat arthritis and rheumatism, as in Western medicine.

§ Ayurvedic doctors believe that chiles are warming to the body. They are also considered a digestive aid.

INGREDIENTS

2½ pounds halibut steaks or firm-fleshed fish fillets such as cod or haddock, skin removed

MARINADE

3   tablespoons rice wine or sake

3 or 4 slices fresh ginger, about the size of a quarter, smashed with the flat side of a knife

1½ tablespoons virgin olive oil

MINCED SEASONINGS

1½ tablespoons minced garlic

1   tablespoon minced fresh ginger

1   teaspoon hot chile paste or ½ teaspoon dried chile flakes

SAUCE (MIXED TOGETHER)

1½ cups Easiest Chicken Broth (page 79) or good-quality reduced-sodium chicken broth

2½ tablespoons soy sauce

1½ tablespoons sugar

2   teaspoons Chinese black vinegar

THICKENER (MIXED TOGETHER)

1   tablespoon cornstarch

2   tablespoons water

2   tablespoons minced scallion greens

FIRST Rinse the fish lightly and drain. Put in a bowl with the Marinade and toss lightly to coat. Cover with plastic wrap and refrigerate 20 minutes.

SECOND Heat a wok, heavy skillet with a lid, or Dutch oven. Add the oil, swirl it around the pan, and heat until very hot but not smoking. Add the Minced Seasonings and stir-fry until fragrant, about 10 seconds. Arrange the fish in the pan, and fry about 15 to 20 seconds to brown lightly. Using a spatula, flip the fish over and pour on the premixed Sauce. Partially cover and bring the liquid to a boil. Reduce the heat to medium and cook for 8 to 10 minutes, partially covered, or until the fish is just cooked.

THIRD Using a slotted spoon or spatula, transfer the fish to a large bowl or a deep platter. Slowly add the Thickener to the sauce, stirring constantly until thickened to prevent any lumps. Pour or spoon the sauce over the cooked fish and sprinkle the top with the minced scallion greens.

Coconut Shrimp with Basil and Lime Leaves

SIX SERVINGS

Taste a spoonful of this dish and your mouth will come alive with an explosion of flavors and sensations. Fresh Kaffir lime leaves may be purchased in Asian markets. If unavailable, substitute lime zest and lime juice.

INGREDIENTS

1½ pounds medium raw shrimp, peeled and deveined

SEASONINGS

- 2 dried red chile peppers, seeds removed, or 1 teaspoon dried chile flakes
- 2 ½-inch slices fresh ginger, peeled
- 6 cloves garlic, peeled
- 1½ teaspoons ground cumin
- ½ teaspoon ground turmeric

2 tablespoons virgin olive oil

1½ red onions, peeled and cut into thin julienne slices

COCONUT SAUCE (MIXED TOGETHER)

- 1½ cups light coconut milk
- 1 tablespoon light brown sugar
- 1½ teaspoons salt, or to taste

5 Kaffir lime leaves, cut into very thin slivers, or juice and chopped zest of one lime

3 tablespoons Thai holy basil or sweet basil leaves, cut into thin slivers

¾ pound snap peas or snow peas, ends trimmed, blanched for 1 minute in boiling water, refreshed in cold water, and drained

FIRST Score the shrimp lengthwise along the back, rinse, and drain thoroughly.

SECOND Drop the Seasonings in descending order into a blender or down the feed tube of a food processor while the machine is running and process to a paste. Pulse several times to get a smooth mixture.

THIRD Heat a casserole or a Dutch oven, add the oil, and heat until hot. Add the seasonings and cook over medium heat, stirring with a wooden spoon for about 3 to 4 minutes, until fragrant.

FOURTH Add the onions and toss over medium heat briefly. Cover and cook about 3 minutes, until the onions are soft. Add the Coconut Sauce and bring to a boil. Add the shrimp and lime leaves and cook for about 2½ to 3 minutes, until the shrimp turn pink and are cooked. Add the shredded basil and the snap peas or snow peas. Cook for about a minute, stirring to mix. Remove from the heat and serve with steamed basmati or jasmine rice.

+ *See "Dr. Jim Duke's Herbal Farmacy" on page 158 for the benefits of basil.*

Garlicky Seafood Cioppino

Cioppino, an Italian seafood stew that was created in San Francisco, was inspired by the Italian *zuppa di pesca* (seafood soup). My recipe has a combination of firm-fleshed fish fillets, shrimp, and scallops, but other seafoods may also be used.

INGREDIENTS

SEAFOOD MARINADE

- ½ cup rice wine or sake
- 6 slices fresh ginger, about the size of a quarter, smashed with the flat side of a knife

- 1 pound firm-fleshed fish fillets, such as haddock or red snapper, skin removed, cut into chunks about 1½ inches thick and square, rinsed and drained
- ¾ pound sea scallops, rinsed and drained
- ¾ pound medium shrimp, peeled, deveined, and cut along the back to butterfly, rinsed and drained
- 3½ tablespoons virgin olive oil

SEASONINGS

- 1½ tablespoons minced garlic
- 1 tablespoon minced fresh ginger
- 1 heaping teaspoon hot chile paste
- 2½ medium onions, peeled and chopped (about 2 cups)
- 2 medium green bell peppers, cored, seeded, ends removed, and chopped

- 1½ cups peeled, seeded, and coarsely chopped tomatoes (about 5), or 1 14½-ounce can peeled tomatoes in juice, chopped coarsely
- 1 tablespoon tomato paste
- 2⅔ cups clam juice (2 bottles) or fish stock
- 1 cup rice wine or sake
- 2 tablespoons chopped fresh basil leaves
- 1 teaspoon dried oregano
- 1½ teaspoons salt
- ¼ teaspoon freshly ground black pepper

FIRST Put the fish and scallops with the shrimp into two separate bowls. Pour a third of the marinade into the fish bowl and the remainder into the scallops and shrimp. Toss lightly and let sit 10 minutes.

SECOND Heat the oil until hot in a 6-quart casserole or a Dutch oven, add the Seasonings and sauté about 6 to 7 minutes over medium heat, stirring occasionally, until the onions and peppers are tender. Add the remaining ingredients (except the seafood) and bring to a boil. Reduce the heat to low and simmer uncovered for about 12 to 15 minutes.

THIRD Add the fish with its marinade to the tomato-pepper mixture, stir to mix, partially cover, and cook for about 7 to 8 minutes, or until the fish is almost cooked. Add the shrimp and scallops with the marinade, stir gently, partially cover, and cook for about 4 minutes, or until the seafood is cooked. Taste for seasoning, adding more salt if necessary. Ladle into bowls and serve with a salad or cooked vegetable and crusty bread.

+ *Tomatoes* *are one of the top foods in the "Seven Colors of Health" chart on page 199.*

Spicy Salmon Curry

SIX TO EIGHT SERVINGS

According to Camellia Panjabi, author of *The Great Curries of India*, "curry," as the word is used in India, simply means gravy. The origin of the word, from *kaari*, is a meat, vegetable, or seafood dish especially suited to (but not always eaten with) rice. This aromatic sauce, with its unique blending of myriad flavors, is quite different from the typical overpowering curry sauce. Other types of seafood, including shrimp, scallops, or other firm-fleshed fish fillets, may be used in place of the salmon.

§ *Ayurveda cautions against eating too many tomatoes, believing that they can be toxic to the body, but it also considers them to be healing when cooked with certain spices. Tomato juice with cumin is recommended for improving digestion.*

INGREDIENTS

SEASONINGS

2   small bird's-eye chiles, ends trimmed and seeds removed*

1   small jalapeño chile, ends trimmed and seeds removed

3   stalks lemongrass, ends trimmed to tender heart and tough outer stalks removed, cut into chunks[†]

8   cloves garlic

1   2-inch length fresh ginger, peeled and cut into small pieces

1   tablespoon ground cumin

1   tablespoon ground coriander

2½ tablespoons virgin olive oil

2   medium onions, peeled and chopped coarsely (about 2 cups)

1   28-ounce can whole tomatoes, seeded and diced, with juice (about 2 cups)

¼   cup unsweetened coconut milk

1½ tablespoons firmly packed light brown sugar

2   pounds salmon fillets, skin removed, cut into 2-inch-wide sections

2   cups fresh peas or thawed frozen peas

1½ teaspoons salt, or to taste

1   teaspoon tamarind pulp dissolved in 2 tablespoons warm water, seeds removed[‡]

3   tablespoons freshly squeezed lemon juice (juice of 1 medium lemon)

*If unavailable, substitute 1½ teaspoons dried chile flakes or to taste.
[†]Fresh lemongrass is available at most Asian markets. You may use dried, but first reconstitute by softening in boiling water to cover for 20 minutes.

[‡]If tamarind pulp is unavailable, use freshly squeezed lime juice or cider vinegar to taste.

FIRST Prepare the Seasonings by dropping the ingredients in descending order down the feed tube of a food processor, or into a blender, with the machine running. Pulse and scrape down the sides of the work bowl with a spatula until you have a rough but even texture. If the lemongrass remains in large pieces, carefully scrape the seasonings onto a cutting board and chop by hand.

SECOND Heat a heavy wok or a Dutch oven or large casserole over medium-low heat until very hot but not smoking. Add the oil and heat until very hot, about 20 seconds. Add the seasonings and stir-fry over medium heat, stirring constantly with a wooden spoon, for 3 to 4 minutes, until very fragrant.

THIRD Add the chopped onions and stir, then cover and cook, stirring occasionally, for about 4 minutes, until soft and translucent. Add the tomatoes, coconut milk, and sugar, and cook, partially covered, for 5 to 7 minutes. Add the salmon, peas, salt, tamarind, and lemon juice, stir together, and cover. Cook until the fish turns opaque and a knife passes through easily, about 6 to 7 minutes. Taste for seasoning and serve on a platter or in serving bowls. Serve with steamed jasmine or basmati rice.

Lucia Douglas
North African / Mediterranean
Spices and Meditation

My dear friend Lucia Douglas is an inspiration to me in the way she lives and cooks. Although Lucia is French, she grew up in Morocco and divides her time between Cassis, France, and Malibu, California. The influence of these places is readily apparent in the way she effortlessly puts together a sumptuous meal of several small dishes or *mezze,* as they are called in the Middle East, that are delicious as well as health-giving.

For Lucia cooking is a form of meditation. "Meditation involves getting connected with yourself," she says as I watch her in her kitchen in the picturesque town of Cassis in southern France. "When I cook, I look at the vibrant colors, I smell the fragrant aromas, and I concentrate on the dish, as if on a mantra."

Her unique food reflects her colorful background. Lucia's natural parents were Italian and her stepfather was Portuguese. She grew up in Morocco, but spent her summers in Spain and Portugal. At the age of seventeen she went to school in Paris, where she lived until the early seventies, when she married and moved to Malibu.

About twenty-five years ago, she began studying Ayurveda, the science of life traditionally practiced by Indian doctors, and she has incorporated these different influences into her own way of life. Her day usually begins with at least ten minutes of breathing exercises to calm the body. Then she meditates, an exercise that focuses and rejuvenates her energy. Several times a week she performs a routine of yoga exercises that keeps her body flexible and her mind balanced.

Spices figure prominently in her cooking, for flavoring as well as for their health-giving attributes. "I grew up surrounded by fabulous spices," she explains. "In Morocco, we have a spice mixture called *ras el hanut,* which is used with meat, couscous, or rice. Each cook has their own recipe, and it may have up to twenty different seasonings, including ginger, turmeric, cinnamon, cardamom, allspice, and galangal."

At fifteen, Lucia could identify by smell or taste each vendor's spice mix in the market. Years later, when she studied Ayurveda, she learned that spices can also be used to balance a dish in terms of its effect on the body.

"You play with the flavors of the food," she says, "mingling sweet with savory, sour with salty, and mild with spicy."

- Let the **MARKET BE THE INSPIRATION** for your meals and don't be afraid to improvise. My husband says that I never cook a dish the same way twice. If the cilantro looks very pretty, I will use a lot of that. If the fresh mint catches my eye, I'll throw that in too. Don't be too rigid; relax and enjoy.

- Your body **NEEDS DIFFERENT FOODS**, depending on the season. If it's winter, when your body is coolish, serve soups and warming foods. In summer, when your body is hot, prepare salads, vegetables, and cooling foods.

- Spices have a **LIMITED SHELF LIFE**. I like to replenish mine every two or three months. Smell them and replace them if they are very old and no longer pungent.

- Try to serve a **DIFFERENT WHOLE GRAIN** with each meal. We eat a lot of couscous, kasha, barley, and rice.

- To be a good cook and **SERVE A GREAT MEAL TO FRIENDS** is very gratifying. Whatever you do, if you do the best you can, the results will surely give you pleasure. There is nothing better than feeling the contentment of your family and friends when you have prepared a delicious and satisfying meal.

Since she was raised on Middle Eastern *mezze* and Spanish tapas, she prefers a meal of small dishes (even for everyday meals) so that those gathered around the table can taste everything informally and eat what they like. The food should be simple, she says, and the flavors must be complementary. Furthermore, she adds, "if you prepare food with six tastes—sweet, sour, salty, spicy, astringent, and bitter—as the Ayurvedic teachings suggest, then your guests will be satisfied and never go hungry."

Lucia's Cooked Pepper and Tomato Relish

FOUR SERVINGS

Lucia likes to serve this vibrantly flavored relish as a condiment for fish or meat. It can be made year-round, but is especially good in the fall, when tomatoes and peppers are at their peak.

INGREDIENTS

3	medium green bell peppers
2	medium red bell peppers
10	plum or 8 vine-ripened tomatoes (about 2 pounds)
1	tablespoon canola or peanut oil
6	cloves garlic, peeled and thinly sliced
1	teaspoon salt, or to taste
¼	teaspoon freshly ground black pepper

FIRST To roast the peppers, prepare a fire for grilling or preheat the broiler. Arrange the whole peppers about 3 inches from the source of heat and roast on all sides, turning occasionally, until blackened. Place in a paper bag and close the bag securely, or wrap tightly in newspaper, and let the peppers steam until cool, about 15 minutes.

SECOND Using a sharp knife, scrape off the skin from the peppers and cut them lengthwise in half. Remove and discard the seeds and cut lengthwise into thin julienne strips.

THIRD Using a sharp knife, core the tomatoes and cut a light X through the skin in the opposite end. Place the tomatoes in a large bowl and pour boiling water over them to cover. Let sit for 5 minutes, then peel away the skin. Cut in half horizontally and scoop out the seeds with a chopstick or your fingers. Cut into ¼-inch dice.

FOURTH Heat a heavy skillet or pot with a lid, pour in the oil, and heat until hot over medium heat. Add the garlic and sauté lightly for 15 seconds, then add the peppers and tomatoes. Stir with a wooden spoon, cover, and cook over medium-low heat until the vegetables are tender, about 20 to 25 minutes. Add the salt and pepper, uncover, and continue cooking until the liquid evaporates and the vegetables are very soft, about 15 to 20 minutes. Spoon the vegetables into a bowl or onto a plate and let cool. Season with more salt if necessary. Serve at room temperature or chilled.

Lucia's Moroccan Sweet and Sour Carrots

FOUR SERVINGS

Lucia makes these delicious carrots as a side dish with meals, but they are so popular, I've started serving them as an hors d'oeuvre with drinks.

INGREDIENTS

5   medium carrots or 1 package baby carrots (about 1 pound)

3   cloves garlic, peeled and cut in half

1   teaspoon salt

DRESSING

1   teaspoon Hungarian sweet paprika

1   tablespoon ground cumin

2   tablespoons good-quality red wine vinegar

2   tablespoons canola or peanut oil

2   tablespoons chopped fresh parsley

FIRST If not using the baby carrots, peel the larger carrots, trim the ends, and cut into sticks about 1½ inches long and ¼ inch thick. Place the sticks or baby carrots in a saucepan with the garlic, salt, and water to cover. Bring to a boil, cover, reduce the heat to medium, and cook the carrots until very tender, about 15 to 20 minutes. Drain off the cooking water, retaining the garlic.

SECOND Scoop the carrots into a bowl. Mash the garlic with a fork or the back of a spoon and add it along with the ingredients of the Dressing to the carrots. Toss lightly, tasting for seasoning and adding more salt if necessary. Let sit until cooled and serve at room temperature or chilled.

Lucia's Baked Moroccan Chicken

FOUR TO SIX SERVINGS

Once baked in the oven, the garlic-cilantro marinade blends with the juices of the chicken to create an exquisite sauce. Lucia likes to cook the chicken until the skin is very crisp and the meat is tender. She likes to serve the chicken with couscous and one or two vegetable dishes.

INGREDIENTS

1   whole roasting chicken, about 3½ pounds, trimmed of fat and cut into 8 serving pieces (2 drumsticks, 2 thighs, 2 wings, and 2 breast halves)

MARINADE

- 4   cloves garlic, peeled
- 1¼ cups fresh cilantro leaves, rinsed and drained
- ¾   cup fresh parsley leaves, rinsed and drained
- ⅓   cup freshly squeezed lemon juice
- 1   teaspoon salt, or to taste
- ¼   teaspoon freshly ground black pepper

FIRST Rinse the chicken and drain. Pat dry, and put the pieces in a mixing bowl.

SECOND Drop the garlic cloves through the feed tube of a food processor fitted with a steel blade while the machine is running, and chop finely. Add the cilantro and parsley and continue to chop finely. Once the herbs are a coarse paste, add the lemon juice, salt, and pepper, then pulse to mix. Spoon the Marinade over the chicken, toss lightly to coat, then arrange skin side up in an ovenproof pan. Cover securely with aluminum foil, and let sit 1 to 2 hours in the refrigerator.

THIRD Preheat the oven to 350 degrees. Bake the chicken for about 1 hour, covered, turning over twice so that the skin side is up again. Increase the oven heat to 375 degrees and continue baking for 30 to 45 minutes, until the skin is very crisp and golden brown. Skim off any excess fat from the liquid using a spoon. Remove from the oven and serve from the pan, spooning the juices over the cooked chicken.

Lucia's Fish with Moroccan Spices

FOUR SERVINGS

The fresh and pungent flavor of this colorful sauce is a superb complement to the sweet flavor of fresh fish. Use a firm, meaty fillet for the best results.

INGREDIENTS

1   pound firm white fish, such as halibut steaks or sea bass fillets, without skin

FISH MARINADE

2 or 3 cloves garlic, peeled

1   cup fresh cilantro leaves, rinsed and drained

½   cup fresh parsley leaves, rinsed and drained

2   teaspoons Hungarian sweet paprika

½   tablespoon ground cumin

1   cup water

1   tablespoon canola or peanut oil

1½ medium white onions, peeled, and cut into sixths

5 or 6 plum or small vine-ripened tomatoes, peeled, seeded, and cut into sixths (see page 124 for how to peel tomatoes)

1½ teaspoons salt, or to taste

¼   teaspoon freshly ground black pepper

2 to 3 tablespoons freshly squeezed lemon juice

FIRST Rinse the fish, drain, and place in an ovenproof gratin dish, pie plate, or quiche pan.

SECOND Using a food processor fitted with a steel blade, drop the garlic cloves down through the feed tube while the machine is on. Chop finely. Add the cilantro, parsley, paprika, and cumin, and continue chopping to a paste. Pour in the water and oil and process until smooth. Spread the mixture evenly over the surface of the fish and let sit for 1 hour at room temperature, or for several hours in the refrigerator.

THIRD Preheat the oven to 375 degrees. Using the food processor, pulse to chop the onions finely, then add the tomatoes and continue pulsing to a coarse paste. Season with the salt and pepper. With a spatula or a spoon, scoop the mixture out and spread around the fish.

FOURTH Bake the fish for about 17 to 20 minutes (depending on the thickness), or until the fish flakes when prodded with a knife. Remove from the oven and squeeze the lemon juice on top. Serve hot with an herbal couscous or rice.

Lucia's Easy Herbal Couscous

FOUR SERVINGS

Lucia enhances the flavor of fast-cooking couscous with the addition of chopped fresh cilantro and fruity virgin olive oil.

INGREDIENTS

- 3 cups water (or amount indicated on the couscous package)
- 1½ cups quick-cooking couscous
- 1 tablespoon fruity virgin olive oil
- 1 teaspoon salt
- 3 tablespoons finely chopped fresh cilantro leaves

FIRST In a heavy saucepan with a lid, bring the water to a rapid boil. Add the couscous and cook for 1 minute, stirring with a spoon or a fork. (If the cooking instructions on the label are very different, follow them instead.)

SECOND Add the olive oil, salt, and cilantro, and stir with a fork to mix. Cover and remove from the heat. Let the couscous sit for about 10 minutes, until the grains are plump and have absorbed all the water. Stir again with a fork and serve warm.

Lucia's Poached Pears with Cinnamon and Prunes

Surprisingly, no sugar is needed in this recipe. The vanilla bean, lemon peel, and prunes add a delightful natural sweetness to the dish.

INGREDIENTS

2 or 3 slightly underripe Anjou pears

10   prunes

1   stick cinnamon

3   cloves

2   strips lemon peel

1   vanilla bean

1¼ cups water

Ground cinnamon for garnish

FIRST Peel the pears with a vegetable peeler or a paring knife. Place in a heavy pot and add the remaining ingredients, except the ground cinnamon.

SECOND Cover tightly and bring the water to a boil. Reduce the heat to low, and cook for about 20 minutes, or until tender. You may test for doneness by piercing a knife through the center of the pears. If it passes through easily, they are cooked. Spoon into serving bowls and sprinkle with the ground cinnamon. Serve warm, at room temperature, or chilled.

main-dish salads

Most people assume, since I have written books about Asian cooking, that our family meals are elaborate productions full of exotic ingredients. But if you were to look through my keyhole, you'd be surprised at how simple and diverse our dinners are. Like many working mothers, I have to consider convenience and time in determining what we are going to eat.

Main-dish salads are a good answer—especially, but not exclusively, in warm weather. I'll vary the ingredients depending on what I happen to have on hand in my pantry and refrigerator. Leftovers can find a new life in salads, and they're satisfying as well as health-giving.

For two years recently I lived in Europe and was exposed to some wonderful Mediterranean food—vibrantly colored platters heaped with grilled and roasted seasonal vegetables, cooked seafood, and meats, all dressed with light, herbal sauces. It inspired me to make such dishes at home for my own family.

I also continue to discover appealing Asian salads on my forays to Thailand, Vietnam, and China, multilayered creations stacked with seafood and meat and crisp sliced vegetables, dusted with fresh herbs, and doused with a hot, sour, and sweet dressing. The flavors and textures collide in your mouth in an exciting burst of sensations. I find the fresh lime- and lemon-based dressings rounded out with garlic, fish sauce, and sugar nicely refreshing, and the more voluptuous sauces, with a peanut or sesame butter base, are equally appealing, especially when contrasted with crisp sliced vegetables.

Main-dish salads demand great ingredients—the best olive oil, ripest tomatoes, and freshest seafood. While these dishes invite spontaneity, they

Chapter opener:
Vietnamese Shrimp
and Fennel Salad

often can be made in advance. I like to mix and match different cooking techniques within one dish for contrasting flavors and textures: Fresh fish or seafood may be grilled or roasted, while vegetables are raw, blanched, or steamed.

Since I often grill or poach extra meat or seafood to have on hand for a salad, I can throw one together rather quickly. And I usually make large batches of dressings to keep in the refrigerator. I often sprinkle fresh herbs on top to complete the visual effect. And as you'll notice from "Dr. Jim Duke's Herbal Farmacy" on page 158, the herbs and spices (as well as the vegetables) provide not just flavor but also a wealth of health-giving and healing properties.

Roasted Tomato Spinach Salad

SIX SERVINGS

Roasting tomatoes really brings out their sweet flavor and the juice provides a flavorful base for this dressing. You can prepare the spinach salad as is or make it more substantial by adding vegetables.

+ See "Seven Colors of Health" chart on page 199 for benefits of tomatoes.

+ **Basil** aids digestion and eases gas. For other health-giving properties, see "Dr. Jim Duke's Herbal Farmacy" on page 158.

INGREDIENTS

12   large tomatoes (about 3½ pounds), preferably vine-ripened

1½ tablespoons minced garlic

1   teaspoon dried chile flakes, or to taste

5 to 6 tablespoons extra-virgin olive oil

About 1 heaping cup large fresh basil leaves, rinsed and drained

1¼ teaspoons salt, or to taste

½   teaspoon freshly ground black pepper

3½ tablespoons balsamic vinegar

1¼ pounds spinach, stems removed, rinsed and spun dry

½   pound feta cheese, crumbled into bits

FIRST Preheat the oven to 425 degrees. Make a small X in the top of each tomato and put in a bowl. Pour boiling water on top to cover, and let stand for 10 minutes, then peel. Cut the tomatoes crosswise in half and scoop out the seeds. Arrange the tomatoes cut side up in a roasting or lasagna pan.

SECOND Sprinkle the minced garlic and chile flakes on top, then sprinkle with half the olive oil. Rip the basil leaves into bits and sprinkle on top, with salt and black pepper. Bake for 50 minutes, remove, and let cool slightly, draining off the liquid into a bowl. Cut the tomatoes into bite-size pieces.

THIRD To make the dressing, pour the balsamic vinegar into the bowl with the baked tomato juice. Slowly add the remaining olive oil while whisking constantly. Taste for seasoning, adjusting if necessary, and pour the dressing into a serving container.

FOURTH Arrange the spinach in a large bowl. Sprinkle the roasted tomatoes on top. Sprinkle the feta cheese bits on top of the salad. Serve with the tomato dressing and crusty bread.

Italian Tuna Salad

SIX SERVINGS

This salad is very simple and quintessentially Italian, so the best ingredients, especially top-quality olive oil, are essential.

INGREDIENTS

- 4 red bell peppers
- 1 19-ounce can cannellini beans, or other type of white beans
- 1 6-ounce can solid-pack tuna, drained
- ⅔ pound mesclun mix (mixed baby greens), rinsed and spun dry
- 1 ounce slivers of freshly grated Parmigiano-Reggiano cheese, or more if desired

SIMPLE VINAIGRETTE

- 2 cloves garlic, minced finely
- 1 teaspoon Dijon mustard
- 2½ tablespoons red wine vinegar
- 8 tablespoons extra virgin olive oil
- 1 teaspoon salt, or to taste
- ⅓ teaspoon freshly ground black pepper

FIRST To roast the peppers, prepare a fire for grilling or preheat a broiler. See Lucia's Cooked Pepper and Tomato Relish (page 124) for roasting and peeling peppers.

SECOND Cut the peeled peppers lengthwise in half. Remove and discard the seeds and cut lengthwise into thin julienne strips. Drain the cannellini beans, blanch in boiling water to cover for 15 seconds, refresh in cold water, and drain thoroughly.

THIRD Break up the tuna with a fork into bite-size pieces. Arrange the mesclun greens in a salad bowl or on a deep round platter. Sprinkle the beans evenly over the greens, then sprinkle the strips of roasted peppers, the tuna, and the cheese slivers on top.

FOURTH Prepare the Vinaigrette by whisking together in a bowl the garlic, mustard, and wine vinegar. Slowly add the oil in a thin stream, whisking vigorously, until the mixture begins to thicken. Add the salt and pepper, whisk lightly, and adjust the seasonings. Drizzle the dressing on top and serve at room temperature or chilled with crusty bread.

+ *Cannellini beans and other beans (legumes), dried and fresh, are rich in soluble fiber. They help lower cholesterol levels, thereby preventing heart disease, and they stabilize blood sugar levels.*

Gado Gado (Indonesian Salad) with Spicy Peanut Dressing

SIX TO EIGHT SERVINGS

Gado Gado is a sumptuous Indonesian salad that usually contains many different types of foods, including tofu, cabbage, string beans, cauliflower, tomatoes, eggs, and potatoes. Prepare the coconut-peanut dressing in advance and heat it until warm before serving. It will keep refrigerated for weeks.

INGREDIENTS

- ½ pound firm tofu, cut through the thickness into ½-inch-thick slices
- 1 pound string beans or snap peas, ends trimmed, and, if long, cut on the diagonal in half
- ½ pound baby carrots
- 1 pound baby white or red potatoes, scrubbed lightly to remove any dirt
- 1 head cauliflower (about 1 pound), stems trimmed, cut into florets
- 3 tablespoons virgin olive oil
- 1 head Boston lettuce, core trimmed, leaves separated, rinsed, and spun dry
- ½ pound bean sprouts, rinsed and drained

INDONESIAN PEANUT DRESSING

- 1½ small fresh red Thai chiles, ends trimmed, seeds removed, or 1½ teaspoons dried red chile flakes
- 4 shallots, peeled
- 3 cloves garlic, peeled
- ¾ cup crunchy peanut butter
- 1 cup light unsweetened coconut milk
- 2 tablespoons firmly packed brown sugar
- 2 tablespoons fish sauce
- 1 tablespoon soy sauce
- 2 teaspoons tamarind pulp, dissolved in ½ cup water*

*Alternatively, you may use 3 tablespoons freshly squeezed lemon juice with ½ cup water.

FIRST Wrap the tofu slices in paper towels or a cotton towel and place a heavy weight, such as a cast-iron skillet, on top. Let stand for 30 minutes to press out the excess water.

SECOND Bring 3 quarts water to a boil in a large pot and separately cook the string beans (about 6 minutes; if using snap peas, just blanch for 20 seconds), carrots (about 5 to 6 minutes), potatoes (12 to 14 minutes), and cauliflower (about 8 to 10 minutes) until just tender, refreshing each vegetable under cold running water once it is cooked and draining thoroughly. Cut the potatoes (with the skins on) into halves or quarters, depending on the size.

THIRD Heat a heavy skillet until hot (about 10 seconds), add the olive oil, and heat to about 375 degrees. Fry the tofu in several batches until golden brown, turning several times to brown on all sides. Remove with a slotted spoon and drain on paper towels. Cut the tofu into matchstick-size pieces about 1½ inches long and ¼ inch thick.

FOURTH Arrange the lettuce leaves in overlapping layers to cover the bottom of a large platter. Arrange the potato pieces and the cauliflower florets over the lettuce leaves, then sprinkle the green beans, baby carrots, tofu pieces, and bean sprouts on top.

FIFTH To prepare the Peanut Dressing: Use a food processor fitted with a steel blade, or a blender, and drop the chiles, shallots, and garlic down the feed tube while the machine is running and chop finely. Add the remaining ingredients one at a time, pulsing after each addition. Pour the dressing into a saucepan and cook over low heat, stirring, for about 2 minutes. Turn off the heat and let sit for a minute to let the flavors marry. Pour the warm dressing into a serving container and serve warm on the side with the vegetables. Once cool, the dressing will keep, tightly covered, in the refrigerator for several weeks.

✳ Asian doctors believe that peanuts lubricate the intestines and harmonize the stomach. They also are credited with increasing the milk supply in nursing mothers.

My Salade Niçoise

My Salade Niçoise is a casual affair in which I often add other seasonal vegetables that may be in the market or in my refrigerator. I also like to mix greens with fresh herbs and flat parsley leaves for a base. I tend to be generous, making enough for dinner and lunch the following day.

INGREDIENTS

1   head Boston lettuce, leaves separated, rinsed, and spun dry

1½ cups flat parsley leaves, rinsed, drained, and spun dry

3   red bell peppers, roasted as directed on page 124

1½ pounds green beans

2   pounds baby new potatoes

5   medium free-range organic eggs, hard-cooked and peeled

1   6-ounce can solid-pack tuna, drained

1   cup pitted black olives

GARLIC VINAIGRETTE

4   cloves garlic, peeled and lightly smashed with the flat side of a knife

1¼ teaspoons Dijon mustard

½   cup good-quality balsamic vinegar

1¾ cups extra virgin olive oil

1¼ teaspoons salt

¼   teaspoon freshly ground black pepper

FIRST To make the Garlic Vinaigrette, drop the garlic cloves down the feed tube of a food processor fitted with a steel blade while the machine is running. Mince finely. Open the lid and add the mustard and vinegar. Pulse to blend, then slowly pour the olive oil down the feed tube in a thin stream with the machine running. The dressing should become thick and creamy. Add salt and pepper, taste, and adjust the seasoning if necessary.

SECOND Trim the stem end of the lettuce, and rip the leaves into big pieces. Toss with the flat parsley, and arrange the greens in the bottom of a large bowl or platter. Cut the roasted peppers into thin strips.

THIRD Bring 1½ quarts water to a boil in a pot. Add the green beans and cook over medium heat until crisp-tender, about 6 minutes. Scoop out with a strainer and refresh in cold water. Drain thoroughly, put in a bowl, and drizzle some of the dressing in, tossing lightly to coat. Add the potatoes to the water and bring to a boil. Cook for about 12 to 14 minutes, drain, refresh in cold water briefly, and cut any large ones in half. Place in a bowl and drizzle some of the dressing on top while still warm, tossing lightly to coat.

FOURTH To assemble the salad, arrange the green beans and potatoes in separate piles or concentric circles over the lettuce. Cut the hard-cooked eggs into thin wedges and arrange them around the beans and potatoes. Break the tuna into bite-size clumps and sprinkle over the beans and potatoes. Sprinkle the roasted peppers and the olives on top and drizzle with a little more dressing, serving any remaining in a bowl on the side. Serve with crusty bread.

+ See the "yellow/ green" category of the "Seven Colors of Health" chart on page 199 for the health-giving properties of green beans.

Five-Treasure Seafood Rice Salad with Basil Dressing

SIX TO EIGHT SERVINGS

Everyone is making pasta salads these days; we seem to have forgotten that rice is an equally versatile medium for a main-dish salad. I often make extra rice when I'm cooking it for dinner. I like to mix and match cooked seafood, meat, and vegetables, adding whatever is in season and varying the fresh herbs to complement the ingredients.

INGREDIENTS

- 1 pound cooked shrimp, peeled and deveined
- ½ pound snap peas, ends snapped and veiny string removed
- ½ small red onion, peeled and finely diced
- 1 yellow, orange, or red bell pepper, cored, seeded, and cut into small dice
- 1 tablespoon minced lemon zest
- 4 cups cold cooked basmati or jasmine rice (about 1½ cups uncooked rice; see page 300)

FRESH BASIL DRESSING

- 1½ tablespoons minced garlic
- 3 tablespoons balsamic vinegar
- 4 tablespoons freshly squeezed lemon juice
- 6 tablespoons extra virgin olive oil
- 1¼ teaspoons salt, or to taste
- ¼ teaspoon freshly ground black pepper
- 2½ tablespoons chopped fresh basil leaves

- 2 cups shredded lettuce leaves or baby spinach for serving (optional)

FIRST Holding a knife or cleaver horizontal with the cutting board, butterfly the shrimp, cutting them in half through the thickness.

SECOND Bring 2 quarts of water to a boil in a pot and add the snap peas. Partially cook for 1½ minutes and drain in a colander. Refresh in cold water, drain thoroughly, and blot dry.

THIRD Put the cooked shrimp, snap peas, red onion, bell pepper, lemon zest, and rice in a large mixing bowl and set aside while preparing the dressing.

FOURTH Prepare the Fresh Basil Dressing by whisking together in a mixing bowl the minced garlic, vinegar, and lemon juice. Slowly pour in the olive oil in a thin stream, whisking vigorously. Add the salt, pepper, and basil and whisk again.

FIFTH Drizzle the basil dressing over the shrimp, vegetables, and rice, tossing lightly. Taste for seasoning, adding salt, pepper, or lemon juice as needed, and toss lightly. Arrange the shredded lettuce or spinach leaves on the bottom of a platter, if using, and spoon the rice salad on top. Serve at room temperature or chilled.

+ *Basil aids digestion and soothes upset stomachs. Steep 1 to 2 teaspoons of dried basil or 2 tablespoons of fresh in 1 cup of hot water for 5 minutes. Strain and drink. See "Dr. Jim Duke's Herbal Farmacy" on page 158 for more health-giving properties.*

Vietnamese Shrimp and Fennel Salad

Shrimp and shaved fresh fennel, with its anisey flavor, are a unique combination that is nicely complemented by the sweet and sour fresh lime dressing. If fennel is unavailable, substitute 1 pound blanched snow peas, sliced in half lengthwise.

INGREDIENTS

- 1 pound raw medium shrimp, peeled and deveined
- 2 tablespoons rice wine or sake (optional)
- 2 pounds fennel bulbs, stalks and root base trimmed, leaving ⅛ inch of the stem to hold the fennel together
- ⅓ pound thin rice stick noodles, softened in hot water and drained
- 3 cups grated carrots
- 5 to 6 tablespoons coarsely chopped fresh cilantro leaves
- ¼ cup finely chopped scallion greens
- 3 tablespoons coarsely chopped fresh basil leaves

SWEET AND SOUR DRESSING

- 1¼ teaspoons dried chile flakes
- Juice of 4 to 5 limes or 2½ lemons (about ⅔ cup)
- ⅓ cup fish sauce, or more to taste
- ⅓ cup sugar
- 1½ tablespoons minced garlic

FIRST Using a sharp knife, slice the shrimp lengthwise along the back in half. Bring 4 cups of water and the rice wine, if using, to a boil, add the shrimp, and cook about 1½ minutes after the water reaches a boil, or until the shrimp are opaque. Drain in a colander and rinse under cold running water. Drain again.

SECOND Holding each fennel bulb securely, cut lengthwise in half, then cut into slices about ¼ inch thick and 1½ inches long.

THIRD In a large stockpot, heat 2 quarts of water until boiling. Add the softened rice stick noodles and swirl in the hot water. Cook for 10 seconds, or until just tender. Remove with a strainer or a slotted spoon and drain thoroughly in a colander. Rinse under cold running water. Drain thoroughly and arrange on a deep serving platter.

FOURTH Bring the water back to a boil. Add the fennel slices and cook about 6 to 7 minutes, until crisp-tender. Drain, refresh under cold running water, and drain again thoroughly. Arrange the fennel slices over the noodles and sprinkle the carrots on top, leaving a slight indentation in the center. Arrange the shrimp in the center. Sprinkle the cilantro, scallion greens, and basil on top.

FIFTH Soak the dried chile flakes in the lime juice for 2 to 3 minutes in a medium bowl. Add the remaining Dressing ingredients, and stir to dissolve the sugar. Spoon the dressing onto the salad or serve on the side. Eat at room temperature or chilled.

+ *Fresh **fennel** is rich with the phytonutrient limonene, which may help prevent certain types of cancer.*

✳ § *Coriander seed and fresh cilantro aid digestion, remove heat from the body, and serve as diuretics. For further information, see "Key to Primary Indian Spices" on page 288.*

Shrimp, Avocado, and Wild Greens with a Charred Tomato Dressing

SIX SERVINGS

Grilling expert Chris Schlesinger, who with John Willoughby has written numerous books on the subject, is the owner of the East Coast Grill in Cambridge, Massachusetts, and a great cook. This recipe, from their *Lettuce in Your Kitchen,* inspired this dish. The surprisingly creamy dressing uses broiled tomatoes as a base, but the lime juice and cilantro enhance its fresh flavor.

INGREDIENTS

CHARRED TOMATO DRESSING

3	medium tomatoes, cored and cut into slices about 1 inch thick
¼	cup plus 2 tablespoons virgin olive oil
2	cloves garlic, smashed with the flat side of a knife and peeled
⅓	cup freshly squeezed lime juice or red wine vinegar
2	teaspoons ground cumin, toasted until fragrant in a dry pan
1	teaspoon salt
¼	teaspoon freshly ground black pepper
	¼ to ½ cup chopped cilantro leaves, rinsed and drained

5	cups mesclun mix or greens of choice, rinsed and spun dry, arranged in a serving bowl
1½	pounds cooked medium shrimp, peeled and deveined
1	avocado, peeled, pitted, and cut into thin slices
3	tablespoons minced red onion for garnish (optional)

FIRST Arrange the tomato slices on a baking sheet. Brush liberally with the 2 tablespoons of olive oil. Broil the tomatoes about 10 minutes on each side and remove.

SECOND Drop the garlic down the feed tube of a food processor fitted with a steel blade while the machine is running. Pulse until it is finely chopped, then drop in the tomatoes and puree, leaving some chunks. While the motor is running, add the lime juice or vinegar and ¼ cup olive oil in a thin, steady stream. Add the cumin, salt, pepper, and chopped cilantro, pulse briefly, then taste for seasoning, adjusting if necessary.

THIRD Arrange the shrimp, then the avocado slices, on top of the greens. Pour some of the Dressing over and put the rest into a sauce bowl. Sprinkle the minced red onion on top, if using, and serve at room temperature.

Grilled Seafood Pasta Salad with Cilantro Vinaigrette

SIX SERVINGS

This "stir-fry" pasta salad has infinite variations. You can simplify the recipe by using only shrimp or scallops, and you may substitute another vegetable for the asparagus, such as broccoli, snap peas, or green beans. I like to serve it warm, but it's equally appealing served at room temperature or chilled.

INGREDIENTS

- ¾ pound raw medium shrimp, peeled and deveined
- ¾ pound sea scallops, rinsed, drained, and sliced in half through the thickness

SEAFOOD MARINADE

- 3 tablespoons soy sauce
- 1½ teaspoons toasted sesame oil
- ½ cup rice wine or sake
- 3 tablespoons peeled and minced fresh ginger

- 20 10-inch bamboo or metal skewers (bamboo soaked in cold water to cover for 1 hour)
- 1½ pounds asparagus, tough woody ends snapped off, peeled if necessary
- ½ pound fusilli (corkscrew pasta)
- 2 teaspoons virgin olive oil
- ¼ cup minced scallions, white part only
- 2 tablespoons rice wine or sake

FRESH CILANTRO VINAIGRETTE (MIXED TOGETHER)

- ⅓ cup soy sauce
- ¼ cup Japanese clear rice vinegar
- 2½ tablespoons toasted sesame oil
- ¼ cup freshly squeezed lemon juice, or to taste
- 1½ tablespoons sugar
- 1 teaspoon salt
- 5 tablespoons chopped fresh cilantro leaves

FIRST Score the shrimp along the back. Put the shrimp and scallops in separate bowls, pour half the Marinade into each bowl, toss lightly, and let sit for 20 minutes. Thread the shrimp and scallops separately onto the skewers, leaving about 1 inch on each end.

SECOND Cut the asparagus on the diagonal into 1½-inch lengths.

THIRD Bring 3 quarts of water to a boil in a large pot, drop in the fusilli, stir, and cook about 9 to 11 minutes, until al dente (or check package for cooking time). Drain the fusilli in a colander and rinse under warm water to remove the starch. Drain again and set aside.

FOURTH Prepare a medium-hot fire for grilling or preheat the broiler. Place the seafood about 3 inches from the source of heat and grill or broil about 4 to 5 minutes on each side, until the seafood is cooked. Remove from the heat and let cool slightly, then take the seafood off the skewers and set aside.

FIFTH Heat a wok or heavy skillet, add the oil, and heat until hot, about 10 seconds. Add the scallions and stir-fry 15 seconds, until fragrant. Add the asparagus and toss lightly over medium heat. Add the rice wine and 2 tablespoons of water, cover, and cook for about 5 to 7 minutes, until just tender, over medium heat, stirring occasionally.

SIXTH Add the cooked fusilli and seafood and pour the Cilantro Vinaigrette over. Toss lightly over high heat to coat. Scoop out into a bowl or onto a platter and serve warm, at room temperature, or chilled.

+ *Asparagus is a natural diuretic. For other health-giving properties, refer to the "white/green" category of the "Seven Colors of Health" chart on page 199.*

Roasted Cumin Salmon with Sweet and Sour Cucumbers

SIX TO EIGHT SERVINGS

Wild salmon is now more readily available, and the flavor is far superior to that of farm-raised salmon. By all means try it if the price isn't too high. This dish is excellent served warm, at room temperature, or chilled.

+ **Cumin** is believed to have anticancer properties, but it is particularly helpful in aiding digestion.

§ Cumin is one of the most popular spices used in Indian cooking. Its Ayurvedic properties include purifying blood and reducing nausea, particularly in pregnant women.

INGREDIENTS

1   **recipe Dad's Sweet and Sour Cucumber Pickle (page 175)**

1½ to 2 pounds skinless center-cut salmon fillets

MARINADE (MIXED TOGETHER)

3   **tablespoons mirin or sweetened rice wine**

2   **tablespoons soy sauce**

2   **tablespoons freshly squeezed lemon juice**

1½ **teaspoons ground cumin**

1   **head butter lettuce or Boston lettuce, leaves separated, rinsed and drained**

2   **teaspoons good-quality virgin olive oil**

3   **tablespoons coarsely chopped fresh dill sprigs for garnish**

FIRST Prepare Dad's Sweet and Sour Cucumber Pickle as directed in the recipe.

SECOND Cut the salmon fillets diagonally through the thickness into slices that are ¾ inch thick. Toss lightly with the Marinade and let sit for about 15 to 20 minutes. Preheat the oven to 475 degrees.

THIRD Trim the core end of the lettuce leaves and flatten with your hand. Arrange in overlapping layers on the bottom of a large shallow serving bowl.

FOURTH Arrange the salmon slices on a cookie sheet that has been lightly brushed with the olive oil. Bake in the preheated oven for 7 to 9 minutes, until just cooked and the edges are golden.

FIFTH Arrange the cooked salmon on top of the lettuce leaves. Spoon the cucumbers on top of the salmon, leaving some of the dressing. Sprinkle with the chopped dill and spoon some of the remaining dressing on top. Serve.

Grilled Garlic Beef over Crunchy Vegetables with a Fresh Thai Dressing

SIX SERVINGS

In his brilliant book *Thai Food,* Chef David Thompson says that the cardinal rule of Thai salads is that the dressing must be strongly flavored with seasonings that complement and unify all the ingredients in the salad. This dressing is a fitting example.

INGREDIENTS

1½ pounds sirloin or rib-eye steak, or left-over Balsamic-Glazed Steak (page 255)

MEAT MARINADE (MIXED TOGETHER)

- 1 tablespoon minced garlic
- 3 tablespoons soy sauce

3 cups grated carrots (about 3 medium)

4½ cups bean sprouts (about 12 ounces), rinsed and drained

1½ cups minced scallion greens

DRESSING (MIXED TOGETHER)

- ½ cup fish sauce
- ½ cup freshly squeezed lime juice (about 6 to 7 limes)
- 6 tablespoons firmly packed light brown sugar, or to taste
- ½ teaspoon freshly ground black pepper
- ½ cup fresh cilantro leaves, chopped coarsely, with 3 tablespoons reserved for sprinkling on top of the salad

FIRST Trim the meat of any fat or gristle and put in a bowl. Pour the Marinade over the meat and rub along the surface to coat. Let sit for 30 minutes.

SECOND Toss the grated carrots, bean sprouts, and scallion greens together in a mixing bowl. Arrange on a platter. Drizzle some of the prepared Dressing on top and pour the rest into a serving container.

THIRD Prepare a medium-hot fire for grilling or preheat the broiler. Arrange the meat about 3 inches from the source of the heat and grill or broil for about 5 to 7 minutes for medium-rare. Remove from the heat and cool slightly.

FOURTH Cut the meat across the grain into thin slices and arrange the slices on top of the vegetables. Sprinkle with the reserved cilantro and serve with the remaining dressing.

Chicken and Black Bean Salad with a Spicy Tomato Salsa

SIX SERVINGS

I make this meal-in-one salad often at home. I often serve it with toasted cornbread or stuffed into a flour tortilla.

INGREDIENTS

3 poached or grilled boneless, skinless chicken breasts (about 1½ pounds)*

SPICY SALSA

1½ jalapeño chiles, ends trimmed and seeds removed

1 tablespoon minced garlic

1 cup minced scallion greens

1 pound vine-ripened tomatoes, rinsed, drained, cored, and cut into large chunks

4 tablespoons freshly squeezed lemon juice (about 1 lemon)

½ cup fresh cilantro leaves

1 teaspoon salt, or more to taste

5 ears shucked sweet corn, fresh or frozen, or 2½ to 3 cups leftover cooked corn

½ head romaine lettuce, outer leaves and core removed, rinsed and spun dry

1 15-ounce can black or pinto beans, blanched briefly in boiling water, refreshed in cold water, and drained

2 ripe but firm avocados, peeled, pitted, and cut into ½-inch cubes

*See Curried Chicken Salad with Mango and Grapes (page 154) or Jesse's Spicy Grilled Chicken Breasts (page 250).

FIRST To prepare the Salsa, drop the jalapeño chiles and garlic down the feed tube of a food processor fitted with a steel blade while the machine is running, or into a blender, and chop finely. Add the scallion greens and pulse to mix. Drop in the tomatoes and pulse until coarsely chopped. Stir in the lemon juice, cilantro, and salt. Pour into a serving bowl and let stand for 30 minutes at room temperature, then refrigerate until ready to serve.

SECOND Cook the corn about 10 minutes, drain, let cool, and cut the kernels from the cobs. (You should have about 2½ to 3 cups.) Cut the poached or grilled chicken meat across the grain into thin slices. Cut the lettuce leaves into ¼-inch julienne strips.

THIRD Sprinkle the lettuce on the bottom of a round serving bowl or platter. Arrange the ingredients in separate concentric circles, starting with the corn, then the black beans, the avocado, and the chicken in the center. Serve the salsa on the side, spooning some on top of each portion.

Hot and Sour Slaw
with Barbecued Pork

SIX SERVINGS

This hot and sour salad is especially good with smoky barbecued pork or chicken. The flavors and textures complement one another well. Scoop it into blanched cabbage leaves or lettuce for an unusual wrap.

INGREDIENTS

1   small head Savoy cabbage (about 1½ pounds)*

1   teaspoon salt

1½ pounds Barbecued Pork (page 317)

1   medium red bell pepper, cored and seeded

2   teaspoons virgin olive oil

1   teaspoon toasted sesame oil

1   teaspoon dried chile flakes

2   tablespoons minced fresh ginger

5   medium carrots, peeled, ends trimmed, and grated (about 4 cups)

2   tablespoons rice wine or sake

HOT AND SOUR DRESSING
(MIXED TOGETHER)

¼   cup soy sauce

½   teaspoon salt

3   tablespoons sugar

3   tablespoons Chinese black vinegar or Worcestershire sauce

1   head leafy lettuce, stem end removed, rinsed, and spun dry (optional)

*If you have extra cabbage, blanch the leaves and use as wrappers.

FIRST Remove the tired outer leaves from the cabbage and discard. Cut the cabbage in half, cut away the core, and slice the leaves into thin julienne shreds (you should have about 8 cups). Put in a bowl, sprinkle in the salt, and let sit 30 minutes. Using your hands, squeeze the cabbage to remove liquid.

SECOND Cut the prepared Barbecued Pork into thin slices and then into pieces about 1½ inches square. Cut the red pepper into ¼-inch dice.

THIRD Heat a wok or a heavy skillet, add the olive and sesame oils, and heat until very hot but not smoking. Add the chile flakes and ginger and stir-fry until fragrant, about 10 seconds. Add the diced red pepper and toss lightly over high heat. Add the cabbage shreds and grated carrots and toss lightly. Pour in the rice wine, toss lightly, and cover. Cook over medium-high heat for 2 minutes, until the cabbage and carrots are almost tender. Add the Hot and Sour Dressing and stir-fry for about 1 minute to blend the flavors.

FOURTH Scoop the slaw out into a bowl or onto a deep platter and let cool slightly. Arrange the barbecued pork slices on top and serve warm or at room temperature. The slaw and pork may be put into blanched cabbage leaves or leafy lettuce leaves as wrappers, or spooned over rice.

+ As a member of the cruciferous family, **cabbage,** particularly Savoy, is full of cancer-fighting nutrients. Since it's also high in beta-carotenes, it helps to prevent cataracts. See the "green" category of the "Seven Colors of Health" chart on page 199.

✳ Cabbage helps digestion and lubricates the intestines. Cabbage soup or cooked cabbage is particularly good for constipation.

Curried Chicken Salad with Mango and Grapes

SIX SERVINGS

Chicken salad can be bland, but imagine it seasoned with a vibrant curry powder and dressed with a fresh ginger–yogurt sauce. It can be served over shredded fresh vegetables or stuffed into pita pockets for a unique lunch. I often grill extra chicken when making Jesse's Spicy Grilled Chicken Breasts (page 250) to have on hand for salads.

INGREDIENTS

- 3 slices fresh ginger, about the size of a quarter, smashed lightly with the flat side of a knife
- 3 tablespoons rice wine or sake
- 2 boneless, skinless chicken breasts (about 1¼ pounds), trimmed of fat
- 4 stalks celery, ends trimmed and cut into ½-inch dice
- ¾ pound red or green seedless grapes, removed from the stem, rinsed, and drained
- 1 large just-ripe mango (about 1¼ pounds), peeled, pitted, and cut into ¼-inch dice
- ¼ cup minced scallion greens

DRESSING

- 2½ teaspoons brown or black mustard seeds (optional)
- 2½ teaspoons top-quality curry powder, preferably Sun brand Madras-style
- 1 2-inch piece peeled fresh ginger, cut into ½-inch pieces (about 2 tablespoons)
- 3 cloves garlic, smashed with the flat side of a knife, and peeled
- 1 cup low-fat plain yogurt
- 1¼ teaspoons salt, or to taste
- ¼ teaspoon freshly ground black pepper

- 1 head romaine lettuce, outer leaves removed, rinsed, drained, and patted dry on paper towels

FIRST Bring 1 quart water, the ginger slices, and the rice wine to a boil in a medium saucepan. Add the chicken breasts, partially cover, and return to a boil. Reduce the heat to medium-low and simmer uncovered about 12 minutes, or until the chicken is cooked. Remove the chicken from the pan and let cool, reserving the broth for another use. Cut the chicken into 1-inch dice.

SECOND Toss the chicken, celery, grapes, mango, and scallion greens in a mixing bowl.

THIRD To prepare the Dressing: Heat a small, heavy skillet until hot. Toss the mustard seeds, if using, and curry powder into the pan and stir with a wooden spoon over medium-low heat until the curry powder is very fragrant and the mustard seeds begin to pop. Scrape out onto a plate to cool. Drop the ginger and garlic down the feed tube of a food processor fitted with a steel blade, or into a blender, while the machine is running. Pulse until they are finely chopped. Add the mustard seeds and curry powder, yogurt, salt, and pepper, and process until smooth. Taste and adjust the seasoning if necessary. Pour the dressing into the bowl with the chicken and stir to coat.

FOURTH Trim the stem end from the lettuce leaves, cut the leaves across into shreds, and arrange on a platter or in a shallow bowl. Spoon the chicken salad on top and serve with crusty bread.

+ *Mangoes are a potent source of beta-carotenes, as well as vitamins C and E and iron.*

+ *Yogurt with active cultures helps to prevent gastrointestinal and urinary tract infections. It also counters the negative effects of antibiotics.*

§ *Ripe mangoes energize the body and are believed to be an aphrodisiac.*

Skewered Lamb with Herbal Cracked Wheat Salad

SIX SERVINGS

Cracked wheat, like bulgur, is made from the whole grain of wheat. It is milled more thoroughly and broken into small pieces, so it cooks very quickly. It is now widely available at supermarkets as well as Middle Eastern markets.

INGREDIENTS

1½ pounds boneless leg of lamb (shank portion) or pre-cut lamb for kebabs

MARINADE (MIXED TOGETHER)

¼ cup soy sauce

2 tablespoons sugar

2½ tablespoons minced garlic

1 tablespoon dried chile flakes

1 teaspoon toasted sesame oil

6 10-inch bamboo or metal skewers (if bamboo, soak in cold water to cover for 1 hour)

1½ cups cracked wheat*

2 cups boiling water, to cover (or as directed on bulgur label)

¾ pound cherry tomatoes, cut into quarters

CRACKED WHEAT SEASONINGS

1 cup minced scallion greens

¾ cup firmly packed chopped fresh parsley leaves

⅓ cup chopped fresh mint leaves

8 tablespoons freshly squeezed lemon juice, or to taste

3 tablespoons wine vinegar

½ cup virgin olive oil

1¼ teaspoons salt, or to taste

*Bulgur, which is made from whole wheat kernels that have been parboiled and dried, may be substituted for the cracked wheat, but it usually takes longer and requires boiling water to cover. Refer to the package for exact cooking instructions.

FIRST Cut the lamb into cubes about 1 inch square and put in a bowl. Pour in the Marinade and toss lightly to coat. Let marinate for 30 minutes at room temperature or overnight in the refrigerator. Thread the lamb onto the skewers.

SECOND Put the cracked wheat into a heatproof bowl and pour in the boiling water. Let stand uncovered until softened, about 15 minutes. (Refer to the package and follow instructions if directed otherwise.) Pour into a strainer and drain off any excess water. Put back into the bowl and add the tomatoes and Cracked Wheat Seasonings. Toss lightly and spoon into the bottom of a serving dish. You may refrigerate this until you are ready to serve.

THIRD Prepare a medium-hot fire for grilling or preheat the broiler. Arrange the skewered meat about 3 inches from the heat source and cook until medium, about 5 to 6 minutes on each side, turning once (or less, if you prefer rare). Remove from the heat and arrange the skewered lamb over the cracked wheat salad.

+ *Whole **wheat** products, like cracked wheat and bulgur, are not only rich in vitamins (particularly vitamin E), minerals, and complex carbohydrates (good source of fiber). They also help improve digestion and reduce the risk of heart disease and cancer.*

Dr. Jim Duke's Herbal Farmacy and Anti-Aging Tips

Dr. Jim Duke is one of the world's foremost authorities on herbs and the best-selling author of *The Green Pharmacy, The Green Pharmacy Herbal Handbook,* and *The Green Pharmacy Anti-Aging Prescriptions.* For thirty years, Dr. Duke was the leading medical botanist for the USDA, and during that time he compiled databases for the Agricultural Research Service that contain the latest scientific studies on herbs, with information on herbal compounds as well as folklore and herbal remedies that have existed for thousands of years (www.ars-grin.gov/duke).

Dr. Duke's vivacious manner and youthful appearance belie his seventy-plus years. It's a testament to his belief that certain herbs and foods hold the key to disease prevention and good health. "One of my life's missions is to gather data to help overcome the resistance to plant remedies," he says. "But I think it's equally important to get the FDA to encourage tests comparing the synthetic drugs with the most competitive herbal alternatives."

In 1998, with the help of friends and volunteers, Dr. Duke created his Green Farmacy Garden, planting about three hundred species of medicinal herbs in eighty plots, each devoted to a disease or an ailment. There's stinging nettle to relieve arthritis; fenugreek for lowering cholesterol and preventing heart disease; and garlic for fungal infections.

Recently, while writing his book on anti-aging prescriptions, Dr. Duke temporarily renamed his garden the Garden of Youth. Working in the garden helps to keep him young, he feels, and the herbs growing there help to prevent or treat many conditions associated with aging. Dr. Duke contends that herbs can help to slow down the aging process, but he also believes that lifestyle changes are equally important. At right are helpful tips for his "herbal farmacy," and the chart opposite lists culinary herbs recommended for their health-giving and healing properties.

TIPS FROM DR. DUKE

- Drink two ANTIOXIDANT HERB TEAS a day, which may help to delay the aging process. Good research suggests that oregano, rosemary, bee balm, lemon balm, peppermint, sage, spearmint, savory, and thyme contain significant levels of antioxidants.

- Eat a variety of FRUITS AND VEGETABLES, as well as herbs, legumes, nuts, and spices.

- Use olive oil and other MONOUNSATURATED OILS, which are better for you than polyunsaturated oils like corn oil and other vegetable oils. Avoid trans fats and hydrogenated oils.

- Engage in regular moderate physical activity. GO FOR A WALK EVERY DAY.

- DON'T SMOKE, and avoid excessive alcohol consumption.

- KEEP STRESS IN CHECK.

- Get adequate REST.

- Take a MULTIVITAMIN and mineral supplement for extra nutritional protection.

- Smell to CHECK FRESHNESS of dried herbs every other year. Replenish if herbs are stale. Buy herbs at a store with frequent turnover or order online (see "Mail-Order and Web Sources").

- Make HERBAL TEA. Most herbs can be used as an infusion or tea. Herbal amounts vary depending on the strength of the herb. For a general recipe for fresh herbal tea, see the fresh peppermint tea recipe on page 161. For a dried herbal tea, see the recipe for cardamom tea on the right.

- Make love regularly with someone you love, or at least EXPRESS YOUR AFFECTION with friends, pets, even plants. Hug a tree; it won't tell on you.

DR. DUKE'S HERBAL FARMACY

BASIL

Basil is a member of the mint family and native to tropical Asia, where it has been cultivated for more than three thousand years, for both culinary and medicinal purposes. It's an ancient folk remedy for warts and preventing plaque.

key benefits:

- Rich in antiviral compounds

- Natural insect repellent

- Eases gas

- Helps fight plaque formation on teeth

CARDAMOM

Cardamom, one of the oldest spices in the world, can be dated back to fourth-century Greece, where it was highly valued for its flavor and medicinal properties. In India, it has been used as a digestive remedy for hundreds of years. Cardamom is one of the best sources of cineole, an antiseptic that eases congestion in the chest and strengthens the central nervous system. To make cardamom tea, lightly smash 1½ tablespoons cardamom pods. Put in a teapot, add 3 cups boiling water, cover, and let steep for 10 minutes.

key benefits:

- Soothes indigestion and relieves gas

- Kills bad breath

- Eases congestion

CAYENNE

Cayenne peppers can be traced back thousands of years to equatorial America, but they are now grown in tropical climates throughout the world. They are the best source of capsaicin, the substance that provides peppers with varying degrees of heat—the more capsaicin, the hotter the pepper. According to Dr. Jim Duke, cayenne and all hot peppers are "therapeutic wonders," and capsaicin ointments alleviate pain for rheumatoid arthritis, psoriasis, and shingles. Taken internally as a diluted tincture, capsaicin keeps blood flowing smoothly and strengthens the cardiovascular system.

key benefits:

- Stimulates circulation

- Prevents respiratory tract infections

- Eases constipation

- Alleviates rheumatoid and osteoarthritis pain

CELERY SEED

Wild celery has been a common plant in Europe and parts of Asia since ancient times, whereas cultivated celery first appeared in Europe in the 1600s. Although both the stalks and the seeds are used in the kitchen, the seeds are more prized for their medicinal properties. The volatile oil found in celery seeds contains more than a dozen natural chemicals that can help the cardiovascular system and improve blood circulation. Add 1 teaspoon of celery seeds to coleslaw, salad dressings such as vinaigrette, and meat marinades for grilling to give extra flavor.

key benefits:

- Improves circulation
- Helps maintain blood sugar balance, so combats diabetes
- Diuretic and antiseptic
- Lowers blood pressure and cholesterol

CINNAMON

Cinnamon is one of the world's most important spices and is the bark of an evergreen tree related to the laurel family. It is a close cousin to cassia bark, which is used in Asia. Pungent and warming, cinnamon has been used in the kitchen and medicinally throughout Asia and the Middle East since ancient times.

key benefits:

- Fights colds, coughs, and fevers
- Relieves gas and indigestion
- Stimulates circulation
- Eases allergies

CLOVES

Cloves are the dried flower buds of an evergreen tree. They were used in China as early as 266 B.C. and have been used in India since ancient times. The spice is usually present in Chinese five-spice powder and in garam masala, an Indian spice blend. Oil of cloves is strongly antiseptic owing to the presence of eugenol, which relieves pain, kills bacteria, and thins blood.

key benefits:

- Antiseptic
- Antispasmodic
- Fights infection
- Relieves toothaches

FENNEL

Fennel, an anise-flavored vegetable native to the Mediterranean, is one of the oldest cultivated plants. Asians valued fennel as a digestive aid, while the Romans enjoyed fennel shoots as a vegetable. The leaves, stalks, and seeds are used for culinary and medicinal purposes. Anethole, the main component of the plant's essential oil, is most concentrated in the seeds.

key benefits:

- Relieves indigestion
- Fights respiratory disease
- Soothes stomach pain
- Helps break up chest congestion

GARLIC

Originally from central Asia, garlic is now grown all over the world and has been revered for more than five thousand years for its medicinal properties. Garlic bulbs contain the compound allicin and volatile oils that are highly antibacterial and antibiotic. According to Dr. Duke, garlic is most beneficial for heart and circulatory conditions.

key benefits:

- Antibiotic against infections
- Improves overall cardiovascular health
- Strengthens body's immune system
- Lowers incidence of cancer in the gastrointestinal system
- Prevents colds and the flu

GINGER

Fresh ginger is a knotty, aromatic rhizome traditionally cultivated in China and India, but now grown in many tropical countries throughout the world. It has been used for medicinal purposes as well as flavor for thousands of years. It is excellent for settling an upset stomach while aiding the digestive process.

key benefits:

- Soothes nausea, and motion and morning sickness
- Aids circulation
- Antibacterial
- Lowers cholesterol levels

LICORICE

Licorice is one of the most exhaustively researched herbs and one of the most commonly used herbal remedies. It is often used to flavor sweets and is found in Chinese five-spice powder. According to Dr. Duke, it prevents inflammation, fights bacteria, and helps to prevent hair loss and enlargement of the prostate in men.

key benefits:

- Anti-inflammatory and antiarthritis
- Soothes stomach inflammation and ulcers
- Lowers cholesterol
- Prevents cataracts and vision deterioration

ONION

Onion, like garlic, is a member of the *Allium* genus. They both contain the phytochemical allicin. However, onions are gentler on the stomach and more effective than garlic in combating diabetes and allergies. Another component, quercetin, which is found in the onion skin, fights allergies and tames high blood sugar levels. Add onion skins when making chicken broth and other soups. Skim away and discard before serving.

key benefits:

- Fights allergies
- Protects capillaries
- Diuretic
- Protects against angina
- Combats diabetes

PEPPERMINT

Peppermint is a member of the extensive mint family and contains menthol. Both menthol and peppermint oil are used to flavor all types of pharmaceutical products, including laxatives, antacids, toothpastes, breath fresheners, and mouthwash. The herb is used to season numerous dishes, from soups to desserts, and is praised for its innumerable medicinal properties. To make fresh peppermint tea, put 5 tablespoons of fresh peppermint leaves or 3 to 4 tablespoons of dried in a teapot. Pour in 3 cups of boiling water, cover, and steep 10 minutes. (For an herbal remedy, Dr. Duke recommends letting the tea steep until cool, straining it, and reheating the liquid until hot.)

key benefits:

- Tames muscle spasms in intestinal tract
- Relieves gas, flatulence, and bloating
- Applied externally, relaxes tight muscles and relieves pain
- Antibacterial
- Dissolves gallstones

THYME

Thyme is a small, hardy evergreen shrub native to the Mediterranean. Its small, aromatic leaves are a staple flavoring in soups, stews, and sauces, but have also been used since the seventeenth century for their medicinal properties. Thyme tea is an excellent remedy for sore throats and infected gums, and also soothes the digestive system and eases flatulence. Steep 1 teaspoon of dried thyme per cup of boiling water for 10 minutes.

key benefits:

- Relieves coughing and bronchial spasms
- Applied externally, relieves muscle spasms and rheumatism
- Fights mucous membrane inflammation

TURMERIC

Turmeric is native to southern Asia, where it has been used as a flavoring, a dye, and a medicine since ancient times. Curcumin in turmeric has powerful anti-inflammatory and antioxidant properties and is responsible for giving turmeric its bright yellow color.

key benefits:

- Relieves arthritic inflammation
- Defends against cancer in the colon, gallbladder, and liver
- Soothes indigestion
- Powerful antioxidant, so retards aging and prevents disease

Dr. Duke's Anti-Fatigue Tea

ONE SERVING

One of Dr. Duke's favorite herbs for boosting energy is licorice root. It contains glycyrrhizin, a compound that stimulates the adrenal glands and prolongs the action of the adrenal hormones, which regulate metabolism.

INGREDIENTS

1½ to 2 teaspoons powdered licorice root (available from an Asian herbalist or at health food stores)

1   cup freshly boiled water

Put the licorice root in a bowl or teacup and pour in the freshly boiled water. Steep 10 minutes, then strain and drink. You can drink as many as 3 cups a day for up to 6 weeks.

Dr. Duke's Stimulating Tea

FOUR SERVINGS

Dr. Duke says that this tea is rich in cineole, a gentle stimulant that is found in certain herbs. It can boost energy and prevent insomnia, and seems to enhance physical and mental performance.

INGREDIENTS

3   tablespoons eucalyptus,* peppermint, rosemary, and spearmint leaves, rinsed, drained, and blotted dry

4   cups freshly boiled water

½   teaspoon ground cardamom

1   teaspoon stevia, or to taste[†]

Put the herbs in a teapot, pour the freshly boiled water on top, cover, and let steep for 10 minutes. Strain into teacups and sprinkle each one with a shake of cardamom floating on top. Drink leisurely. You may add a little stevia to taste, if desired. Refrigerate any leftover tea for later use.

*Available at health food stores. If unavailable, omit.
[†]Stevia is a natural sweetener. If unavailable, substitute honey or omit.

Opposite:
Rosemary

pleasures from the garden

For me, there is no greater pleasure than eating freshly picked vegetables from the garden. The crisp-tender textures, vibrant flavors, and gorgeous colors are a feast for the senses. Every year, I wait anxiously for that magical time when local produce is at its peak. There's just nothing better than popping cherry tomatoes still warm from the sun into your mouth. They need no seasoning—their sweet, delicious flavor explodes in your mouth. And don't get me thinking about sweet corn . . .

Cooking is a pleasure at that time of year. Planning dinner doesn't even seem a chore. I often wing it and see what's available and appealing at the market. Usually I just love to *look* and savor the experience. I often go a little crazy, heaping my shopping basket full, inspired by the beauty of the ingredients.

I'd like to say that I'm a top-notch gardener, but I have to admit that after a few attempts over the years, I've recognized that my talents lie elsewhere. Nonetheless I do try to keep a few pots of herbs around. And I am a passionate shopper at local farmers' markets and roadside stands. (In the off season, I regularly travel a fair distance to find a good selection of organic produce.) A good number of vegetables need no cooking. Tomatoes can be sliced and served with a sprinkling of fresh basil and a dousing of vinaigrette. Diced cucumbers, folded into a bit of yogurt and dusted with ground cumin, are a delightful and refreshing counterpoint to spicy dishes, which they are often served with.

When I do cook vegetables, I usually choose the simpler preparations: Roasting, steaming, stir-frying, and grilling accentuate and highlight vegetables' inherently good flavors. I often prefer them unadorned, with just a brush-

Chapter opener: A platter of vegetables, clockwise from top: Steamed Asparagus with Cardamom Butter; Spicy Broccolini with Red Pepper; Roasted Beets with Ginger and Balsamic Vinegar

ing of good olive oil. More often than not I like to pair them with a complementary herb or seasoning. Almost any green vegetable is great with garlic;
roasted beets taste sweeter with a bit of chopped or grated ginger; a curry
seasoning with hot chile pepper enriches the sweet flesh of pumpkin, squash,
and sweet potato.

Almost all vegetables inspire me, as you'll see from the variety of the
following recipes. Most of these dishes are meant to be served with meats
and seafood from other chapters to make a meal. Or you can cook several
vegetables, as I do, and serve them with steamed rice, couscous, or crusty
bread for a satisfying dinner. Leftovers are just as delicious cold at lunch the
next day, or you can add them to soups to enliven their flavors. Vegetables not
only taste delicious, but as recent research has shown, as well as David Heber's
"Seven Colors of Health" chart on page 199, they contain a variety of phytonutrients that may prevent or reduce the risk of a number of cancers and
chronic diseases.

Stir-Fried Spinach, Snow Pea Shoots, or Leafy Greens

SIX SERVINGS

This master recipe may be used for all leafy vegetables. The key is to organize everything before you start cooking and to not be afraid to use high heat and get your pan really hot. When preparing snow pea shoots, my friend Wilson Wong, who owns the Sun Sun Market in Boston, recommends discarding the top of the plant with the tendrils and pinching the stem joints to see if they are hard, then snapping off the tender new shoots to use.

INGREDIENTS

1½ pounds tender snow pea shoots, water spinach, baby spinach, or other leafy greens*

1   teaspoon virgin olive oil

2   tablespoons rice wine, sake, or very good-quality dry sherry

1   tablespoon minced garlic

½ to ¾ teaspoon sea salt

FIRST Trim away any tough ends from the stalks and leaf tips of the snow pea shoots and spinach. If you are using mature snow pea shoots, snap off and use only the new shoots where they branch off of the main stalk. (Discard the stalks with the tendrils since they are usually tough.) Put the greens in the sink in water to cover and rinse thoroughly. Throw the leaves in a salad spinner and spin dry.

SECOND Heat a wok or a deep skillet until very hot, then pour in the oil and heat until near smoking. *(Don't be afraid to get the pan really hot. This will give the dish its special flavor.)* Add the greens, rice wine, garlic, and salt, and toss lightly over high heat about 1½ minutes, or until the greens are slightly wilted but still bright green. Scoop out the greens, arrange them on a serving platter, and spoon the juice on top. Serve immediately or at room temperature.

*Snow pea shoots and water spinach (also called water convolvulus) are available at Asian markets.

Stir-Fried Bok Choy, Broccoli, or Flowering Rape

SIX SERVINGS

I like to stir-fry all types of green vegetables and use them as an edible garnish around seared, grilled, or steamed meats or seafood. They are excellent hot or cold, and if seared properly over high heat will keep their vibrant green color.

INGREDIENTS

- 1½ pounds bok choy, broccoli, flowering rape, snow or snap peas, cauliflower, string beans, etc.*
- 1 teaspoon virgin olive oil
- 2½ tablespoons rice wine, sake, or very good-quality dry sherry
- 1½ tablespoons minced garlic
- 1 teaspoon sea salt

FIRST Trim off any tough leafy ends and peel away any tough skin from the stalk. Cut the stalk on the diagonal into 1½-inch lengths. Separate any florets. Rinse the vegetable thoroughly and drain.

SECOND Bring 4 quarts water to a boil in a large pot and add the stalky, tougher part of the vegetable. Cook about 2 minutes, or until nearly tender. Add the leafy sections or florets and cook for another minute. Drain in a colander and rinse under cold running water. Drain. (You can do this in advance.)

THIRD Heat a wok or a deep skillet until very hot, then pour in the oil and heat until near smoking. *(Don't be afraid to get the pan really hot. This will give the dish its special flavor.)* Add the vegetable, rice wine, garlic, and salt, and toss lightly over high heat for about a minute. Scoop out the vegetable, arrange it on a serving platter, and spoon the liquid on top. Serve immediately or at room temperature.

*Bok choy, flowering rape, pak choi, and choy sum are all cruciferous vegetables. They may be purchased at Asian markets and many produce markets.

+ *Green vegetables such as **broccoli** and cabbage are rich in anticancer nutrients and are an excellent source of iron and beta-carotene. See the "green" category of the "Seven Colors of Health" chart on page 199 for other health-giving properties.*

✳ § *Asian doctors believe that broccoli removes heat from the body.*

Steamed Asparagus with Cardamom Butter

SIX SERVINGS

Rich Vellante, the talented executive chef of Legal Sea Foods restaurants, developed this wonderful recipe during the "Spices of Life" project when we were working with Chef Suresh Vaidyanathan from the Oberoi Hotel group in India.

§ *Ayurvedic doctors credit cardamom with stimulating the heart and aiding digestion. Cardamom, cinnamon, and bay leaves together are referred to as the "Three Aromatics." The combination is believed to aid in the absorption of medicine. See "Key to Primary Indian Spices" on page 288 for more health-giving properties.*

INGREDIENTS

- 2 tablespoons whole cardamom pods (about 50), smashed with the flat side of a knife
- ¼ cup virgin olive oil
- ¼ cup unsalted butter
- 2 pounds fresh asparagus, tough woody stems snapped off
- ½ teaspoon salt

FIRST Toast the cardamom pods in a heavy skillet for about 5 minutes over low heat, shaking the pan from time to time until the cardamom is very fragrant. Add the olive oil and butter and slowly heat to infuse the oil and butter with the cardamom flavor for about 10 to 15 minutes while the asparagus is cooking.

SECOND Rinse the asparagus stalks and arrange in a heatproof plate, such as a pie or quiche pan, or in a steamer basket. (If using bamboo, line the basket with a piece of parchment or wax paper.)

THIRD Fill a large pot or a wok with several inches of water and heat until boiling. If using a plate, set it on a tuna fish can with both top and bottom removed. Or, set the steamer basket in the wok. Steam the asparagus 5 to 6 minutes, or until just tender. Remove and arrange on a serving plate.

FOURTH Pour the cardamom butter and sprinkle the salt over the asparagus and serve.

Grilled Hot and Sour Zucchini

SIX SERVINGS

Although grilling vegetables may not be the traditional cooking method favored in China, I find that it complements the flavor and improves the texture of watery vegetable varieties, especially zucchini and other summer squash.

INGREDIENTS

5 medium zucchini (about 2 pounds), rinsed and drained

1 tablespoon virgin olive oil

HOT AND SOUR DRESSING (WHISKED TOGETHER)

6 tablespoons light soy sauce

3½ tablespoons Chinese black vinegar or Worcestershire sauce

1 tablespoon minced fresh ginger

3 tablespoons water

1 teaspoon hot chile paste, or to taste

FIRST Trim the ends of the zucchini and discard. Cut the zucchini on the diagonal into ¼-inch-thick slices and put in a bowl. Pour in the olive oil and toss lightly with your hands to coat.

SECOND Prepare a medium-hot fire for grilling and place the grill 3 to 4 inches from the heat. Arrange the zucchini slices on the grill (you may have to cook them in batches), and grill about 5 minutes on each side. Remove the slices from the grill and put them on a serving platter.

THIRD Pour the Hot and Sour Dressing over the zucchini and serve warm, at room temperature, or chilled.

Spicy Broccolini with Red Pepper

SIX SERVINGS

This recipe is excellent for broccolini, rapini, broccoli, cauliflower, and bok choy. Most supermarkets offer broccolini, which looks similar to rapini but has a flavor that is less bitter. You can steam, boil, or stir-fry broccolini or rapini.

INGREDIENTS

2   pounds broccolini, rapini, Chinese or Western broccoli, or flowering rape

2   tablespoons virgin olive oil

1   teaspoon dried chile flakes

1   small red bell pepper, cored, seeded, and cut into ¼-inch dice

6   cloves garlic, smashed with the flat side of a knife, peeled, and sliced thinly

Juice of ½ lemon (about 2½ tablespoons)

1   teaspoon salt, or to taste

FIRST Cut off the tough ends of the broccolini or rapini and peel away the tough outer skin from the stems. Cut the stalks into 1-inch lengths and separate the florets, if using broccoli. Separate the stalks or tougher part of the vegetable from the more tender part (florets).

SECOND Bring 3 quarts water to a boil, add the stalky, tougher part of the vegetable, and cook for about 2 minutes, or until almost tender but al dente. Add the remaining part of the vegetable and cook for another minute, or until the vegetable is tender. Drain and refresh briefly in cold water. Drain again.

THIRD Heat a wok or a heavy skillet, add the oil, and heat until hot but not smoking. Add the chile flakes, red pepper, and garlic. Stir-fry over medium-high heat for 2 minutes, or until the red pepper is slightly tender. Add the broccolini and toss lightly over high heat to mix for a minute. Add the lemon juice and salt and toss lightly to mix. Stir together and taste for seasoning, adjusting if necessary. Scoop onto a platter or into a bowl, and serve hot, at room temperature, or chilled.

+ *Broccoli is one of the stars in the "Seven Colors of Health" chart on page 199.*

Cucumber Raita

SIX SERVINGS

Raitas (yogurt salads) are served at Indian meals to provide a refreshing, cool complement to spicy dishes. Look for natural, ethnic, and whole-milk yogurts for the best, richest flavor.

+ **Yogurt** *may reduce the risk of heart disease and has been used successfully to treat diarrhea. Yogurt also encourages the intestines to produce good bacteria, which prevent the growth of harmful bacteria.*

§ *According to Ayurvedic belief, yogurt is a digestive stimulant, is nourishing, and increases strength.*

INGREDIENTS

- 2 medium English seedless or 5 small pickling cucumbers (about 1½ pounds), rinsed and drained
- 2 cups chilled plain yogurt
- ½ teaspoon ground cumin
- 3 tablespoons finely chopped fresh cilantro leaves
- 1½ teaspoons salt, or to taste

FIRST Trim the ends of the cucumbers. Slice them in half lengthwise and scoop out the seeds with a spoon. Cut into very small cubes, or grate with a food processor or by hand. Using your hands, squeeze out any excess water from the grated cucumbers.

SECOND Mix together the cucumbers, yogurt, cumin, cilantro, and salt in a bowl. Cover with plastic wrap and let sit for 10 minutes before serving so that the flavors will marry. If preparing in advance, you may refrigerate the seasoned yogurt, but chill the cucumbers on the side and mix together before serving. (The salt will draw out the water in the cucumbers.) Serve as a side dish or with Indian dishes.

Dad's Sweet and Sour Cucumber Pickle

SIX SERVINGS

Cantonese chefs make a simple pickle by marinating carrots, cucumbers, and daikon radishes with equal amounts of vinegar and sugar. My dad's favorite, especially during the summer, is this recipe made with English or pickling cucumbers. To increase the flavor and crisp the pickle, let it sit for an hour in the refrigerator.

INGREDIENTS

2 pounds English seedless or pickling cucumbers, rinsed and drained

SWEET AND SOUR DRESSING

1 cup Japanese clear rice vinegar

1 cup sugar

1 teaspoon salt

1½ tablespoons minced fresh ginger

FIRST Trim the ends of the cucumbers. Slice them in half lengthwise, scoop out the seeds with a spoon, and cut on the diagonal into slices about ¼ inch thick. Put the slices in a bowl.

SECOND Mix together the Sweet and Sour Dressing. (You may add 1 teaspoon dried chile flakes or 1½ teaspoons hot chile oil for extra flavor.) Add the dressing to the cucumbers and toss lightly with a spoon to coat. Cover with plastic wrap and let sit for 30 minutes, or longer in the refrigerator. Serve chilled.

§ *Because of their coolish nature, cucumbers are especially popular in the summer, since they dissipate heat. They are also considered to have diuretic and laxative effects. To soothe a scratchy throat or laryngitis, drink some cucumber soup.*

Rainbow Slaw with Curried Yogurt Dressing

SIX SERVINGS

I often make this spicy slaw to serve with grilled seafood or meats. It's equally good the following day with leftover grilled dishes for lunch or a light dinner.

INGREDIENTS

- ½ small head green or Savoy cabbage (about ¾ pound)
- ½ small head red cabbage (about ¾ pound)
- 2 teaspoons salt
- 2 medium carrots, peeled and ends trimmed
- 2 teaspoons top-quality curry powder, preferably Sun brand Madras-style

CURRIED YOGURT DRESSING

- 1 cup plain yogurt
- 1½ tablespoons minced fresh ginger
- ½ tablespoon minced garlic
- 1 teaspoon Dijon mustard
- ¼ cup light cream
- ¼ teaspoon salt, or to taste
- ¼ teaspoon freshly ground black pepper

1½ cups raisins

FIRST Remove the tough outer leaves from the cabbage and cut each in half. Cut out the core. Separate and stack the leaves together and cut into fine julienne strips. (You should have about 12 cups.) Put in a bowl, sprinkle in the salt, toss lightly, and cover with a plate with a heavy pot on top. Let sit for about 1 hour and drain in a colander. Grate the carrots.

SECOND Heat a small, heavy skillet until hot. Put the curry powder in the pan and stir with a wooden spoon over medium-low heat until the curry powder is very fragrant. Scrape out onto a plate to cool.

THIRD To make the Curried Yogurt Dressing, put the yogurt in a mixing bowl and add the curry powder and the remaining ingredients of the dressing, whisking lightly after each addition. Taste and adjust the seasoning if necessary.

FOURTH Put the drained cabbage, carrots, and raisins in a bowl. Pour in the dressing and toss lightly to coat. Cover with plastic wrap and refrigerate for at least 1 hour, tossing occasionally. Serve.

+ *See the "Seven Colors of Health" chart on page 199 for the health-giving properties of cabbage.*

+ *Dr. Jim Duke, an expert on herbs (see page 158), eats coleslaw often, since recent research shows it may prevent colon cancer, which runs in his family.*

§ *Ayurvedic doctors believe that white cabbage removes toxins from the body.*

Roasted Mediterranean Vegetables

SIX SERVINGS

The simple technique of roasting accentuates the natural delicious flavor of vegetables. I like to vary the vegetables in this dish, using fall or winter root vegetables like pumpkin or sweet potato, eggplant, or fennel. The dish is especially good served over couscous or rice.

INGREDIENTS

2 medium zucchini, ends trimmed

2 medium yellow summer squash, ends trimmed

2 red bell peppers, cored and seeded

1 large red onion, peeled

1 pound cherry tomatoes

3 tablespoons virgin olive oil

1½ tablespoons minced garlic

4 tablespoons fresh basil leaves (about 7 or 8), rinsed and blotted dry

1¼ teaspoons salt

¾ teaspoon freshly ground black pepper

1 tablespoon balsamic vinegar

4 ounces feta cheese, crumbled into small pieces

FIRST Preheat the oven to 475 degrees. Diagonally cut the zucchini and yellow squash into slices about 1 inch thick. Cut the bell peppers and onion into 1-inch dice.

SECOND Put the cut vegetables and cherry tomatoes in a roasting pan, pour in the olive oil, sprinkle in the garlic, tear the basil leaves into small pieces, and sprinkle them on top along with the salt and pepper. Toss lightly to coat and spread out in a single layer. Bake for 30 to 40 minutes, until the vegetables are brown at the edges and very tender. Let cool slightly.

THIRD Add the balsamic vinegar and feta cheese to the vegetables and toss lightly. Taste for seasoning and adjust if necessary. Serve warm, at room temperature, or chilled.

Sliced Tomatoes and Basil with Garlic Vinaigrette

SIX SERVINGS

The appearance of this dish in my house heralds the arrival of the best part of summer, when tomatoes are at their peak. I love to make this salad with yellow and orange tomatoes, which can be very sweet. We like to make tomato-basil sandwiches with toasted seven-grain bread for lunch or a light dinner.

INGREDIENTS

GARLIC VINAIGRETTE

- **4 cloves garlic, peeled and lightly smashed**
- **1¼ teaspoons Dijon mustard**
- **½ cup balsamic vinegar**
- **1¾ cups extra virgin olive oil**
- **1¼ teaspoons salt**
- **½ teaspoon freshly ground black pepper**

6 to 7 medium vine-ripened tomatoes (about 1½ pounds) (yellow and orange tomatoes are wonderful, if available)*

12 to 15 fresh basil leaves, stems removed

FIRST To make the Garlic Vinaigrette, drop the garlic cloves down the feed tube of a food processor fitted with a steel blade while the machine is running. Mince finely. Open the lid and add the mustard and vinegar. Pulse to blend, turning the machine on and off, and slowly pour the olive oil down the feed tube in a thin stream with the machine running. The dressing should become thick and creamy. Add salt and pepper, taste, and adjust the seasoning if necessary. This will keep refrigerated for months.

SECOND Cut out the stem of each tomato and cut into ¼-inch slices. Arrange on a plate. Rinse the basil leaves and blot dry with paper towels. Tear into thin pieces with your hands and sprinkle over the tomatoes. Pour some of the vinaigrette on top and serve some remaining on the side. Serve the tomatoes at room temperature or cold.

+ *According to Dr. Jim Duke, basil is rich in antiviral compounds, eases gas, and prevents the buildup of plaque on teeth. See his "Herbal Farmacy" on page 158 for other health-giving properties.*

*Alternate slices of fresh mozzarella with the tomato, if desired.

Sesame Grilled Eggplant

Recipes often call for salting the eggplant before cooking to remove any bitter flavor, but if you choose smaller eggplants, they are rarely bitter and you can omit the tedious salting step.

INGREDIENTS

3½ pounds medium eggplants, rinsed and drained

¼ cup fruity virgin olive oil

SESAME SAUCE (MIXED TOGETHER)

5½ tablespoons soy sauce

¼ cup balsamic vinegar

1½ teaspoons toasted sesame oil

FIRST Remove the stem end of the eggplants and cut them lengthwise into ¼-inch-thick slices.

SECOND Prepare a medium-hot fire for grilling and place the grill 3 to 4 inches from the heat. Lightly brush both sides of the eggplant with the olive oil and arrange on the grill (you may have to cook it in batches). Grill about 8 minutes on the first side and about 5 minutes on the second side with the lid down.

THIRD Remove the eggplant and arrange on a platter, overlapping edges. Pour the Sesame Sauce over the eggplant and serve hot, at room temperature, or chilled.

Roasted Hoisin Squash or Pumpkin

SIX SERVINGS

Hoisin sauce, seasoned generously with garlic, fresh ginger, and chiles as in this dish, accentuates the sweet flavor of different winter squashes and pumpkin. Baking the squash in a shallow pool of water prevents any spilled sauce from burning and creates steam, making the squash juicier.

INGREDIENTS

3½ to 4 pounds acorn, butternut, pumpkin, or other type of winter squash

SPICY HOISIN SAUCE (MIXED TOGETHER)

6 tablespoons hoisin or sweet bean sauce

3 tablespoons soy sauce

2½ tablespoons rice wine or sake

2½ tablespoons sugar

1½ tablespoons minced fresh ginger

1 tablespoon minced garlic

1 teaspoon hot chile paste or dried chile flakes (optional)

2 tablespoons water

2 tablespoons minced scallion greens for garnish

FIRST Preheat the oven to 425 degrees. Rinse the squash and drain. Cut in half and scoop out the seeds with a spoon. Arrange in a roasting pan with the cut edges up. Spoon the Hoisin Sauce over the squash and fill the hollows.

SECOND Pour about ½ inch of boiling water in the pan and place the squash on the middle shelf of the oven. Bake for about 40 to 45 minutes, until the squash is tender. A knife pierced through the center should come out easily. Remove from the oven and sprinkle the top with scallion greens. Cut the squash into serving portions if necessary, or serve in the middle of the table. Diners can scoop out squash with the sauce themselves. Serve with steamed rice.

+ *Most varieties of **squash** contain coumarins, which can help to prevent certain types of cancers, and their antioxidants help to protect against colds and the flu.*

✳ *Winter squashes are considered warming to the body and are believed to reduce inflammations and improve the circulation of energy in the body.*

Grilled Rainbow Peppers with Chile Oil Dressing

SIX SERVINGS

Roasting peppers not only helps to remove the skin, but accentuates their sweet flavor. I often like to blacken them only partially (especially with this recipe) so that their texture remains firmer.

INGREDIENTS

CHILE OIL DRESSING

3 to 4 small dried red Thai chiles (reconstitute in hot water for 15 minutes), or ½ teaspoon dried chile flakes

¼ cup virgin olive oil

1½ teaspoons toasted sesame oil

4 cloves garlic, peeled and minced

½ cup Japanese clear rice vinegar

3 tablespoons soy sauce

3 red bell peppers, rinsed and drained

3 orange bell peppers, rinsed and drained

3 sweet Italian peppers

FIRST Trim the ends and stems from the chiles, remove the seeds, and coarsely chop by hand. Heat the olive oil and the toasted sesame oil in a saucepan until very hot, about 400 degrees. Remove from heat. Carefully add the chiles, cover, and let sit for 5 minutes. Uncover and drop in the minced garlic, cover, and let sit until warm. Pour in the rice vinegar and soy sauce, stir, and taste for seasoning, adjusting if necessary.

SECOND Prepare a medium-hot fire for grilling and place the grill about 3 inches above the heat source. Arrange the peppers on the grill and cook for about 6 to 7 minutes, or until tender and charred at the edges. They will not be totally blackened. Turn the peppers over and cook for 3 to 4 minutes longer, or until charred at the edges. (You can also grill the peppers under a broiler or over a gas burner.) Put the peppers in a paper bag, close securely, and allow to cool. Pull most of the skin off the peppers, using a small paring knife.

THIRD Cut the stems off the peppers and cut each in half lengthwise. Scrape out the seeds and cut each half into thirds. Put in a bowl, pour in the Chile Oil Dressing, cover with plastic wrap, and let sit about 20 minutes. Serve.

+ See the "Seven Colors of Health" chart on page 199 for the health-giving properties of peppers.

Roasted Beets with Ginger and Balsamic Vinegar

SIX SERVINGS

Roasting accentuates the sweet flavor of beets. In this recipe, their juice, mixed with the balsamic vinegar and ginger, reduces to produce an extraordinary glaze. Serve these as a side dish or, chilled, alone or in a salad. You may roast different-colored beets if available.

+ *Beets are rich in phytonutrients that may prevent cancer.*

INGREDIENTS

2½ pounds medium fresh beets with stems (about 10)

FLAVORINGS (MIXED TOGETHER)

2   tablespoons extra-virgin olive oil
1½ tablespoons minced fresh ginger
2½ tablespoons balsamic vinegar

FIRST Preheat the oven to 450 degrees. Trim the beet stems to 1 inch if necessary, and scrub the beets. Arrange on a cookie sheet that has been lined with aluminum foil. Cover the top with the foil and roast the beets for 25 minutes. Let cool enough to handle and rub off the skin.

SECOND Cut the beets in half, rearrange on the cookie sheet with the cut edges up, and brush all parts of the beets except the stems with the Flavorings. Return, uncovered, to the oven and continue roasting until they are very tender, another 20 to 25 minutes. Arrange on a platter, cool slightly, and serve warm, at room temperature, or chilled.

Glazed Green Beans

When I lived in Taipei, we shopped almost every day in open-air markets, and the variety of vegetables was extraordinary. We usually cooked them very simply, allowing the natural fresh flavors to dominate. Here is our family's home-style recipe for green beans. I find the beans equally good hot from the pan or at room temperature the next day.

INGREDIENTS

2   pounds green beans, Chinese long beans, or French haricots verts

1½ tablespoons virgin olive oil

½   cup minced scallions, white part only

SAUCE (MIXED TOGETHER)

¼   cup soy sauce

3   tablespoons rice wine or sake

1½ tablespoons sugar

½   cup water

FIRST Trim the ends of the beans, and cut the beans into 3-inch lengths or, if not too long, leave whole.

SECOND Heat a wok or a heavy skillet until hot, add the oil, and heat until very hot but not smoking. Add the scallions and stir-fry over high heat for about 15 seconds, until fragrant. Add the green beans and stir-fry over high heat for about a minute. Pour in the Sauce and bring to a boil. Reduce the heat to medium-low, cover, and cook for about 9 to 10 minutes, or until the beans are tender. Uncover, increase the heat to high, and continue to cook, stirring occasionally, until the sauce has reduced to a glaze. Toss lightly and scoop the beans onto a serving platter. Serve hot or at room temperature.

Roasted Cherry Tomatoes

I was introduced to roasted cherry tomatoes by a friend in London who often served them with their stems as an attractive and delicious side dish. I like to season them with oregano, but other herbs, like thyme or basil, are equally good.

INGREDIENTS

1½ **pounds cherry or grape tomatoes (or 2 pints), rinsed and drained**

1½ **tablespoons dried oregano**

2½ **tablespoons virgin olive oil**

1 **teaspoon salt**

¼ **teaspoon freshly ground black pepper**

FIRST Preheat the oven to 400 degrees. Arrange the tomatoes in one layer in a nonreactive pan (not aluminum). Prick them lightly with the tip of a small knife or a fork.

SECOND Sprinkle the oregano and drizzle the olive oil evenly over the tomatoes. Season with salt and pepper. Roast for 30 to 35 minutes, until soft and tender. Spoon into a bowl or serve on plates.

Braised Garlic Mushrooms

SIX SERVINGS

Once cooked to render their natural juices, mushrooms soak up flavors. Fresh shiitake mushrooms tend to be more dry than most mushrooms, so they absorb the fragrant braising mixture. You may use porcini mushrooms, but first cook longer to render their liquid, then prepare the dish as directed.

INGREDIENTS

2   pounds fresh shiitake mushrooms, rinsed lightly and drained

1   teaspoon virgin olive oil

1½ tablespoons smashed garlic, peeled and thinly sliced

6   whole scallions, ends trimmed, cut into ½-inch lengths (reserve enough greens to make 2 tablespoons minced)

BRAISING SAUCE (MIXED TOGETHER)

1   cup good-quality reduced-sodium chicken broth

¼   cup soy sauce

3   tablespoons rice wine or sake

1   tablespoon oyster sauce

1   tablespoon sugar

1   teaspoon toasted sesame oil

1   teaspoon cornstarch

FIRST Trim the stem ends of the mushrooms and discard. Cut the large mushroom caps in half.

SECOND Heat a casserole, wok, or heavy skillet with a lid, add the oil, and heat until hot. Add the shiitakes, garlic, and scallions and stir-fry for about a minute over high heat. Pour in the Braising Sauce and bring to a boil. Reduce the heat and simmer the mushrooms uncovered for about 10 minutes, or until they have absorbed almost all the liquid, stirring occasionally.

THIRD Scoop the mushrooms into a bowl, spoon the sauce on top, and sprinkle the reserved minced scallion greens on top. Serve hot.

+ *Shiitake* **mushrooms** *contain lentinan, a component that strengthens the immune system and helps to combat and prevent disease.*

Curried Coconut Sweet Potato

SIX SERVINGS

Too many cooks overlook sweet potatoes except during the winter holidays, when they are often candied to a cloying sweetness. What many don't realize is that their firm texture makes them perfect for stewing and braising, and their sweet flavor makes them a perfect complement to spicy dishes such as this curry. I often serve it with rice for a light but satisfying dinner.

INGREDIENTS

5   sweet potatoes (about 3¼ pounds)

CURRY SEASONINGS

3   dried red chiles, or 1 teaspoon dried chile flakes

2   ½-inch slices fresh ginger, peeled

1½ teaspoons ground cumin

1½ teaspoons ground coriander

½   teaspoon freshly ground black pepper

1   teaspoon salt

1½ tablespoons virgin olive oil

2   medium red onions, peeled and cut into small dice

SAUCE (MIXED TOGETHER)

1½ cups light coconut milk

3   tablespoons fish sauce

1½ tablespoons sugar

½   cup fresh basil leaves cut into thin shreds (optional)

FIRST Peel and cut the sweet potatoes in half lengthwise, then cut each half into 1- to 1½-inch pieces.

SECOND Drop the Curry Seasonings down the feed tube of a food processor fitted with a steel blade while the machine is running. Pulse to chop the seasonings evenly and mince to a coarse powder.

THIRD Heat a heavy casserole or a Dutch oven with a lid. Add the oil and heat until hot. Add the Curry Seasonings and red onions, stirring over medium-low heat with a wooden spoon for about 3 minutes, until the onions are tender and the seasonings are fragrant. Add the Sauce and bring to a boil. Add the sweet potatoes and stir to coat the potatoes with the sauce. Bring the mixture back to a boil, reduce the heat to low, cover, and cook for about 20 to 25 minutes, or until the sweet potatoes are tender. Sprinkle in the fresh basil, if using, and toss lightly for a few seconds to coat. Scoop the potatoes and sauce into a serving bowl. Serve with steamed rice.

New Potato Salad with Scallion-Oil Vinaigrette

SIX SERVINGS

Potatoes are a versatile medium with which you can try a number of different dressings. This recipe has a base of scallion-flavored oil with some balsamic vinegar. Pour on the vinaigrette while the potatoes are still warm and they will absorb more flavor. I leave the skins on, but you may prefer to remove them.

INGREDIENTS

SCALLION-OIL VINAIGRETTE

- **10 whole scallions, rinsed and drained**
- **½ cup virgin olive oil**
- **3 tablespoons toasted sesame oil**
- **¼ cup balsamic or good-quality wine vinegar**
- **1½ teaspoons salt, or to taste**
- **1½ teaspoons freshly ground black pepper, or to taste**

- **2 pounds red or white new potatoes**
- **¼ cup minced scallion greens or chives for garnish**

FIRST Trim the ends from the scallions. Mince 3 tablespoons of the greens for the salad and reserve. Cut the remaining scallions in half and smash lightly with the flat side of a knife.

SECOND Heat the oils in a small saucepan with a lid until near smoking, about 400 degrees. Add the smashed scallions, cover, and remove the pan from the heat. Let stand for 15 minutes, then strain the oil through a fine-mesh strainer, pressing down on the scallions to remove as much oil as possible. Discard the scallions. Add the vinegar, salt, and pepper, and mix together.

THIRD Put the potatoes in a large pot with water to cover and bring to a boil. Reduce the heat to medium and cook uncovered for 20 to 25 minutes, until tender. Drain and cool slightly.

FOURTH Cut the potatoes in half or quarters, depending on their size, and put in a bowl. Pour in the Scallion-Oil Vinaigrette and the reserved 3 tablespoons of minced scallion greens. Toss to coat, cover with plastic wrap, and let sit at room temperature for 30 minutes. Before serving, sprinkle with the ¼ cup minced scallion greens for garnish.

+ *Chinese doctors have prescribed scallion-ginger tea as a remedy for the common cold for thousands of years.*

Myrtle and Darina Allen at Ballymaloe: Good Food from the Good Earth

For Myrtle Allen of Ballymaloe House in Southern Ireland and her daughter-in-law Darina Allen, who with her husband Tim founded the Ballymaloe Cookery School, the keys to good cooking are simplicity and using fresh, local ingredients. Supporting local farmers and sustainability have become common themes among chefs today, but Myrtle and her late husband Ivan, when they opened an inn and restaurant four decades ago, were pioneers in promoting these practices.

I first read about Myrtle and Ballymaloe House, with its adjoining 350-acre farm, in Gourmet magazine in the seventies. Later, in the mid-eighties, I started hearing about the school, which was gaining an international reputation. But it wasn't until I visited both places, which are surrounded by some of the most beautiful countryside in Ireland, that I was able to appreciate the extent of the Allens' commitment and understand their influence in Europe in promoting their beliefs.

Myrtle's sensibility was shaped by sheer survival. Ivan Allen, who began cultivating fruits in the thirties but later diversified into tomatoes, mushrooms, and cucumbers, had been one of Ireland's most progressive farmers. Originally his products were sent to England during the Second World War, but in the years after, he bought the Ballymaloe farm and broadened still further into raising cows, sheep, pigs, and grain. In the sixties Myrtle, who was a self-taught cook, opened a small restaurant in their big country house. Rather than trying to produce sophisticated continental cuisine, Myrtle cooked simple country dishes, using all local foods and letting the ingredients speak for themselves. It was the first restaurant of its kind in Ireland.

"Although my husband was not an organic farmer, he was a very progressive thinker," explains Myrtle. "After the Second World War, we started traveling to learn about farming and to taste good food in Europe. Our trips made us appreciate how good our own food was. So in our restaurant we presented food simply that was fresh and good, which was quite different from what other places were doing. We had fresh vegetables from our own gardens, meat, and our own milk and cream."

DARINA'S SHOPPING TIPS

- Note the variety and source when buying vegetables and fruit. Whenever possible, BUY LOCALLY GROWN PRODUCE. It's fresher, supports local farmers, and puts money back into the community.

- ASK QUESTIONS about the breed and name of the producers of meat and poultry. You don't want to eat food for which animals have suffered under inhumane conditions.

- Seek out FREE-RANGE, ORGANIC produce whenever possible.

- BUY WITH THE SEASONS—foods usually are fresher and cheaper.

- Buy pots or plant window boxes with commonly used FRESH HERBS so you can just snip some whenever you need them.

- TASTE whenever possible. Be observant and uncompromising in your pursuit of quality. People forget that the health, energy, and vitality of their family depends on what they put into their basket at the market.

Myrtle's passion inspired Darina, who is the author of eleven cookbooks and has become one of Ireland's most celebrated cooks. Their shared philosophy is a key influence in the curriculum of the twelve-week Ballymaloe cookery course. Students are taught not only cooking technique and recipes, but also butchering and organic gardening.

"On the very first day of the twelve-week course, we introduce students to the farm managers and gardeners who grow much of the food cooked at the school," says Darina. "Their first recipe is how to make compost. I show them a barrow full of rich soil and tell them to remember that this is where it all starts—in the good earth. We walk through the gardens and past the herbs, vegetables, and fruits, and we remind them of the simple fact that if you don't have clean, fertile soil, you won't have good food or pure water."

Myrtle and Darina are ardent promoters of farmers' markets and local, artisanal producers. Darina acknowledges that not everyone can have their own vegetable garden, but since she believes that the quality of the ingredients is so vital to the success of the dish, shopping is as important for her as cooking.

A DARINA ALLEN DINNER MENU
(Pages 192–197)

Darina's Risotto with Broad Beans, Peas, Green Asparagus, and Sugar Snaps

Darina's Pan-Grilled Chicken with Parsley Salad and Sun-Dried Tomatoes

Darina's Roasted Potatoes

Darina's Strawberry-Rhubarb Crumble

Darina's Risotto with Broad Beans, Peas, Green Asparagus, and Sugar Snaps

This sumptuous risotto is generously studded with a medley of spring vegetables, preferably fresh. Darina prefers her risottos soft and soupy, so she adds even more chicken broth and cooks them longer. I've adjusted the broth and found a happy medium. Cook according to your own taste.

INGREDIENTS

½ pound unshelled broad beans, preferably fresh (if unavailable, increase the amount of snap peas and asparagus by one-third)*

2 teaspoons salt, or to taste

⅓ pound snap peas, ends snapped and veiny strings removed

8 stalks asparagus, tough woody ends snapped off

½ pound peas (about 1¾ cup), preferably fresh, but if frozen defrosted to room temperature

5½ to 6 cups good-quality reduced-sodium chicken broth, preferably homemade

3 tablespoons unsalted butter

1 onion, peeled and chopped finely

1½ cups Arborio rice

⅓ cup dry white wine

½ cup freshly grated Parmigiano-Reggiano cheese, plus a little extra for serving

¼ teaspoon freshly ground black pepper

*Shelled broad beans are available frozen in many supermarkets. If using, defrost and add at the last minute.

FIRST Bring 2 quarts of water to a boil in a saucepan, add the broad beans and 1 teaspoon of salt, and if using fresh beans, cook for 2 to 3 minutes, or until almost tender. Remove with a slotted spoon and refresh in cold water. Drain again and, using your fingers, slip the beans out of their skins. Bring the water again to a boil and cook the snap peas for about 2 minutes, remove with a slotted spoon, and refresh in cold water. Do the same for the asparagus and the peas, cooking the asparagus for 4 to 5 minutes and the peas for 3 to 4 minutes, if fresh (defrosted frozen peas do not need to be precooked; add in step 3). Refresh in cold water and drain. Cut the asparagus on the diagonal into 1-inch lengths.

SECOND Bring the chicken broth to just under a boil in a saucepan and keep at a slow simmer. Melt 1½ tablespoons of the butter in a large, heavy saucepan. Add the chopped onion and cook over medium heat until soft but not colored. Add the rice and 1 teaspoon of salt and stir for about 2 to 3 minutes, or until the edges of the rice become translucent, then increase the heat to high and add the white wine.

THIRD Keep stirring, and when the wine has evaporated, pour in a couple ladlefuls of chicken broth, reducing the heat to medium. Continue stirring, and when the liquid has almost been absorbed (after about 6 to 8 minutes), add another ladleful of broth. Continue to ladle in more broth and keep repeating until the rice is just cooked. Add the beans, sugar snaps, and peas, and taste the rice to see if it is cooked. If not, continue cooking and adding a little more broth. Stir in the remaining butter, the freshly grated cheese, the asparagus, and the black pepper. Stir in a little more broth if necessary; the risotto should be moist. Taste the risotto for seasoning, adding more salt if necessary. Spoon into heated bowls with extra freshly grated cheese on top. Serve immediately.

Darina's Pan-Grilled Chicken with Parsley Salad and Sun-Dried Tomatoes

SIX SERVINGS

This dish is so easy and yet so good! The combination of fresh parsley, sun-dried tomatoes, cooked chicken, and fresh basil dressing is superb. Add a few roasted potatoes and you have a delicious and filling meal.

INGREDIENTS

BASIL DRESSING

1   shallot, peeled, ends trimmed, and smashed with the flat side of a knife

3   cloves garlic, smashed with the flat side of a knife and peeled

1¼ cups fresh basil leaves, rinsed, drained, and blotted dry

⅓   cup Japanese clear rice vinegar

1   cup virgin olive oil

1¼ teaspoons salt, or to taste

¼   teaspoon freshly ground black pepper

3   whole boneless, skinless chicken breasts

2   teaspoons virgin olive oil

⅓   teaspoon salt

¼   teaspoon freshly ground black pepper

4   cups curly parsley leaves, rinsed and drained

6   sun-dried tomatoes, cut into small dice

⅓   cup slivers or shavings of Parmigiano-Reggiano cheese

FIRST To make the Basil Dressing, drop the shallot and garlic down the feed tube of a food processor fitted with a steel blade, or into a blender, while the machine is running. Add the basil and continue chopping until you have a paste, scraping down the sides with a rubber spatula. Pour in the vinegar and slowly pour in the olive oil in a very thin, steady stream while the machine is running. Add the salt and pepper.

SECOND Divide each whole chicken breast in two and flatten with the heel of your hand. Brush with the olive oil and sprinkle with salt and pepper. Heat a cast-iron grill or skillet until very hot but not smoking. Place the chicken breasts on the grill (you may have to do this in two batches) and cook, covered, at medium-high heat for about 4 to 5 minutes. Turn the chicken breasts over and continue cooking for another 4 to 5 minutes, until they are cooked through. (If they are very thick, continue cooking.) Remove the chicken breasts to a platter, and let sit for 5 minutes. Cook any remaining chicken. Cut on the diagonal into thin slices, keeping each breast half together.

THIRD Toss the parsley and sun-dried tomatoes in a bowl with a third of the dressing, then arrange on six serving plates. Place the chicken on top of the parsley. Spoon some basil dressing over the top and sprinkle with the cheese slivers. Serve warm or at room temperature with roasted potatoes (see the following recipe).

Darina's Roasted Potatoes

Darina shares my belief that good-quality, seasonal vegetables taste best when cooked simply.

INGREDIENTS

1¼ pounds smallish russet (Idaho) or Yukon Gold potatoes

1   tablespoon virgin olive oil

1   teaspoon sea salt

FIRST Preheat the oven to 400 degrees. Lightly rinse the potatoes to remove any soil and drain thoroughly. Dry with paper towels. Do not peel. Cut the potatoes into quarters or smaller pieces. Put in a bowl and toss lightly with the oil and salt. Spread the potatoes out in an even layer on a cookie sheet.

SECOND Bake for 25 to 30 minutes, or until crisp and a deep golden brown color. Remove and transfer to a serving platter or portion onto individual plates. Serve hot.

Darina's Strawberry-Rhubarb Crumble

SIX TO EIGHT SERVINGS

Rhubarb and strawberries are a classic spring combination. Rhubarb may be very tart, so adjust the sugar accordingly.

INGREDIENTS

- 1 pound red rhubarb, ends trimmed, cut into 1-inch chunks
- ½ to ¾ cup sugar, or to taste
- 2 tablespoons water
- 1 pint strawberries, rinsed lightly, stems removed, cut in half

Juice of ½ lemon

CRUMBLE TOPPING

- 4 tablespoons unsalted butter, cut into small pieces
- 1 cup all-purpose flour, preferably unbleached
- ¼ cup sugar

½ cup light brown sugar and 1½ cups whipped cream for garnish

FIRST Preheat the oven to 350 degrees. Put the rhubarb, ½ cup of the sugar, and the water into a nonreactive saucepan (not aluminum). Stir, cover, and bring to a boil. Reduce the heat and simmer about 10 minutes. Remove from the heat and taste to see if it needs an additional ¼ cup of sugar. Stir in the strawberries and lemon juice. Put into a 9-inch round or square pan.

SECOND For the Crumble Topping, rub the butter into the flour just until the mixture resembles coarse bread crumbs. Add the sugar and sprinkle the topping over the rhubarb and strawberries. Bake for 20 to 25 minutes, turn up the heat to 375 degrees to brown and crisp the top, and bake for 15 minutes more, until the topping is cooked and golden. Serve warm with a sprinkling of light brown sugar and whipped cream.

David Heber and His "Seven Colors of Health"

David Heber has long been a pioneer in exploring the relationship between food and health. In 1983, he became the founding director of the Division of Clinical Nutrition in the Department of Medicine at UCLA, and in 1995 he became the founding director of the renowned UCLA Center for Human Nutrition. Since its opening, the center's groundbreaking research has promoted and strengthened the role of nutrition in preventing and treating common diseases, including cancer, heart disease, and obesity.

Lately Dr. Heber has been intent on adding color to our plates. In his best-selling book *What Color Is Your Diet?,* he and his coauthor, nutritionist Susan Bowerman, introduce a revolutionary "Seven Colors of Health" eating plan, which incorporates seven different color groups of fruits and vegetables that can protect our genes, vision, and hearts, reduce inflammation in the body, and help prevent common forms of cancer.

Dr. Heber contends that the majority of the most common diseases are caused by the imbalance between our modern diet and our genes. By eating a variety of specified fruits and vegetables, we can strengthen our immune systems, reduce the risk of common diseases, increase our longevity, and lose weight. Dr. Heber organizes fruits and vegetables into seven color groups by their health-giving phytochemicals, the disease-fighting nutrients found in plants that can also protect humans. According to the color-coded food plan, men and women should eat one serving (at least ½ cup of a cooked vegetable or fruit or at least 1 cup of a raw vegetable or fruit) from each of the seven color-coded groups of fruits *or* vegetables every day, as well as some protein, whole grains, and taste enhancers at each meal. To make it simpler, he suggests filling two-thirds of your plate with fruits and vegetables of different colors and reducing the meat portion to 3 to 6 ounces.

The chart opposite gives a detailed breakdown of each color group and the specific health-giving benefits of the fruits and vegetables belonging to it. This chart was compiled from information contained in *What Color Is Your Diet?,* by David Heber and Susan Bowerman; *Food & Fitness Advisor,* a newsletter published by the Weill Medical College of Cornell University (December 2002); and *The Color Code,* by James A. Joseph, Ph.D., Daniel A. Nadeau, M.D., and Anne Underwood.

SOME HELPFUL DEFINITIONS

ANTIOXIDANTS
red/purple vegetables

Antioxidants are positively charged molecules that snag the negatively charged free radicals in the body, making them harmless. Many fruits and vegetables have antioxidant properties. They protect against cancer and heart disease, and are believed to slow the aging process.

CAROTENOIDS
red, orange, yellow/green vegetables

Carotenoids are chemical compounds that absorb light and determine the color in fruits and vegetables. In our bodies, carotenoids make their way to specific tissues and organs, where they have been shown to protect against DNA damage, thereby preventing heart disease and certain cancers.

FREE RADICALS
Free radicals are unstable molecules that damage healthy cells as they travel through the body. They are produced naturally by the body as it uses oxygen to convert digested food into energy. Liver spots, cataracts, cancer, and other degenerative diseases are all the result of free-radical damage.

	FRUITS AND VEGETABLES	MAIN PHYTONUTRIENTS AND THEIR BENEFITS	MAIN VITAMINS/ MINERALS
RED	Tomatoes and tomato products, pink grapefruit, watermelon, ketchup	Lycopene is one of the most potent free-radical scavengers in nature. It has been shown to prevent heart and lung disease, as well as prostate cancer.	Vitamin C, Potassium
RED/ PURPLE	Red grapes, blueberries, blackberries, cherries, plums, prunes, raisins, eggplant, raspberries, red beets, red peppers, strawberries, red apples, cranberries	Anthocyanins are powerful antioxidants that strengthen skin and other tissues, tendons, and ligaments. They also seem to prevent heart disease by keeping blood clots from forming.	Vitamin C, Potassium
ORANGE	Apricots, acorn and winter squash, butternut and yellow squash, carrots, mangoes, cantaloupes, pumpkins, sweet potatoes	Alpha- and beta-carotene are carotenoids and very effective antioxidants. They protect against cancer by preventing oxidation damage, reducing the multiplication of cancer cells, and eliminating tumors.	Vitamin A, Beta-carotene, Vitamin C, Magnesium, Potassium
ORANGE/ YELLOW	Clementines, mandarin oranges, oranges and orange juice, peaches, pineapples and pineapple juice, nectarines, papayas, tangerines, tangelos, lemons, limes	Beta cryptothanxin is another carotenoid, which plays an important role in fighting heart disease and may help to prevent cervical cancer.	Vitamin C, Folate, Potassium
YELLOW/ GREEN	Collard greens, green and yellow peppers, green beans, kale, mustard and beet greens, spinach, green peas, avocados, honeydew melons, yellow corn	Lutein and zeaxanthin are pigments that become concentrated in the eye, where they help reduce the risk of cataracts and age-related macular degeneration.	Vitamin C, Vitamin K, Calcium, Folate
GREEN	Broccoli and broccoli sprouts, bok choy, brussels sprouts, cabbage, Chinese cabbage, kale, cauliflower	Sulforaphane, isothiocyanate, and indoles fight numerous diseases by eliminating toxic waste (carcinogens) from the body.	Vitamin C, Folate, Potassium
WHITE/ GREEN	Asparagus, celery, chives, endive, garlic, leeks, mushrooms, pearl onions, pears, shallots, artichokes	Allicin, which is found in members of the onion family, is known to lower cholesterol and blood pressure and have antitumor effects. Flavonoids are powerful cancer-fighting antioxidants.	Selenium, Folate

- To implement this concept in your daily diet, try adding more different-colored FRUITS AND VEGETABLES to every meal. Fill two-thirds of your plate with fruits and vegetables and reduce the meat portion to 3 to 6 ounces.

- Eat a different fruit or two EACH MORNING with your breakfast.

- After food shopping, clean vegetables, precut or prepare them for cooking, then wrap in paper towels and put in bags in the refrigerator READY TO USE.

- Try UNUSUAL COMBINATIONS and new foods to get more color in your diet. Toss some dried cranberries or mandarin oranges into a spinach salad, or add colorful baby Swiss chard to a salad.

- Visit your LOCAL FARMERS' MARKETS whenever possible. Frequently there are unusual varieties of fruits and vegetables that are not available in the supermarket, and the seasonal produce is picked at its nutritional peak, offering a wealth of phytonutrients.

- Make getting your COLORS CONVENIENT—search the freezer, salad bar, and produce section for prewashed, presliced, prechopped vegetables and fruits to put meals together more quickly.

- Serve FRUIT FOR DESSERT instead of high-fat and high-sugar items.

Opposite: Sage

versatile stir-fries and sautés

I've always been fascinated with stir-frying, even before I went to Asia to study Chinese cooking. As a child, I loved to peek into the kitchen of my local Chinese restaurant and watch transfixed as the chef would toss different foods into a pan, then casually flip them about over a roaring flame. In a flash, the dish was done and sent steaming to the table, ready to eat. The whole thing seemed so magical.

Years later at French cooking school, as a chef tossed some shallots, wine, and French beans in a sauté pan over a sizable flame, I realized how much sautéing and stir-frying have in common. "The term 'sauté' comes from the French verb meaning to jump," he told us, "as cooks often throw or toss food in the pan to prevent it from burning and encourage it to cook evenly."

It is precisely the speed, versatility, and convenience that make these two cooking methods so appealing to the home cook. The quick cooking sears in flavor, so that in the finished dish, vegetables are vibrant yet crisp-cooked. Meat is juicy and seafood is tender. You can also tailor the methods to your dietary preferences: Whereas in restaurants most chefs precook meats and seafood for stir-fried dishes by deep-frying them in oil, home cooks can adapt the recipe and roast, steam, or boil foods.

When sautéing you can replace butter with olive oil (or use a little of both), and with either cooking method the quantity of meat and seafood can be decreased while the variety and amount of vegetables may be increased to make dishes healthier. Stir-frying and sautéing also lend themselves nicely to improvisation depending on what is on hand and in season. Leftovers can be transformed into a feast with very little effort and a bit of ingenuity.

Both techniques are not so much magical as methodical. Success depends on organization. Here are some suggestions that cooks may find useful:

- All preparation should be completed before the cooking begins.
- Arrange everything necessary near the stove.
- Seasonings that are going to be added at the same time can be combined in one bowl. (The same is true for liquids.)
- Set the heat on the highest setting and get the pan really hot before adding oil, which prevents food from sticking. Never add cold oil to a cold pan.
- Heat the oil until hot. To test the temperature, sprinkle a little chopped scallion or ginger into the pan. If it sizzles, the oil is hot enough to proceed with the stir-frying. If the seasonings burn, the oil is too hot, so clean out the pan and start over.
- Use a heavy sauté pan, skillet, or wok that conducts heat evenly and efficiently.

Good cooks have been stir-frying and sautéing for centuries now, and both methods are good for accentuating the natural flavors of ingredients. So it is important to choose foods that are fresh and of the best quality. As my French chef used to say, "A dish is only as good as its ingredients," a message echoed by my Chinese chef: "Select your ingredients as if they were your future daughter-in-law."

Wilted Greens with Garlic

SIX SERVINGS

Stir-frying is one of the best techniques for cooking leafy vegetables since it accentuates fresh flavors and brings out vibrant colors. I like to make large batches of this recipe and serve some for dinner with a grilled or steamed main dish and rice. The rest I'll add to a soup for lunch the next day.

INGREDIENTS

- 1¾ to 2 pounds baby spinach or regular spinach, arugula, or other leafy vegetable
- 1½ teaspoons virgin olive oil

GARLIC DRESSING (MIXED TOGETHER)

- 3½ tablespoons soy sauce, or to taste
- 3½ tablespoons rice wine or sake
- 1½ tablespoons minced garlic
- 1½ teaspoons sugar
- 1 teaspoon hot chile paste (optional)

FIRST Tear the stems, if they are tough, from the spinach and discard. Throw the leaves into a colander and rinse thoroughly under cold running water. Spin dry.

SECOND Heat a large wok or a skillet, add the oil, and heat until near smoking. *(Don't be afraid to get the pan very hot. This will give the dish its appealing flavor.)* Add the greens and Garlic Dressing, and toss lightly over high heat about 1½ minutes, or until the greens are slightly wilted but still bright green. Scoop out the greens, arrange them on a serving platter, and spoon the juice on top. Serve immediately, at room temperature, or chilled.

+ *Spinach is one of the richest sources of lutein, one of the main antioxidants for the eye. For more information, see the "yellow/green" category of the "Seven Colors of Health" chart on page 199.*

Spicy Sichuan-Style Green Beans

SIX SERVINGS

This spicy Sichuan sauce is delicious not only with green beans, but with many other types of vegetables, including broccoli, snow peas or snap peas, and Chinese greens like broccoli and bok choy.

+ *Refer to the "yellow/green" category of David Heber's "Seven Colors of Health" chart on page 199 for the health-giving properties of green beans.*

✽ *Green beans strengthen the spleen and pancreas. Chinese doctors recommend that diabetics eat them, since they are believed to quench thirst.*

INGREDIENTS

2½ pounds green beans, rinsed and drained

2½ tablespoons virgin olive oil

SEASONINGS

1½ tablespoons minced scallions, white part only

2 tablespoons minced garlic

1 teaspoon hot chile paste or dried chile flakes, or to taste

SPICY SAUCE (MIXED TOGETHER)

¾ cup good-quality reduced-sodium chicken broth, or water

3 tablespoons soy sauce

2½ tablespoons rice wine or sake

1½ tablespoons sugar

1 teaspoon toasted sesame oil

2 teaspoons Chinese black vinegar or Worcestershire sauce

1¼ teaspoons cornstarch

½ cup toasted sliced almonds for garnish (optional)

FIRST Trim the ends of the beans and cut the beans into 3-inch lengths or, if not too long, leave whole.

SECOND Bring 2 quarts of water to a boil in a pot or large saucepan. Add the green beans and bring to a boil again. Reduce the heat to medium and cook uncovered for about 8 minutes, or until almost cooked but still crisp. Drain in a colander and refresh in cold water. Drain again.

THIRD Heat a wok or a deep skillet, add the oil, heat until hot, and add the Seasonings. Stir-fry briefly, about 15 seconds, then add the Spicy Sauce. Bring to a boil, stirring continuously to prevent lumps, until thickened. Return the cooked green beans to the pan, toss lightly to coat, and scoop onto a serving platter. Sprinkle with the toasted almonds, if using, and serve with steamed rice, couscous, or quinoa, and grilled seafood or meat, or more vegetables.

Françoise's Sautéed Mushrooms

SIX SERVINGS

Françoise Fetchko, my dear friend and brilliant recipe tester, is a master of the sauté (perhaps the fact that she's French helps). She and her husband often forage for fresh chanterelles, or she gets superb fresh shiitake mushrooms from her friend Toshio Hashimoto, who owns Shiitake Farms in Rumford, Maine. Both varieties are good in this recipe.

INGREDIENTS

- 1½ **pounds fresh shiitake or chanterelle mushrooms**
- 2 **tablespoons virgin olive oil**
- 1½ **teaspoons salt, or to taste**
- ¼ **teaspoon freshly ground black pepper**
- 2 **tablespoons chopped garlic**
- 1½ **cups chopped flat-leaf parsley**

FIRST Trim the stem ends of the mushrooms, rinse lightly, and drain thoroughly. Cut the mushrooms into thin slices.

SECOND Heat a heavy 10-inch skillet or sauté pan until hot. Pour in the oil and heat until hot, about 10 seconds. Add the mushrooms and stir-fry over medium-high heat for about 4 minutes, until they have rendered their liquid. Sprinkle in the salt and pepper.

THIRD Turn up the heat slightly and add the garlic. Toss lightly and sauté for about a minute. Add the parsley and toss lightly to mix together. Taste for seasonings, adjusting if necessary. Scoop into a bowl or a platter and serve.

✳ Shiitake mushrooms have tremendous immune-enhancing properties. Japanese doctors have isolated the phytonutrient lentinan and synthesized it, and it is used in fighting certain forms of cancer, AIDS, and chronic fatigue syndrome.

Kung Pao Chicken with Peanuts

SIX SERVINGS

This Sichuanese chicken dish with peanuts has become a stir-fry classic. All the ingredients should be uniformly cut to the same size so that they cook evenly and the dish looks attractive. It's a perfect "rice-sending" dish along with a steamed, sautéed, or stir-fried vegetable.

+ *Recent research has shown that **nuts** help to strengthen the immune system and lower cholesterol. They also may reduce the risk of heart disease.*

INGREDIENTS

1½ pounds boneless, skinless chicken meat

MARINADE

2   tablespoons soy sauce

2   tablespoons rice wine or sake

1   teaspoon toasted sesame oil

1   teaspoon cornstarch

4½ tablespoons virgin olive oil

SEASONINGS

2   tablespoons minced scallions, white part only

1½ tablespoons minced fresh ginger

1½ tablespoons minced garlic

1   teaspoon hot chile paste or dried chile flakes, or to taste

1½ cups thinly sliced water chestnuts (about 8 ounces), blanched for 10 seconds, then refreshed in cold water and drained

SAUCE (MIXED TOGETHER)

½   cup good-quality reduced-sodium chicken broth or water

2½ tablespoons soy sauce

2   tablespoons rice wine or sake

1   teaspoon toasted sesame oil

1   tablespoon Chinese black vinegar or Worcestershire sauce

1¼ teaspoons cornstarch

1   cup ½-inch lengths scallion greens (optional)

1¼ cups unsalted dry-roasted peanuts

FIRST Trim the chicken of any fat or gristle and cut into ½-inch cubes. Place in a bowl. Add the Marinade and toss lightly to coat. Cover with plastic wrap and refrigerate for 20 minutes.

SECOND Heat a wok or a skillet, add 2½ tablespoons of the oil, heat until very hot, and add the chicken. Cook over high heat until the chicken becomes opaque and is cooked, about 3 to 4 minutes. Remove with a strainer and drain. Wipe out the pan.

THIRD Add the remaining oil and heat until hot. Add the Seasonings and stir-fry briefly, about 15 seconds, then add the water chestnuts and stir-fry over high heat for about 1½ minutes to heat through. Add the Sauce and cook, stirring continuously to prevent lumps, until thickened. Return the cooked chicken to the pan and add the scallion greens, if desired, and the peanuts. Toss lightly to coat and heat through. Scoop up everything onto a serving dish or platter. Serve with steamed rice.

⁕ According to Traditional Chinese Medicine, peanuts lubricate the intestines and are prescribed to increase the milk supply in nursing mothers.

§ Ayurvedic doctors recommend a tea made boiling peanut shells and water for lowering blood pressure.

Seared Garlic Beef with Rainbow Peppers in Black Bean Sauce

SIX SERVINGS

Usually the most tender cuts of meat or poultry are used for stir-fried dishes: For beef dishes, flank steak, London broil, sirloin, or tenderloin is used. You may substitute chicken breast meat, center-cut pork loin, or turkey tenderloin for the beef in this dish, if you prefer.

INGREDIENTS

1¼ pounds flank steak or boneless sirloin steak, about 1 inch thick

MARINADE (MIXED TOGETHER)

2 tablespoons soy sauce

2 tablespoons minced garlic

1 teaspoon toasted sesame oil

¾ pound snap peas

3½ tablespoons virgin olive oil

SEASONINGS (MIXED TOGETHER)

3½ tablespoons fermented or salted black beans, rinsed, drained, and minced

3 tablespoons minced garlic

2½ tablespoons peeled and minced fresh ginger

1 teaspoon dried chile flakes, or to taste

2 red onions, peeled and cut into thin julienne slices (about 3 cups)

1 red bell pepper, cored, seeded, ends removed, and cut into julienne strips

2 orange or yellow bell peppers, cored, seeded, ends removed, and cut into julienne strips

2 tablespoons rice wine or sake

SAUCE (MIXED TOGETHER)

1 cup good-quality reduced-sodium chicken broth or water

6 tablespoons soy sauce

3 tablespoons rice wine or sake

1½ tablespoons sugar

2 teaspoons cornstarch

FIRST Trim away any fat or gristle and put the meat in a bowl. Pour in the Marinade, toss lightly to coat, and cover with plastic wrap. Let marinate for 20 minutes, or longer if possible.

SECOND Bring 1½ quarts of water to a boil. Add the snap peas and cook for about 1½ minutes, or until crisp-tender. Drain in a colander and refresh under cold running water. Drain again.

THIRD Prepare a medium-hot fire for grilling or preheat a broiler. Brush or spray the grill with oil and place the meat about 3 inches from the source of heat. Grill or broil for about 5 minutes on each side for medium-rare (grill longer if you want the meat well done). Take off the heat and let sit for 10 minutes. Cut the meat across the grain into thin slices about 1½ inches long.

FOURTH Heat a wok or a heavy skillet, add the oil, and heat until hot, about 15 seconds. Add the Seasonings and red onions, and cook for about 1 minute, then add the peppers and stir-fry for another minute. Pour in the rice wine and toss lightly. Cover and cook for 2 minutes, until the peppers are tender. Add the blanched snap peas and the Sauce and cook until thickened, stirring to prevent lumps. Add the cooked beef and toss lightly in the sauce. Scoop onto a serving platter and serve with steamed rice.

ALL-PURPOSE
RECIPE

Spicy Shrimp with Basil

SIX SERVINGS

Thai cooks have integrated the stir-fry technique from China into their cuisine with great success, as exemplified by this dish. You can substitute other types of seafood or meat for the shrimp. Serve with a green vegetable and steamed rice or, for a change, try quinoa.

+ For the health-giving properties of **basil**, see "Dr. Jim Duke's Herbal Farmacy" on page 158.

§ *In India, an infusion of basil leaves and ginger is one of the most popular remedies for children's stomachaches.*

INGREDIENTS

1½ pounds medium shrimp, peeled and deveined

MARINADE (MIXED TOGETHER)

3 **tablespoons rice wine or sake**

2 **tablespoons soy sauce**

1 **tablespoon minced fresh ginger**

½ **pound snow peas, ends snapped, veiny strings removed, blanched, refreshed, and drained**

2½ tablespoons virgin olive oil

SEASONINGS

1 **teaspoon dried chile flakes**

2 **tablespoons chopped garlic**

2 **medium red onions, peeled and cut into thin julienne slices (about 3 cups)**

SAUCE (MIXED TOGETHER)

3 **tablespoons fish sauce**

1½ **tablespoons soy sauce**

1 **tablespoon sugar**

1½ **tablespoons water**

1½ cups fresh Thai holy basil or sweet basil leaves, rinsed, drained, and coarsely shredded

FIRST Rinse and drain the shrimp. Toss the shrimp with the Marinade in a bowl and let sit 20 minutes.

SECOND Heat a wok or a heavy skillet. Add 1 tablespoon of the oil and heat until near smoking. Swirl the oil around the pan. Add the shrimp and toss lightly over high heat for 2½ minutes, until the shrimp have changed color and are *just* cooked. Drain in a colander. Wipe out the pan.

THIRD Reheat the pan, add the remaining oil, and heat until very hot. Add the Seasonings and stir-fry over high heat, about 3 minutes, or until the onions are tender. Pour in the Sauce mixture and bring to a boil. Add the cooked shrimp, snow peas, and fresh basil, and mix. Scoop the shrimp onto a serving platter and serve with rice or another staple.

Vegetarian Roll-Ups

SIX SERVINGS

Vegetarian roll-ups are a satisfying and healthy meal by themselves, with their vibrant stir-fried filling and steamed wrappers. I vary the vegetables, substituting garlic chives for leeks and half the amount of dried black mushrooms for the fresh shiitakes. To save time, wrap the wrappers in a damp cloth napkin and steam briefly in a microwave oven.

INGREDIENTS:

18 to 20 Mandarin pancakes or flour tortillas

2½ tablespoons virgin olive oil

1　large egg, lightly beaten

SEASONINGS (MIXED TOGETHER)

3　tablespoons minced garlic

3　tablespoons minced fresh ginger

3½ cups leeks (about 3), cleaned, ends trimmed, and cut into thin julienne shreds

¾　pound fresh shiitake mushrooms, stems trimmed, rinsed, drained, and cut into thin slices

1½ cups grated carrots (about 3)

5　cups Napa cabbage, stem sections separated, cut into thin julienne shreds

2½ tablespoons rice wine or water

3½ cups bean sprouts

SAUCE (MIXED TOGETHER)

3½ tablespoons light soy sauce

3½ tablespoons rice wine or sake

½　teaspoon sugar

⅓　teaspoon freshly ground black pepper

1　teaspoon cornstarch

¾　cup hoisin sauce, mixed with 2½ tablespoons water in a serving dish

FIRST Separate the pancakes or tortillas, fold them into quarters, and place in a steamer tray. Cover and set over a wok or pan of boiling water. Steam them for 10 minutes. Set aside, covered, to keep warm.

SECOND Heat a wok or a heavy skillet. Add 1 tablespoon of oil and heat until hot. Add the egg and stir-fry over high heat to scramble, then remove to a plate.

THIRD Pour in the remaining 1½ tablespoons of oil, heat until very hot, and add the Seasonings. Stir-fry for 10 seconds, until fragrant, then add the leeks, mushrooms, and carrots. Toss lightly over high heat for 1½ minutes, then add the cabbage stems and rice wine or water and continue stir-frying over high heat for another minute. Add the leafy cabbage sections, and cook until the vegetables are crisp-tender, about 1 minute. Add the cooked egg to the pan, stir, then add the bean sprouts and Sauce. Toss lightly to thicken, stirring constantly to prevent lumps. Scoop onto a serving platter.

FOURTH To serve, arrange a pancake or a tortilla on a plate, smear a tablespoon of the hoisin sauce on it, spoon some of the stir-fried mixture on top, and eat.

+ *Refer to the "Seven Colors of Health" chart on page 199 for the health-giving properties of carrots, leeks, and cabbage.*

Pork Lo Mein with Garlic Chives and Bean Sprouts

SIX SERVINGS

"Lo mein" dishes are cooked noodles stir-fried in a sauce with seafood, meat, or chicken, and vegetables. The noodles generally are made of wheat flour and water and may be flat like linguine or fettuccine or round like spaghetti. My family loves them, and the leftovers are easy to reheat by stir-frying the next day or later for lunch or dinner.

INGREDIENTS

1½ pounds boneless center-cut pork loin

GARLIC MARINADE (MIXED TOGETHER)

2   tablespoons soy sauce

1½ tablespoons rice wine or sake

1   teaspoon toasted sesame oil

1½ tablespoons minced garlic

9   ounces Chinese flour-and-water noodles or linguine

4   tablespoons virgin olive oil

MINCED SEASONINGS (MIXED TOGETHER)

3   tablespoons minced fresh ginger

2½ tablespoons minced garlic

4   cups 1-inch lengths garlic chives, ends trimmed (or 4 cups cleaned leeks cut into 1-inch lengths plus 2 tablespoons minced garlic)

2   tablespoons rice wine or sake

SAUCE (MIXED TOGETHER)

2¼ cups good-quality reduced-sodium chicken broth

4   tablespoons oyster sauce

3   tablespoons soy sauce

3   tablespoons rice wine or sake

1½ teaspoons toasted sesame oil

1   teaspoon sugar

¼   teaspoon freshly ground black pepper

1½ tablespoons cornstarch

14   ounces (or 5 cups) bean sprouts, rinsed and drained

FIRST Trim the pork of any fat or gristle. Holding the knife on the diagonal, cut into very thin slices and then into very thin julienne shreds. Place in a bowl, and add the Garlic Marinade. Toss lightly to coat.

SECOND Heat 4 quarts of water until boiling, add the noodles, and cook until near-tender (about 2½ to 4 minutes if fresh, or 7 to 9 minutes if dried), drain in a colander, rinse lightly to remove the starch, and drain again thoroughly.

THIRD Heat a wok or a skillet, add 2½ tablespoons of the oil, and heat until very hot but not smoking. Add the pork and toss lightly over high heat until the meat slices change color and separate. Remove with a strainer and drain. Wipe out the pan.

FOURTH Reheat the pan, add the remaining oil, heat about 20 seconds, and add the Minced Seasonings. Stir-fry over medium-high heat for about 10 seconds, until fragrant. Add the garlic chives, and stir-fry about 1½ minutes, until tender, adding the 2 tablespoons of rice wine. Add the Sauce mixture and bean sprouts, and cook, stirring continuously to prevent lumps, until thickened. Add the noodles and pork, and toss lightly. Transfer the lo mein onto a warm platter and serve immediately.

Pad Thai

Pad thai is one of the most popular of Thai noodle dishes, and rightfully so. The flat silken rice noodles soak up the sweet and sour sauce and provide a superb foil to the tender tofu and crunchy bean sprouts. Although this dish is often served with others in a Thai restaurant, my family is very happy to eat it as a meal by itself.

INGREDIENTS

1 pound medium shrimp, peeled and deveined

3½ tablespoons virgin olive oil

2 large eggs, lightly beaten

2 tablespoons minced garlic

SAUCE, (MIXED TOGETHER)

¼ cup fish sauce, or to taste

5 tablespoons ketchup

1½ tablespoons sugar

3 tablespoons water

⅜ to ½ pound Chinese rice stick noodles or rice vermicelli, softened in hot water and drained

2½ cups bean sprouts, rinsed lightly and drained

TOPPING

3 tablespoons minced scallion greens

½ teaspoon dried chile flakes

3½ tablespoons coarsely chopped fresh cilantro leaves

¼ cup finely chopped dry-roasted peanuts

2 limes, cut into six wedges each

FIRST Rinse the shrimp and pat dry. With a sharp knife, score the shrimp along the back, then rinse and drain thoroughly.

SECOND Heat a wok or a heavy skillet, add 1 tablespoon of the oil, and heat until near smoking, about 30 seconds. Swirl the oil around the pan. Add the shrimp and toss lightly over high heat for 2½ minutes, until the shrimp have changed color and are *just* cooked. Drain in a colander. Wipe out the pan.

THIRD Reheat the pan, add the remaining oil, and heat until hot, about 20 seconds. Add the eggs, stirring to scramble, over medium-high heat. Move the eggs to the side of the pan and add the garlic. Stir-fry for about 10 seconds, until fragrant, add the Sauce mixture and the rice stick noodles, and toss over medium-high heat. Cook for about 3 to 4 minutes, until the noodles are tender and the liquid has been absorbed.

FOURTH Add the bean sprouts and shrimp and toss to mix. Scoop out onto a serving platter. Sprinkle with the prepared Topping ingredients. Arrange the lime wedges on the side and serve. Diners squeeze the lime onto their individual portions before eating.

Like rice, noodles tone the body, energize, and strengthen the spleen.

Pan-Roasted Salmon with Minty Snap Peas

SIX SERVINGS

The ginger-soy-balsamic marinade gives the seared salmon a lovely flavor and color, and the simple mint dressing is a light and refreshing complement to snap peas. I like to serve this dish hot, or at room temperature with rice pilaf for a festive buffet.

INGREDIENTS

6 **salmon fillets with skin on (each about 6 ounces)**

MARINADE (MIXED TOGETHER)

2 **tablespoons minced fresh ginger**

3 **tablespoons soy sauce**

3 **tablespoons balsamic vinegar**

1½ pounds snap peas

MINT DRESSING

3 **tablespoons fruity extra-virgin olive oil**

2 **tablespoons lemon juice, or to taste**

6 **tablespoons chopped mint leaves**

1 **teaspoon salt**

½ **teaspoon freshly ground black pepper**

2 **tablespoons virgin olive oil**

FIRST Lightly toss the salmon with the Marinade in a bowl and let sit at room temperature.

SECOND Bring 2 quarts of water to a boil in a saucepan and add the snap peas. Cook for 2 minutes, or until crisp-tender. Drain in a colander and refresh in cold water. Drain again and blot dry on paper towels.

THIRD Whisk the ingredients of the Mint Dressing together in a mixing bowl. Add the snap peas and toss lightly to coat.

FOURTH Heat the 2 tablespoons olive oil in a large frying pan over high heat until very hot. Rub the marinade all over the salmon and place in the pan, skin side down. Partially cover, and fry about 5 to 6 minutes over high heat (depending on the thickness), until the skin is crisp and the salmon meat has started becoming opaque. Carefully flip over with a spatula and cook for another 3 to 4 minutes, or until just cooked.

FIFTH Arrange the salmon on a serving platter and spoon the snap peas around. Serve with a rice pilaf or steamed rice.

+ *For the health-giving properties of mint, refer to the "Peppermint" category of "Dr. Jim Duke's Herbal Farmacy" on page 158.*

Seared Scallops with Asparagus, Shallots, and White Wine

SIX SERVINGS

This is one of those simple dishes where only the best ingredients should be used. I generally use sea scallops, but when bay scallops are in season, they are excellent in this recipe. Just reduce the cooking time slightly. Other vegetables such as snap peas and broccoli may be used instead of asparagus.

+ *Asparagus has long been recognized as an effective diuretic. Eating several servings one week to ten days prior to menstruating may prevent premenstrual bloating. David Heber classifies asparagus in the "white/green" category of his "Seven Colors of Health" chart on page 199.*

INGREDIENTS

3   tablespoons virgin olive oil

1½ pounds sea scallops or bay scallops, rinsed, drained, and blotted dry on paper towels

¾   teaspoon salt

½   teaspoon coarsely ground black pepper

1½ pounds fresh asparagus, tough woody ends snapped off, and cut into 1-inch lengths

1   tablespoon unsalted butter

⅓   cup minced shallots

¾   cup dry white wine

Juice of ½ lemon

FIRST Heat 2 tablespoons of the oil until very hot in a large, heavy skillet over medium-high heat. Sprinkle the scallops with salt and pepper. Sear half the scallops until brown and just opaque in center, about 1½ minutes per side. For bay scallops, sauté half at a time until opaque, stirring frequently, about 1½ minutes per batch. Scoop onto a serving platter and set aside. Save the pan and scallop juices.

SECOND Bring 2 quarts water to a boil in a saucepan or pot, add the asparagus, and cook for about 5 minutes, or until crisp-tender. Drain in a colander and refresh in cold water. Drain again.

THIRD Reheat the skillet until hot, add the remaining tablespoon of oil and the butter, and heat until the foam begins to subside. Add the shallots and sauté over medium heat until softened, about 3 to 5 minutes. Pour in the wine and increase the heat slightly. Cook for about 5 minutes, stirring occasionally, to reduce the liquid. Add the asparagus, scallops, and the reserved pan and scallop juices, and squeeze the lemon juice over the top. Toss lightly to mix everything together and coat with the sauce. Scoop onto a serving platter and serve immediately with crusty bread.

Sautéed Chicken with Cherry Tomatoes

SIX SERVINGS

This dish is equally good for family or guests. I serve it with steamed rice, but my father loves it over mashed potatoes. A simple salad or vegetable on the side is nice, but not essential.

INGREDIENTS

- 3 tablespoons extra-virgin olive oil
- 1½ pounds boneless, skinless chicken breasts*
- 4 cloves garlic, peeled, smashed with the flat side of a knife, and chopped coarsely
- 6 shallots, peeled and chopped coarsely
- 1½ pounds cherry or grape tomatoes (or 2 pints), rinsed and drained
- 1½ tablespoons dried oregano
- ¾ cup dry white wine
- 1 teaspoon salt
- ¼ teaspoon freshly ground black pepper

FIRST Heat a 12-inch skillet, a Dutch oven, or a casserole with a lid, pour in the oil, and heat until quite hot. Line the pan with a batch of chicken breasts and fry over high heat until golden brown on one side, about 2½ to 3 minutes. Turn over and brown on the other side. Remove with tongs and continue browning the remaining pieces. Set the chicken aside.

SECOND Reduce the heat to medium, put the garlic and shallots in the pan, and sauté until fragrant, about 15 seconds. Add the cherry tomatoes, oregano, white wine, salt, and pepper and sauté uncovered about 4 to 4½ minutes, shaking the pan from time to time. Return the chicken to the pan, cover, and cook about 10 to 12 minutes, or until the chicken is cooked. Taste for seasoning and adjust if necessary.

THIRD Scoop the chicken out onto a platter and serve with rice or over mashed potatoes.

*You can substitute boneless chicken thighs for the boneless breasts. After returning the chicken to the pan in the second step, cook for about 15 to 20 minutes, or until cooked. Serve as directed.

Uby Munoz
A Balanced Lifestyle and Disease Prevention

Uby Munoz specializes in acupuncture and shiatsu massage. After spending one hour enveloped in her serene presence, being gently manipulated by her strong, capable hands, I had no doubt that she was a healer.

I first met Uby in London, when she treated me for perimenopausal symptoms (insomnia, mood swings, and anxiety). Over the next two years, I saw her on a regular basis. The weekly ritual of acupuncture, massage, and talk not only alleviated my symptoms but helped me to feel better in general.

Uby diagnosed me as having a weak kidney, a condition that my body had developed over time, but which is also routinely symptomatic of the aging process. "According to Chinese medicine, we are born with the essence of energy, which is stored in the kidneys," she told me. "This life essence, or qi, should be kept intact. The food you eat and the air you breathe should provide the energy that you need. But if you work long hours and eat improper food, you will start to deplete your body's vital energy. Exhaustion and anxiety will be accompanied by frustration and irritability."

Uby recommended that I eat foods like adzuki beans, corn, seaweed, string beans, and quinoa, which tone and strengthen the kidneys. She also stressed the importance of a revision of my exercise routine and lifestyle. I was not surprised when she told me that I needed more balance, considering our recent hectic move to London and a strenuous work period.

Uby was raised in Santiago, Chile, and was influenced at an early age by her grandmother's natural, holistic approach to health. "My grandmother believed very strongly in the importance of taking care of your body for good health and well-being. We always ate good food that was in season."

It was later, when she was twenty-four, while helping to translate several books on macrobiotics (an extreme diet that is based on concepts of Traditional Chinese Medicine), that she learned about the yin and yang of foods and the importance of balance. She was also fascinated by the idea that the mind, body, and health were all interrelated. She moved to London and began a three-year training program at the College of Integrative Chinese Medicine. She now has a busy practice and teaches at one of England's foremost schools of acupuncture.

UBY'S BREATHING EXERCISE

FIRST SIT comfortably in a chair with your spine **STRETCHED** as if there were a fine silk thread connecting the top of your head with the sky. Feel the weight of your body evenly in the seat. Rest your hands on your lap just touching the belly.

SECOND BREATHE IN, silently counting to four, feeling the air enter your nostrils and go down through the throat, esophagus, and diaphragm, and finally expanding into your belly (check that your shoulders are relaxed).

THIRD Without any pause, **BREATHE OUT**, again counting to four, following the same route but in reverse, feeling the air going up from the belly through the diaphragm, esophagus, throat, back of the nose, and out through the nostrils. Repeat this exercise ten times to begin, and try to do it as many times during the day as possible.

- **EAT AND DRINK IN MODERATION.** Take the time to smell and taste food, and you won't overeat. The next time you fancy a snack, ask yourself, "Does my body really need this, or is it my mind that wants this food?"

- A reasonable amount of exercise is needed to maintain a healthy body, but an excessive amount will diminish your energy, or qi. Cardiovascular exercise, like running and aerobics, is fine in moderation. It burns calories and provides a mental uplift. Pilates, swimming, fast walking, and the more energetic types of yoga help build stamina and keep the body flexible. The **BEST EXERCISES TO HELP RESTORE THE BODY'S ENERGY** are Tai Chi and Qi Gong (two forms of Chinese exercise that manipulate qi), breathing exercises, and meditation.

- Chinese doctors believe that **A POSITIVE ATTITUDE TOWARD LIFE** is important in maintaining good health and happiness. Try to have an open mind and be flexible. When you are feeling anxious or troubled, make a list of the positive things you have done or focus on the positive things in your life, such as a loved one or a beloved pet. This is an especially good exercise before you are going to bed so that you will go to sleep with a positive mind-set.

Uby reminded me that throughout the centuries Chinese doctors have advised that the key to disease prevention and good health is in maintaining a balance between three critical elements in our lives: diet, exercise, and our spiritual well-being. Any long-term imbalance can weaken the immune system and cause disease.

Above are some of Uby's lifestyle suggestions that she feels will help maintain good health.

east-west barbecue

Although Westerners think of stir-frying and steaming as the quintessential Asian cooking methods, they may be surprised to learn that Asians relish grilled foods almost as much as Americans. Asia's streets and alleys are filled with the enticing aromas of grilled foods, and each country has its specialty: In Beijing and other parts of China, *shashlik* (skewered grilled lamb) and *kao rou* (Mongolian beef) are popular dishes. The Japanese savor yakitori (skewered chicken, seafood, or vegetables) with beer and sake; *pulgogi* (grilled sliced beef and pork) is the national dish of Korea; and the Vietnamese love to barbecue pork, beef, and seafood, wrap them in lettuce or spring roll wrappers with vegetables, fresh herbs, and rice noodles, and dip them in *nuoc cham,* a fresh lime and herb dipping sauce.

Not surprisingly, since I'm an American, grilling is one of my favorite cooking methods. Gas grills make it even more effortless. (Grilling purists may disagree, but I can vouch for the difference, since I have put in my share of time building up and waiting for charcoal fires to be ready.)

Grilling gives me the opportunity to be creative and invent dishes that are a blending of East and West. As you'll see from the recipes in this chapter, I love to marry grilled seafood and meats with salsas, pickles, and chutneys. They can be served with rice, but they also make great roll-up meals. I like to take a portion of the grilled food, generously slather it with salsa or salad, and bundle it all up in a steamed flour tortilla or soft lavash wrap. You can lightly brush some toasted sesame oil on the wrap to give it a more distinctive flavor.

Barbecued foods taste just as appealing as leftovers the next day as they do hot off the grill. I often double the recipe for seafood, meats, and vegetables

Chapter opener:
Seared Wasabi
Tuna with Pickled
Ginger Cucumber

to use them in salads, stir-fried dishes, or soups. In fact, I often prefer to pre-cook foods for stir-fries by grilling them, since the seared, slightly charred flavor adds another dimension to the dish.

These Asian-influenced dishes are not unlike their Western counter-parts. Marinades and spice rubs are used regularly to tenderize food, provide flavor and color, and protect the body from the potential harmful effects of grilling. (Refer to Melanie Polk's grilling tips on page 256.) Marinades are simple to make with seasonings like garlic, ginger, scallions, and a little sugar for color.

Cooking food over an open fire is the most basic process known to man, and good-quality ingredients are essential. As it is with stir-frying, organiza-tion is critical: Finish all of the preparation before you start cooking. Make batches of the master marinades in advance and keep them in jars in the refrigerator so that the dish can be prepped easily and conveniently for cook-ing. I usually like to keep a jar of the Ginger Teriyaki on hand, as well as a batch of the Jerk Spice Rub for easy grilling. Fruit salsas and side dishes can be assembled quickly once you have the ripe fruit. Have fun improvising, mixing and matching grilled foods with the different salsas and salads. Some of the most memorable dishes are the ones that are spontaneous.

Spicy Asian Marinade

FOR 1½ TO 2 POUNDS OF CHICKEN, TURKEY, PORK, TOFU, OR SEAFOOD

This all-purpose marinade can be used for chicken or turkey breast, pork cutlets, firm-pressed tofu, and seafood. If you prefer to omit the chile flakes or paste, use 5 or 6 slices of smashed fresh ginger instead.

+ Marinades not only give flavor, they prevent negative side effects that may be caused by eating grilled food. See Melanie Polk's grilling tips on page 256.

INGREDIENTS

- **3   tablespoons soy sauce**
- **2   tablespoons rice wine or sake**
- **1   tablespoon minced garlic**
- **1   teaspoon dried chile flakes or hot chile paste**
- **1   tablespoon virgin olive oil**

Mix together all the ingredients in a bowl and use as directed in the recipe or for other foods.

Five-Spice Marinade

FOR 2 TO 3 POUNDS OF POULTRY, PORK, TOFU, OR VEGETABLES

Five-spice powder is a spice blend sold in Asian markets. The spice mix varies according to the manufacturer, but usually includes star anise, ground cinnamon, ground cloves, and powdered licorice root. (See page 15 for a homemade recipe.) I particularly like this marinade for seasoning squash, pumpkin, and sweet potatoes.

INGREDIENTS

- **1½ tablespoons minced fresh ginger**
- **1½ tablespoons minced garlic**
- **3   tablespoons soy sauce**
- **3   tablespoons rice wine or sake**
- **1   teaspoon toasted sesame oil**
- **1   teaspoon dried chile flakes (optional)**
- **½   tablespoon sugar**
- **1   teaspoon five-spice powder**

Mix together all the ingredients in a bowl and use as directed in the recipe or for other foods.

Ginger Teriyaki Marinade

FOR 1½ TO 2 POUNDS OF SEAFOOD OR CHICKEN

I often double this recipe and keep the extra in the refrigerator to have on hand for marinating all types of seafood for grilling, including shrimp, squid, salmon, and other firm fish fillets.

INGREDIENTS

⅓ cup soy sauce
⅓ cup water
⅓ cup rice wine or sake
7 tablespoons sugar
1½ tablespoons minced fresh ginger
1 teaspoon dried chile flakes
1½ tablespoons cornstarch

Mix together all the ingredients in a heavy medium saucepan and heat until thickened, stirring constantly over medium heat with a wooden spoon to prevent lumps. Remove from the heat and cool slightly. Use as directed in the recipe or for other foods.

ALL-PURPOSE RECIPE

+ For the health-giving properties of ginger, see "Dr. Jim Duke's Herbal Farmacy" on page 158.

Ginger Honey Marinade

FOR 1½ TO 2 POUNDS OF FISH FILLETS OR SEAFOOD

This simple marinade is excellent for six to eight servings of salmon or other fish and seafood, including halibut, cod, haddock, and scallops. I sometimes like to substitute maple syrup for the honey, which gives the marinade an appealing alternative flavor.

INGREDIENTS

½ cup orange juice
¼ cup soy sauce
2 tablespoons minced fresh ginger
2 tablespoons honey
1 teaspoon toasted sesame oil

Mix all the ingredients in a saucepan and bring to a boil. Reduce the heat slightly and simmer 5 minutes. Use as directed in the recipe or for other foods.

ALL-PURPOSE RECIPE

✲ Honey has been used by Chinese doctors for thousands of years. It is believed to harmonize the liver, relieve pain, and neutralize toxins. It is often added to hot drinks for treating sore throats and coughs.

Jerk Spice Rub

FOR 1½ TO 2 POUNDS OF MEAT, SEAFOOD, VEGETABLES, OR TOFU

I first fell in love with "jerk" seasonings when I went to Jamaica many years ago. Jerk is a tradition of slow-roasting marinated meat that originated there. Since then I have developed my own recipe for a spice rub that is excellent for meat, seafood, vegetables—even tofu.

+ *For the health-giving properties of chile peppers, see "Key to Primary Indian Spices" on page 288.*

INGREDIENTS

2 to 3 small fresh habanero chile peppers, ends trimmed and seeds removed*

3   tablespoons minced scallions, white part only

2   tablespoons minced fresh ginger

1   tablespoon minced fresh thyme or 1½ teaspoons dried

1½ teaspoons ground allspice

2   tablespoons Japanese clear rice vinegar

1½ tablespoons packed light brown sugar

½   teaspoon freshly ground black pepper

2   tablespoons virgin olive oil

Drop all the ingredients down the feed tube of a food processor fitted with a steel blade while the machine is running. Pulse until you have a thick paste. Use as directed in the recipe or for other foods.

*Traditionally Scotch bonnet peppers are used, but you can substitute small Thai peppers or 1 teaspoon dried chile flakes.

Mango Salsa

MAKES ABOUT 3 CUPS

This mango salsa is superb with all types of grilled seafood and meats. You can substitute different fruits for the mango, such as peaches and pineapple. It will keep for about 3 to 4 days in the refrigerator.

INGREDIENTS

4   ripe mangoes (each about 1 pound)
1   medium red onion, peeled and minced
1   teaspoon ground cumin
Juice of 2 limes (about 6 tablespoons)
¼   cup chopped fresh cilantro leaves
1   teaspoon salt
¼   teaspoon freshly ground black pepper

FIRST Stand the mango upright on one of the pointed ends. Cut off the two fleshy cheeks on the sides, cutting as close to the pit as possible. Cut the flesh into ¼-inch dice. Scrape the flesh from the skin with a spoon and drop into a bowl.

SECOND Add the remaining ingredients to the mango. Toss gently to mix, and let sit briefly while you prepare the meal.

+ *Mangoes aid digestion and are an excellent source of beta-carotene, so they may help to prevent cancer.*

Opposite: Mango Salsa (front), Pineapple Salsa (upper left), and Avocado Tomato Salsa (upper right)

Avocado Tomato Salsa

MAKES ABOUT 5 TO 6 CUPS

This salsa is delicious, easy, and versatile. I serve it with many grilled foods, including seafood, pork, and chicken. It's also excellent as a dip with tortilla chips. To preserve the salsa and prevent it from darkening, bury the avocado pits in it, cover tightly, and store in the refrigerator. It will keep for 3 to 4 days.

+ **Avocados** help to lower cholesterol and regulate blood pressure, and are good for the skin.

INGREDIENTS

¾ pound ripe tomatoes, rinsed and drained, stems removed

2 avocados, peeled, pit removed, cut into ¼-inch dice

Juice of about 1½ limes (about 4½ tablespoons)

1 jalapeño chile, cored and seeded, or to taste

1 tablespoon minced garlic

1 cup minced scallion greens

2 tablespoons fruity extra-virgin olive oil

½ cup fresh cilantro leaves, chopped coarsely

1 teaspoon salt

FIRST Cut the tomatoes in half and scoop out the seeds. Cut into ½-inch dice and put in a serving bowl.

SECOND Add the remaining ingredients and carefully stir to mix evenly. Taste for seasoning and adjust if necessary. Use as directed in the recipe or serve with any type of grilled meat, seafood, or vegetable.

Pineapple Salsa

MAKES ABOUT 6 CUPS

Pineapple salsa is an excellent accompaniment to any grilled or pan-fried meat, seafood, or vegetable dish, or to a curry. I especially love the hot food–cold salsa contrast. This will keep refrigerated for 5 days.

INGREDIENTS

1   ripe pineapple (about 4½ pounds)

1   medium red bell pepper, cored, seeded, and cut into ¼-inch dice

1   small red onion, peeled and minced

1   teaspoon ground cumin, or to taste

Juice of 1½ limes (about ¼ cup)

¼   cup orange juice

⅓   cup chopped fresh cilantro leaves

¾   teaspoon salt, or to taste

¼   teaspoon freshly ground black pepper

FIRST Cut away the stem and bottom from the pineapple, then place it upright on a cutting board and cut down all around to remove the skin. Cut the flesh away from the stem and slice into ¼-inch dice, or chop in a food processor fitted with a steel blade, pulsing until you have even-sized small pieces.

SECOND Put the pineapple in a bowl and add the remaining ingredients. Toss lightly to mix together, and let sit briefly. Serve with meat, seafood, or vegetables.

+ **Pineapples** *are an excellent source of vitamin C, aid digestion, and help heal ulcers, arthritis, and tissue damage from disease or surgery.*

❊ *Chinese doctors believe that pineapples dispel heat from the body. Pineapple juice is recommended for heatstroke and indigestion.*

Grilled Radicchio Drizzled with Sesame-Vinegar Dressing

SIX SERVINGS

Usually radicchio is used in salads, lending a bitter flavor. But the leaves take on a lovely flavor when they are charred on the grill. I like to arrange them as a vegetable accompaniment with grilled fish, chicken, or steak—even spareribs.

INGREDIENTS

- 3 heads radicchio (about 1 pound)
- ¼ cup virgin olive oil

SESAME-VINEGAR DRESSING
(WHISKED LIGHTLY)

- 6 tablespoons soy sauce
- ¼ cup freshly squeezed lemon juice
- ¼ cup balsamic vinegar
- 2 tablespoons toasted sesame oil
- 1 teaspoon sugar
- 1 teaspoon salt
- ¼ teaspoon freshly ground black pepper

FIRST Rinse the radicchio and drain. Remove any loose outer leaves and trim the bases, leaving the heads intact. Quarter each head lengthwise. Blot dry on paper towels. Brush the radicchio lightly with the olive oil.

SECOND Prepare a medium-hot fire for grilling or preheat a gas grill (the fire is ready when you can hold your hand 5 inches above the rack for only 3 to 4 seconds) and place the radicchio 3 to 4 inches from the heat. Cover and grill about 6 minutes on one side and 4 minutes on the other, until the outer leaves are browned and the hearts are tender.

THIRD Arrange the radicchio on a platter and drizzle the Sesame-Vinegar Dressing on top.

Julie's Charred Cherry Tomatoes with a Basil-Balsamic Glaze

SIX SERVINGS

My dear friend Julie Lutts, who has been helping me test recipes for my last five books, is a talented cook in her own right and often contributes ideas for my recipes. She likes to grill cherry tomatoes year-round. Try them with a reduced balsamic glaze and a sprinkling of fresh basil.

INGREDIENTS

- ¾ cup balsamic vinegar
- 1½ pounds (or 2 pints) cherry tomatoes, rinsed, drained, and blotted dry on paper towels
- 5 or 6 10-inch bamboo or metal skewers (if bamboo, soak in water to cover for 1 hour)
- ¼ cup fruity extra-virgin olive oil
- 12 large fresh basil leaves, shredded finely
- 1 teaspoon salt
- ¼ teaspoon freshly ground black pepper

FIRST Pour the balsamic vinegar into a heavy nonreactive saucepan. Bring to a boil, reduce the heat to low, and simmer about 20 minutes, until it is reduced to ¼ cup.

SECOND While the vinegar is cooking, thread the cherry tomatoes on the skewers and brush lightly with the olive oil.

THIRD Prepare a medium-hot fire for grilling or preheat a gas grill, and arrange a rack 3 to 4 inches from the heat. Put a batch of tomatoes on the grill and grill for 2 to 3 minutes, until slightly charred. Carefully turn once and grill for a minute, then remove from the heat, take the tomatoes off the skewers, and arrange them on a serving platter. Drizzle the reduced balsamic on top and sprinkle the basil, salt, and pepper over before serving.

+ *Tomatoes* are one of the stars of David Heber's vegetable pantry. They are full of lycopene, one of the most potent phytonutrients, which has been shown to prevent heart and lung disease as well as prostate and breast cancer.

Sweet and Sour Shrimp Kebabs with Pineapple and Bell Peppers

SIX SERVINGS

This dish is festive and excellent for entertaining, since the kebabs can be prepared in advance and cooked quickly at the last minute. Substitute scallops or chicken for the shrimp if you like.

+ Orange and yellow **peppers** are rich in Vitamin C, folate, and potassium, which fights heart disease.

INGREDIENTS

1½ pounds large raw shrimp, peeled and deveined

1   small ripe pineapple, peeled and cut into 1-inch chunks, or 2 cups drained canned pineapple chunks

2   red or orange bell peppers, cored, seeded, and cut into 1-inch cubes

15   10-inch bamboo or metal skewers (if bamboo, soak in water to cover for 1 hour)

SWEET AND SOUR GLAZE (MIXED TOGETHER)

½   cup ketchup

⅓   cup light brown sugar

¼   cup Japanese clear rice vinegar

2   tablespoons soy sauce

1½ tablespoons minced garlic

2   tablespoons olive oil (for oiling the grill)

FIRST Rinse the shrimp thoroughly, drain, and pat dry. Alternately thread shrimp, pineapple chunks, and pieces of bell pepper onto the skewers. Brush liberally with the Sweet and Sour Glaze. Let sit 10 to 15 minutes.

SECOND Prepare a medium-hot fire for grilling or preheat a gas grill, and arrange a rack 3 to 4 inches from the heat. Brush the grill with the olive oil and arrange the skewered shrimp on top. Cook about 3 to 4 minutes per side, brushing with the glaze until the shrimp are cooked through. Take them off the fire and remove from the skewers. Arrange the cooked food on a serving platter. Pour any remaining glaze on top. Serve the shrimp with steamed rice, or rolled up in lettuce leaves, steamed flour tortillas, or Mandarin pancakes.

Ginger-Honey-Glazed Salmon

The combination of honey and orange juice gives the salmon a lovely glaze. To prevent the salmon from sticking, brush or spray oil generously on the grill and use a firm hand with your spatula. I like to make any leftovers into a main-dish salad the next day for lunch or dinner.

INGREDIENTS

1   recipe Ginger Honey Marinade (page 233)

6   salmon steaks (about 6 ounces each and about 1 inch thick), rinsed and drained

3   tablespoons virgin olive oil (for oiling the grill)

FIRST Pour half of the Ginger Honey Marinade into a bowl and cool slightly. Keep the other half warm.

SECOND Put the salmon in one layer in a shallow pan, pour half the marinade on top, and turn the fish so that all sides are coated. Cover with plastic wrap and let sit for 30 minutes.

THIRD Prepare a medium-hot fire for grilling or preheat a gas grill, and arrange a rack 3 to 4 inches from the heat. Brush the grill with the olive oil and arrange the salmon steaks on top. Cook, brushing with the marinade, until the flesh is just opaque, about 6 to 7 minutes per side. Carefully slide the fish off the grill and serve with the remaining marinade spooned on top of each steak. Serve with Grilled Radicchio (page 240) or a stir-fried green vegetable and steamed rice or rice pilaf.

+ Eating oily fish two to three times a week may reduce the risk of heart disease and blood clots. If wild **salmon** is available and reasonably priced, it is preferable to the farmed variety.

Mahimahi Wraps with Avocado Tomato Salsa

SIX SERVINGS

I first tasted freshly caught grilled seafood with salsa right on the beach in a small restaurant in Mexico. Wrapped in warm flour tortillas, it makes an ideal lunch or dinner. But you can skip the tortillas and serve this dish with another staple such as rice or quinoa.

INGREDIENTS

1½ pounds mahimahi steaks (about 1 to 1½ inches thick), or a firm-fleshed fish fillet such as cod, haddock, or swordfish, rinsed lightly and drained

MARINADE (MIXED TOGETHER)

2 tablespoons soy sauce

3 tablespoons dry white vermouth or white wine

3 tablespoons virgin olive oil (for oiling the grill)

1 recipe Avocado Tomato Salsa (page 238)

18 flour tortillas, brushed lightly with toasted sesame oil

FIRST Put the fish in a bowl. Add the Marinade and toss lightly to coat.

SECOND Put the Avocado Tomato Salsa into a serving bowl and cover tightly.

THIRD Fold the flour tortillas in half or in quarters, arrange on a heatproof plate, and cover with a damp cloth. Heat briefly in a steamer, oven, or microwave oven, and set aside.

FOURTH Prepare a medium-hot fire for grilling or preheat a gas grill, and place the rack about 3 inches from the heat. Brush the grill with the olive oil. Arrange the fish on the grill and cook, covered, until the flesh turns opaque, basting with the marinade, for about 7 to 8 minutes on each side, depending on the thickness.

FIFTH Carefully slide the fish off the grill onto plates and serve. Each diner puts some fish on a flour tortilla, spoons some of the salsa on top, rolls it up, and eats it with his or her fingers.

Grilled Sea Bass with Mango Salsa

This dish is wonderful for feeding your family or for entertaining guests. You can prepare the salsa and marinate the fish in advance, making it an easy last-minute dish to cook and serve.

INGREDIENTS

- 1   recipe Mango Salsa (page 237)
- 2   pounds striped bass fillets (about 1 inch thick), or another firm fish such as halibut, grouper, or swordfish
- 2½ tablespoons virgin olive oil
- 1   teaspoon salt
- ½   teaspoon freshly ground black pepper

FIRST Prepare the Mango Salsa as directed in the recipe. Let it sit while the fish cooks.

SECOND If possible, cut the fish into 6 equal pieces. Rub the surface of the fillets with the olive oil and sprinkle with salt and pepper. Prepare a medium-hot fire for grilling or preheat a gas grill, and arrange a rack 3 to 4 inches from the heat. Arrange the fish fillets on the grill and cook, covered, for about 4 to 5 minutes per side, until the flesh is opaque. Slide the fillets off the grill and onto a platter or individual plates. Spoon some of the mango salsa on top and serve with steamed rice and a vegetable.

*+ **Mangoes** are a great source of vitamin C and beta-carotene.*

Seared Wasabi Tuna with Pickled Ginger Cucumbers

SIX SERVINGS

This unusual fresh tuna plate is made by mixing pickled ginger with thin slices of cucumber and arranging them next to the grilled tuna. The gingery cucumber slices are a lively side dish that can be prepared quickly and will keep in the refrigerator for several days.

✚ *For the health-giving properties of ginger, see "Dr. Jim Duke's Herbal Farmacy" on page 158 or "Key to Primary Indian Spices" on page 288.*

INGREDIENTS

6   *very fresh* tuna steaks (about 6 to 8 ounces each and about 1 inch thick), rinsed and drained

FISH SEASONINGS

¼   cup rice wine or sake

6 to 8 slices fresh ginger, about the size of a quarter, smashed with the flat side of a knife

1   teaspoon toasted sesame oil

2   English seedless or 6 Kirby cucumbers (about 1½ pounds)

2   teaspoons salt

1½ cups pickled ginger with juice (or 1 12-ounce jar)*

3   tablespoons wasabi powder*

3½ tablespoons boiling water

½   cup good-quality soy sauce for serving

3   tablespoons virgin olive oil (for oiling the grill)

*Wasabi powder and pickled ginger can be purchased at Asian markets. If pickled ginger is unavailable, serve the tuna with Dad's Sweet and Sour Cucumber Pickle (page 175).

FIRST Put the tuna steaks in a bowl with the Fish Seasonings and toss lightly to coat. Let sit while preparing the cucumbers.

SECOND Trim the ends of the cucumbers. Slice them in half lengthwise, scoop out the seeds with a spoon, and cut on the diagonal into slices about ⅛ inch thick. Put the slices in a bowl, add the salt, toss lightly, and let sit for 30 minutes. Drain thoroughly and put in a serving bowl with the pickled ginger. Toss lightly and chill until ready to serve the tuna.

THIRD Put the wasabi powder in a serving bowl, add the boiling water, and stir to make a smooth paste. Cover with a dish. Before serving, pour the soy sauce into a serving bowl.

FOURTH Prepare a medium-hot fire for grilling or preheat a gas grill, and place the rack about 3 inches from the heat. Arrange the tuna steaks on the grill and cook, covered, for about 4 to 5 minutes on each side, depending on the thickness (the steaks should still be rare). Carefully slide the fish off the grill, cut it into slices, and arrange them on individual plates. Spoon some of the pickled cucumber salad on the side. Give everyone their own small serving bowl, into which they will pour some soy sauce and mix in a little wasabi paste so that they can dip the tuna into the sauce.

Spicy Teriyaki Scallops with Garlic Snow Peas

Scallops are one of my favorite seafoods, and this ginger-teriyaki sauce complements their sweet flavor beautifully. You can also use kebabs of a firm-fleshed fish such as swordfish, or try shrimp or chicken.

INGREDIENTS

1   recipe Ginger Teriyaki Marinade (page 233)

1½ pounds large sea scallops, rinsed and drained

10 scallions (mostly the white part), ends trimmed, cut into 1-inch lengths

8 or 9 10-inch bamboo or metal skewers (if bamboo, soak in water to cover for 1 hour)

1¼ pounds snow or snap peas, ends snapped off and any strings removed

4   tablespoons virgin olive oil

1½ tablespoons minced garlic

2½ tablespoons rice wine or sake

FIRST Prepare the Ginger Teriyaki Marinade as directed in the recipe. Let it cool slightly.

SECOND Alternately thread scallops and scallions on the skewers, starting and ending each skewer with a scallop. Put the skewered seafood in a deep dish and pour half the teriyaki marinade on top, keeping the remaining marinade warm. Cover and let marinate for 1 hour in the refrigerator.

THIRD Bring 4 quarts water to a boil in a large pot and add the snow or snap peas. Boil 1½ minutes, then drain in a colander and refresh in cold water. Drain again.

FOURTH Heat a wok or a deep skillet until very hot. Pour in 1 tablespoon of the olive oil and heat until near smoking. Toss in the snow or snap peas, garlic, and rice wine and stir-fry for about 1 minute. Arrange on a serving platter with a slight well in the middle for the scallops and scallions.

FIFTH Prepare a medium-hot fire for grilling or preheat a gas grill, and arrange a rack generously brushed with the remaining olive oil 3 to 4 inches from the heat. Arrange the skewered scallops on the grill. Cook for about 3 to 4 minutes per side, brushing with the teriyaki marinade until the scallops are cooked through. Carefully lift the scallops off the grill and remove them from the skewers onto the snow peas. Pour the remaining marinade on top. Serve with steamed rice.

Opposite: Snow pea shoots

Jesse's Spicy Grilled Chicken Breasts

My son Jesse loves the spicy flavor of this grilled chicken. I often prepare extra chicken, serving some for dinner and using the rest later in noodle dishes, salads, and stir-fried dishes.

INGREDIENTS

- **3**   **boneless, skinless chicken breasts (about 1½ pounds)**
- **1**   **recipe Spicy Asian Marinade (page 232)**
- **2**   **tablespoons virgin olive oil (for oiling the grill)**

FIRST Prepare the Spicy Asian Marinade as directed in the recipe. Put the chicken breasts in a bowl, pour in the Spicy Asian Marinade, and toss lightly to coat. Cover with plastic wrap and refrigerate for an hour, or longer if possible.

SECOND Prepare a medium-hot fire for grilling or preheat a gas grill or the broiler. If grilling, brush the rack with olive oil and place the meat 3 inches from the source of heat. Grill, covered, 5 to 7 minutes per side, or until the chicken is opaque all the way through. Alternatively, you can heat a nonstick skillet until very hot over high heat and sear the chicken until done, about 8 to 10 minutes, turning once. Remove from the heat and cool slightly. Cut the chicken meat across the grain into thin slices. Serve with a vegetable and rice or noodles, or use as directed in salads or stir-fried dishes.

Five-Spice Chicken Legs

SIX SERVINGS

The five-spice marinade is great for chicken, pork, turkey, tofu, or different vegetables such as zucchini and eggplant. I suggest serving the grilled chicken legs with Mango Salsa, but you can mix and match and serve it with Pineapple Salsa (page 239), Pickled Ginger Cucumbers (page 246), or Mint-Yogurt Dressing (page 253).

INGREDIENTS

- 1 **recipe Five-Spice Marinade (page 232)**
- 2½ **pounds chicken legs and thighs (about 5 or 6), rinsed and drained***
- 1 **recipe Mango Salsa (page 234)**
- 2–3 **tablespoons virgin olive oil (for oiling the grill)**

FIRST Prepare the Five-Spice Marinade as directed in the recipe. Put the chicken legs in a bowl, pour in the marinade, and toss lightly to coat. Cover and let marinate for 1 hour, or overnight in the refrigerator if possible. Prepare the Mango Salsa as directed and put in a serving dish.

SECOND Prepare a medium-hot fire for grilling or preheat a gas grill, and place the rack about 3 inches from the source of heat. Brush the grill with the olive oil and arrange the chicken on top. Cover and cook for about 12 to 13 minutes per side. To test, pierce the thickest part of the leg with a sharp knife: The juice should run clear and the meat should be opaque all the way through. Place the legs on a platter and serve with the mango salsa and a side vegetable.

*You may substitute chicken breasts for the legs and grill 5 to 7 minutes on each side, or until the meat is opaque and the juice is clear when the chicken is pierced with a knife.

Tandoori Chicken Roll-Ups

SIX SERVINGS

This Indian-inspired yogurt-based marinade tenderizes and flavors the chicken and provides a cooling (albeit spicy) contrast to the cooked meat. If you want, tuck a few lettuce greens into the roll-ups. This dish is also delicious with turkey and seafood.

INGREDIENTS

1½ pounds boneless, skinless chicken breasts, trimmed of fat and gristle

TANDOORI MARINADE (MIXED TOGETHER)

1¾ cups low-fat plain yogurt

2½ tablespoons minced fresh ginger

1½ tablespoons minced garlic

1 teaspoon dried chile flakes, or to taste

1¼ teaspoons ground cumin

1¼ teaspoons dried oregano

1 teaspoon salt

½ teaspoon freshly ground black pepper

3 tablespoons virgin olive oil

MINT-YOGURT DRESSING (MIXED TOGETHER)

1½ cups whole-milk plain yogurt

½ teaspoon ground cumin

3 tablespoons chopped fresh mint leaves

1 teaspoon salt, or to taste

18 flour tortillas, folded in half or in quarters and wrapped in a damp cloth and steamed briefly

FIRST Toss the chicken breasts in the Tandoori Marinade to coat and let marinate for 30 minutes, or longer covered in the refrigerator. Brush the grill with olive oil.

SECOND Prepare a hot fire for grilling or preheat a gas grill. Arrange the meat 3 inches from the source of heat, cover, and grill the meat until cooked through, about 6 to 7 minutes per side, depending on the thickness. Remove from the heat and let cool slightly.

THIRD While the chicken is cooking, pour the Mint-Yogurt Dressing into a serving bowl and arrange the flour tortillas on a serving plate. Cut the cooked chicken into thin slices and arrange on a platter. To serve, arrange slices of chicken in a flour tortilla, spoon some of the dressing on top, roll up, and eat with your fingers.* Serve with a side vegetable or a salsa.

*You may also stuff some romaine or leafy lettuce and shredded carrots in the tortilla with the chicken.

+ **Yogurt** *helps to strengthen the immune system and prevent gastrointestinal, yeast, and urinary tract infections.*

Jerk Pork Cutlets with Pineapple Salsa

SIX SERVINGS

Making jerk pork or chicken always seemed to me to be too labor-intensive—that is, until I decided to make it. With the aid of a food processor or blender, it's really quite easy. I make a double batch and use the spice rub to flavor pork, chicken, tofu, and vegetables like squash and sweet potato. Any leftovers are eaten as is or served in main-dish salads.

✳ Chinese doctors recommend eating pork to relieve dryness in the body.

INGREDIENTS

1   recipe Jerk Spice Rub (page 234)

1½ pounds center-cut pork cutlets, trimmed of fat and gristle

2–3 tablespoons virgin olive oil (for oiling the grill)

1   recipe Pineapple Salsa (page 239)

FIRST Prepare the Jerk Spice Rub as directed in the recipe.

SECOND Put the pork cutlets in a bowl or a dish, spoon the spice rub onto the chicken, and toss to coat with a rubber spatula. Cover and let stand at room temperature for 1½ hours, or refrigerate overnight if desired.

THIRD Prepare a medium-hot fire for grilling or preheat a gas grill, and place the rack about 3 inches from the source of heat. Brush the rack with the olive oil and arrange the pork cutlets on top. Cook, covered, for about 7 minutes on each side, turning several times so that they cook evenly. Remove with tongs and let rest for 5 minutes. Cut into thin slices and serve with the Pineapple Salsa.

Balsamic-Glazed Steak with Grilled Rainbow Peppers

SIX SERVINGS

My family and I are not big meat eaters, but every now and then I get a craving for a good steak, and then I try to buy the best meat available, especially when I make this recipe. Leftovers are put to good use in stir-fried dishes or sandwiches.

INGREDIENTS

- 2 pounds porterhouse or sirloin steak (about 1 inch thick)
- 3 tablespoons virgin olive oil
- 3 tablespoons balsamic vinegar
- 4 cloves garlic, peeled and smashed with the flat side of a knife
- 1 teaspoon salt
- ½ teaspoon freshly ground black pepper
- 1 recipe Grilled Rainbow Peppers with Chile Oil Dressing (page 183)

FIRST Trim the meat of any excess fat and put in a shallow pan or bowl. Pour the olive oil and vinegar over the steaks and add the garlic, salt, and pepper. Rub the mixture all over the meat and let sit a few minutes. Prepare the Grilled Rainbow Peppers.

SECOND Prepare a medium-hot fire for grilling or preheat a gas grill, and place the rack about 3 inches from the source of heat. Arrange the steaks on the rack and grill them about 5 to 6 minutes on each side for medium-rare. Remove the beef to a platter or cutting board and cut into thin slices. Serve with the Grilled Rainbow Peppers, a green vegetable, and crusty bread.

✳ Asians credit beef with warming the body, so it is often eaten in cold weather.

Melanie Polk
of the American Institute
for Cancer Research
Grilling Tips

Recent findings confirm that grilling or broiling red meat, poultry, and seafood produces potentially cancer-causing compounds called heterocyclic amines (HCAs), which may increase the risk of breast, colon, stomach, and prostate cancer. That is the reason I went to talk to Melanie Polk, the director of nutritional education at the American Institute for Cancer Research. According to Melanie, "Fat from these foods which drips onto hot coals forms other potentially cancer-causing substances called polycyclic aromatic hydrocarbons, or PAHs."

Melanie Polk is not only a registered dietitian with more than twenty years of experience as a nutrition educator and counselor, she is also a mother and she likes good food. She describes her role as "translating the latest nutrition research into practical strategies that can be applied to our daily lives to lower the risk of certain diseases and promote general health, without ever forgetting the joy of eating."

According to Melanie, grilling and broiling can be enjoyed. Grilled vegetables, fruits, and vegetarian foods like tofu and tempeh present a much lower risk. Meats are the main concern. At right are her recommendations for reducing the risk.

HEALTHIER GRILLING TIPS

■ MARINATING meats and seafoods BEFORE GRILLING may significantly reduce the amount of HCAs. Studies have shown that even briefly marinating can prevent as much as 92 to 99 percent of HCAs. The protective powers may lie in the ingredients, such as herbs, spices, citrus juices, vinegar, and olive oil.

■ TRIM THE FAT as much as possible from meats. Remove the skin from chicken, and avoid high-fat meats like sausages.

■ AVOID letting juices drip into the flames or coals, which causes SMOKE AND FLARE-UPS. Use tongs or a spatula to turn meat instead of piercing with a fork.

■ If you are cooking thick meats or hamburgers, FLIP THEM OVER FREQUENTLY. Recent research has shown that cooking hamburgers at a lower temperature helps prevent the formation of HCAs and kills bacteria.

■ TRIM away charred or BURNT PORTIONS of food before eating.

irresistible vegetarian

Before my first visit to the Far East more than thirty years ago, I thought that most vegetarian food was bland, brown, and boring. As I was soon to discover, this is not the case, especially in Asia. There vegetarian cooks are especially generous with pungent seasonings like ginger, garlic, cumin, curry leaves, hot chile peppers, and mustard seeds. Dishes are vibrant with fresh herbs like cilantro, Thai holy basil, dill, and mint. Ingenious mock meat dishes are created out of simple ingredients. Even die-hard carnivores get up from the table feeling satisfied.

Asia is not the only place where vegetarian dishes shine. The Middle East and the Mediterranean offer outstanding vegetarian food. A visit to any open-air market provides ample inspiration. Freshly picked vegetables heaped in piles often simulate beautiful still-life paintings (no shrink-wrapped plastic cartons here). The smell of fresh herbs and spices assails the senses and piques the appetite. It makes you want to cook and eat—one of the reasons I urge everyone to seek out their local farmers' market.

These days I can't claim to be a total vegetarian, but more and more I find myself planning vegetarian meals. Not only am I aware of the mounting medical evidence that fruits and vegetables contain powerful health-giving nutrients, but my palate has been seduced by great vegetarian dishes and I find myself craving these foods.

The key to great vegetarian cooking—of no matter what ethnic persuasion—is not only in the quality of the ingredients (which should be the very best) but in the seasoning of the dish as well. Herbs and spices are especially

Chapter opener: Spicy Vegetable Sambal

important: Flavors should be generous and used in such a way that they complement and highlight the ingredients.

Learning more about herbs and spices was the goal of my last two trips to India. It was there that a talented Indian chef introduced me to the enticing flavors of South Indian cooking, where spices are so integral to the character of each dish. Chef Suresh Vaidyanathan skillfully and subtly used seasonings that many Western cooks may take for granted, like black pepper, even salt, to give dishes extra dimension. (You can read more about Chef Suresh and his recipes on page 280.)

I was also able to visit an Ayurvedic retreat, where Dr. U. K. Krishna, a prominent authority on Ayurveda, explained to me the Indian holistic system of medicine, including the therapeutic properties of herbs and spices. (For a fuller discussion of Ayurveda and more about Dr. Krishna, see page 292.) In addition to enjoying soothing Abhyanga massages, I sampled superb, simple vegetarian food prepared by the retreat's kitchens. The food was enhanced with such vibrant and intriguing flavors that it reminded me once again, as do the recipes in this chapter, that vegetarian food can be exciting and satisfying.

Grilled Peppers
with Chickpeas on Bruschetta

SIX SERVINGS

When we were living in London, my family developed a passion for bruschetta, which is grilled bread with toppings—some as basic as a rubbing of garlic and a drizzle of olive oil. I like to grill and cook different vegetables for toppings. Bruschetta are usually served as an appetizer, but we eat them with soup or a salad for lunch or dinner.

+ *Refer to the "red/ purple" category of the "Seven Colors of Health" chart on page 199 for the health-giving properties of red peppers.*

INGREDIENTS

6   **medium red bell peppers**
1   **15- or 19-ounce can chickpeas, drained, blanched briefly, refreshed, and drained**

SEASONINGS

3   **tablespoons fruity extra-virgin olive oil**
1½   **tablespoons balsamic vinegar**
1   **teaspoon salt**
½   **teaspoon dried chile flakes**
¼   **teaspoon freshly ground black pepper**
1   **tablespoon freshly squeezed lemon juice**

1   **loaf country-style sourdough bread**

FIRST Grill and peel the red peppers as directed in the recipe for Grilled Rainbow Peppers (page 183) and remove their skins. Cut the stems off the peppers and cut each in half lengthwise. Scrape out the seeds and cut each half into large pieces, then coarsely chop into a rough ¼-inch dice in a food processor fitted with a steel blade. Put the peppers in a mixing bowl.

SECOND Mix the chickpeas with the grilled peppers and add the Seasonings. Taste for seasoning and adjust if necessary.

THIRD Cut the bread into ½-inch-thick slices. Heat a broiler and arrange the slices on a baking sheet about 3 inches from the source of heat. Toast until golden brown on both sides, turning once. (You can also do this on a grill over a medium-hot fire.)

FOURTH Arrange the toasted bread slices on a platter and generously spoon some of the pepper-chickpea mixture on top. Serve.

Roasted Tomato Bruschetta with Lentils or Greens

SIX SERVINGS

This bruschetta topping is made with roasted cherry tomatoes and lentils, or you can substitute a bunch of arugula for the lentils. It's a great appetizer or vegetable side dish. I often brush a little olive oil on the toasted bread so that the topping won't make the bread soggy.

INGREDIENTS

1   cup French green lentils*

4   cloves garlic, smashed with the flat side of a knife and peeled

½   teaspoon salt

1   recipe Roasted Cherry Tomatoes, prepared as directed (page 186)

SEASONINGS

3   tablespoons extra-virgin olive oil

1   tablespoon red wine vinegar

1   teaspoon salt

¼   teaspoon freshly ground black pepper

1   loaf country-style sourdough bread

FIRST Put the lentils, garlic cloves, and ½ teaspoon salt in a saucepan and pour in enough water to cover by about 2 inches. Bring the water to a boil and reduce the heat to low. Simmer uncovered until the lentils are just tender, about 30 to 40 minutes.

SECOND Strain the cooked lentils and put them and the garlic in a food processor fitted with a steel blade and pulse 4 or 5 times to break them up. Then mix them with the Seasonings.

THIRD Cut the bread into ½-inch-thick slices. Heat the broiler and arrange the slices on a baking sheet about 3 inches from the source of heat. Toast until golden brown on both sides, turning once. (You can also do this on a grill over a medium-hot fire.) Spoon and spread a generous portion of the cooked lentils on the toast.

FOURTH Arrange the toasted bread slices on a platter and generously spoon some of the roasted tomato mixture on top. Serve.

+ **Lentils** are a member of the broad family of legumes, which are believed to reduce the risk of heart disease, help control blood sugar levels, and prevent certain forms of cancer. They are sold at well-stocked supermarkets and many health food stores or supermarkets.

*You may omit the green lentils and substitute ½ pound fresh arugula, rinsed lightly and spun dry.

Grilled Tempeh with Saté Sauce

SIX SERVINGS

Tempeh is a fermented soybean cake that I like to mix with different grains such as rice or millet, or with peanuts. Like tofu, it becomes more palatable if it is marinated and then cooked. I like to serve these roll-ups as an appetizer or with a vegetable as a light meal.

+ Like other soybean products, **tempeh** is rich in isoflavones, which are believed to prevent cancer and inhibit its growth.

INGREDIENTS

TEMPEH MARINADE (MIXED TOGETHER)

- 5 tablespoons soy sauce
- 4 tablespoons rice wine or sake
- 10 slices fresh ginger, about the size of a quarter, smashed with the flat side of a knife
- 5 cloves garlic, smashed with the flat side of a knife, peeled, and cut into thin slices
- 1 teaspoon toasted sesame oil

1½ pounds tempeh

8 to 10 scallions, mainly white part, ends trimmed, cut into 1½-inch lengths

9 or 10 10-inch bamboo or metal skewers (if bamboo, soak in water to cover for 1 hour)

SATÉ SAUCE

- ¾ cup smooth peanut butter
- 1¼ cups light coconut milk
- 3 tablespoons fish sauce
- 3½ tablespoons peeled and minced fresh ginger
- 3 tablespoons firmly packed light brown sugar
- 1 tablespoon soy sauce
- 1¼ teaspoons dried chile flakes, or to taste

2 heads Boston lettuce, separated, rinsed, and spun dry

2 tablespoons virgin olive oil

FIRST Pour the Tempeh Marinade into a medium shallow pan. Place the tempeh flat in the marinade and let sit about 30 minutes, turning after 15 minutes. The tempeh should soak up the marinade. Cut the tempeh into 1-inch cubes. Thread the tempeh and scallions alternately onto the skewers.

SECOND Place all the Saté Sauce ingredients in the bowl of a food processor fitted with a steel blade, or put them in a blender, and mix until smooth. Pour the sauce into a serving bowl. Trim away the stem portions of the lettuce leaves and press the leaves lightly with a knife to flatten. Arrange in a basket or in a serving bowl.

THIRD Heat the broiler or prepare a fire for grilling, and brush the grill with the olive oil. Arrange the skewers about 3 inches from the source of heat. Broil or grill about 10 minutes on each side, turning once and brushing with the marinade. Remove the tempeh and scallions from the skewers, place on a serving platter, and serve. Diners put two tempeh cubes in a lettuce leaf, spoon some of the saté sauce on top, roll it up, and eat with their fingers.

Purple basil

Vietnamese Cabbage Rolls

SIX SERVINGS

These lovely vegetarian rolls are fresh and light. Choose a leafy Napa cabbage with firm, unblemished outer leaves to use as wrappers. You can serve the rolls with the Vietnamese dipping sauce below or the spicy Saté Sauce on page 51.

INGREDIENTS

1 medium to large head Chinese (Napa) cabbage (about 3 pounds), outer leaves intact

¼ pound thin rice stick noodles, softened in hot water to cover and drained

VIETNAMESE DIPPING SAUCE
(MIXED TOGETHER AND POURED INTO
A SERVING DISH)

1¼ teaspoons dried chile flakes, or to taste

⅔ cup freshly squeezed lime juice (about 6–7 limes)

⅓ cup fish sauce, or more to taste

⅓ cup sugar

1½ tablespoons minced garlic

2 medium carrots, peeled and grated (about 2 cups)

1½ cups bean sprouts, rinsed and drained

½ cup chopped fresh cilantro leaves

½ cup coarsely chopped fresh basil leaves

½ cup dry-roasted peanuts, chopped (optional)

FIRST Carefully separate the cabbage into individual leaves, rinse, drain, and pat dry. Make a small V in the bottom of 17 or 18 leaves and cut away the stem sections. Bring 3 quarts of water to a boil in a large pot, drop in the cabbage leaves, and cook for 1 minute. Remove with a handled strainer and refresh in cold water, then drain thoroughly.

SECOND Bring the water to a boil again and drop in the rice stick noodles. Swirl in the water and cook for 10 to 15 seconds. Drain thoroughly in a colander, rinse, and drain again. Clip the noodles into 3-inch lengths and put in a mixing bowl.

THIRD Mix together the noodles, carrots, bean sprouts, cilantro, basil, peanuts (if using), and about 3 tablespoons of the Vietnamese dipping sauce. Toss lightly and place about 3 tablespoons of the noodle filling in a thin strip across the cabbage leaf. Fold in the sides and roll over the ends to make a roll and completely enclose the noodles. Arrange the rolls on a serving platter and serve with the remaining dipping sauce or with Saté Sauce.

Five-Spice Hoisin Tofu

SIX SERVINGS

I marinate tofu in a fragrant, garlicky marinade, bake it, and then use it in place of meat or seafood in stir-fried dishes, stews, and soups. The marinade is also very good without the five-spice powder.*

INGREDIENTS

1½ pounds firm tofu, drained and cut in half through the thickness

MARINADE (MIXED TOGETHER)

- **¾ cup hoisin sauce**
- **⅓ cup rice wine or sake**
- **3 tablespoons soy sauce**
- **1½ tablespoons minced garlic**
- **1 teaspoon five-spice powder***
- **1 teaspoon toasted sesame oil**

FIRST Place the tofu in a bowl. Pour the Marinade over it and carefully toss to coat. Let sit for an hour at room temperature. Preheat the oven to 375 degrees.

SECOND Arrange the tofu on a cookie sheet that has been lined with aluminum foil. Pour the marinade on top and bake for 35 minutes, then remove from the oven and cool slightly. Cut into pieces that are ½ inch thick, 2 inches long, and 1 inch wide. Spoon some of the cooked marinade on top and serve, or use as directed in recipes.

ALL-PURPOSE RECIPE

+ *According to the latest research, **tofu**, and other soy foods, may not reduce the risk of heart disease. Soy foods do contain phytoestrogens, which may reduce some symptoms of PMS, perimenopause, and menopause.*

*To make plain Barbecued Tofu, omit the five-spice powder and prepare the recipe as directed.

Hoisin-Drenched Stir-Fried Vegetables

SIX SERVINGS

Use this recipe as a blueprint, substituting different vegetables such as broccoli, bok choy, or green beans and precooking them before adding to the final stir-fry.

INGREDIENTS

1   recipe Five-Spice Hoisin Tofu (page 267)

1½ tablespoons canola or olive oil

3   tablespoons minced scallions, white part only

2   tablespoons minced garlic

1½ teaspoons hot chile paste, or to taste

1   large red bell pepper, cored, seeded, and cut into thin julienne strips

1   large yellow or orange bell pepper, cored, seeded, and cut into thin julienne strips

½   pound snow peas, ends snapped and veiny strings removed

2   tablespoons rice wine or sake

SAUCE (MIXED TOGETHER)

3½ tablespoons soy sauce

1½ tablespoons sugar

1   teaspoon toasted sesame oil

2   cups scallion greens, cut into ½-inch lengths

FIRST Prepare the Five-Spice Tofu as directed in the recipe.

SECOND Heat a large wok or a deep, heavy skillet until very hot over high heat. Pour in the oil and heat until hot. Add the scallions, garlic, and chile paste, and stir-fry until fragrant, about 15 seconds. Scatter in the bell peppers and toss lightly for a minute. Toss in the snow peas and rice wine and continue cooking, tossing lightly over high heat until the snow peas are tender, about 2 to 3 minutes. (If you need longer, cover briefly and cook until tender.) Pour in the Sauce and scallion greens and toss lightly to cook. Fold in the tofu slices, still coated with the hoisin marinade, and carefully stir to mix evenly and heat through. Scoop the stir-fry onto a warm serving platter and serve with steamed jasmine or basmati rice.

Malay Barbecued Tofu

SIX SERVINGS

While Westerners have begun to appreciate the health-giving properties of tofu, they have been slow to recognize its culinary potential. Once grilled or baked, the tofu can be served with rice and a vegetable as a satisfying meal, or used in place of meat or seafood in any dish. I even use it in stews (see Hearty Miso Cabbage Stew on page 270).

INGREDIENTS

BARBECUE SAUCE (MIXED TOGETHER)

7 tablespoons oyster sauce
3 tablespoons soy sauce
3 tablespoons ketchup
2½ tablespoons light brown sugar
2 tablespoons minced garlic
1½ tablespoons minced fresh ginger
1½ teaspoons hot chile paste or dried chile flakes

1½ pounds firm tofu, cut into 1-inch-thick slices

FIRST Add the Barbecue Sauce to the tofu slices. Carefully toss to coat. Cover and let marinate for 1 hour at room temperature.

SECOND Preheat the broiler. Arrange the tofu slices on a cookie sheet that has been lined with aluminum foil. Broil for 8 to 9 minutes, or until the edges are brown and slightly crisp. (Or bake in a 425-degree oven for 15 minutes per side.) Carefully flip over the pieces with a spatula and broil another 8 to 9 minutes on the other side. Serve with a vegetable and staple, or substitute for cooked meat, chicken, or seafood in salads, stir-fries, soups, and most other dishes.

Hearty Miso Cabbage Stew

SIX SERVINGS

Fortunately miso paste has become widely available in many supermarkets and health food stores. I like to use it to season soups and stews, such as this dish, and to flavor marinades for grilled fish and vegetables. There are many different types of miso, but I prefer the flavor of the light-colored or "white" miso paste ("shinshu miso" or "shiro miso").

INGREDIENTS

1	recipe Malay Barbecued Tofu (page 269)
1	head Chinese (Napa) cabbage, outer leaves discarded (about 1½ pounds)
1	tablespoon virgin olive oil
6	cloves garlic, smashed lightly with the flat side of a knife, and peeled
6	slices fresh ginger, about the size of a quarter, smashed lightly with the flat side of a knife and cut into thirds
¾	cup rice wine or sake
8	cups water
½	cup light-colored ("white") miso paste, or to taste
3	tablespoons soy sauce, or to taste

FIRST Prepare the Malay Barbecued Tofu as directed in the recipe. Once the tofu has cooled, cut into ¼-inch dice.

SECOND Rinse the cabbage lightly and drain. Cut away the core section. Separate the cabbage leaves. Make a small V in the bottom of the leaves, then cut them into 2-inch squares, separating the tougher sections from the leafy, tender ones.

THIRD Heat a large pot or casserole, pour in the olive oil, and heat until hot, about 10 seconds. Lightly drop the garlic and ginger into the oil, and stir briefly. Add the harder cabbage sections, stir, cover, and cook for a few minutes over medium-high heat. Pour in the rice wine, cover, and cook for several minutes more. Toss in the remaining cabbage sections and the water, cover, and bring to a boil. Reduce the heat to low and simmer uncovered for 15 to 20 minutes. Add the diced tofu, stir, and cook for 5 minutes.

FOURTH Put the miso paste in a small bowl, and slowly pour in ½ cup of the cooking liquid, stirring until smooth. Add a little more of the liquid if the mixture seems too thick.

FIFTH Add most of the miso mixture and the soy sauce to the stew. Stir to blend and taste for seasoning, adding more miso if needed. Portion the stew into bowls and serve.

Opposite: Sweet basil

Warm Roasted Winter Vegetable Salad

SIX SERVINGS

This warm salad is especially appealing because the squash, fennel, sweet potatoes, and onions roast in a hot oven and acquire a caramelized glaze. Serve it with rice, couscous, or another staple, as a main dish, or as a vegetable side dish with other vegetables, meats, or seafood.

+ *Fennel bulb aids digestion and is rich in potassium, which prevents and reduces high blood pressure. For information on the health-giving properties of squash and sweet potatoes, see the "Seven Colors of Health" chart on page 199.*

INGREDIENTS

1   large acorn squash (about 1¼ pounds)
2   medium fennel bulbs (about 1½ pounds with stalks), rinsed and trimmed, leaving ⅛ inch of the root base to hold the fennel together
2   sweet potatoes (about 1¾ to 2 pounds)
2   medium red onions, peeled

FLAVORINGS (MIXED TOGETHER)

½   cup extra-virgin olive oil
½   cup balsamic vinegar
3   tablespoons minced fresh ginger

2   tablespoons virgin olive oil for greasing the cookie sheet

DRESSING (MIXED TOGETHER UNTIL THE SUGAR DISSOLVES)

3   tablespoons soy sauce
5 to 6 tablespoons water
1   tablespoon minced garlic
2   teaspoons sugar

FIRST Preheat the oven to 425 degrees. Rinse the squash and drain. Cut in half and scoop out the seeds with a spoon. Cut each half into 3 or 4 wedges and put in a large bowl.

SECOND Cut each fennel bulb lengthwise in half, then cut the fennel into slices about ¼ inch thick and 2 inches long. Put in the bowl with the squash.

THIRD Peel the sweet potatoes and cut each in half. Cut each half into 3 or 4 wedges and put in the bowl. Cut the red onions in half, then cut each half lengthwise into ¼-inch-thick slices. Put in the bowl with the other vegetables.

FOURTH Pour in the Flavorings and toss lightly to coat. Brush or spray a cookie sheet liberally with olive oil. Arrange the vegetables on the cookie sheet. (Alternatively, you can arrange the vegetables on the oiled cookie sheet and brush liberally with the Flavorings.) Bake the vegetables about 45 to 50 minutes, flipping them over after 30 minutes. The vegetables should be tender when pierced with a knife, and the tops should be brown and slightly crisp at the edges.

FIFTH Arrange the vegetables randomly on plates, in a serving bowl, or on a platter. Spoon the Dressing on top. Serve warm or at room temperature.

Curried Rice Noodles in Lettuce Packages

SIX SERVINGS

In India, what we know as curry powder is called "garam masala," meaning "warming spices" in Hindi. The formula varies with each cook and region. Traditionally coriander, cumin, cinnamon, clove, cardamom, and black pepper are included. Garam masala is especially important in Northern India, where the "hot" spices counteract the cool climate.

+ Spices of curry powders such as cumin, cinnamon, cardamom, and black pepper are all credited with having health-giving properties. Refer to the "Key to Primary Indian Spices" on page 288.

INGREDIENTS

½   pound thin rice noodles or rice sticks (rice vermicelli)

2   heads Boston lettuce, cores trimmed

1½   tablespoons virgin olive oil

CURRY SEASONINGS (MIXED TOGETHER)

3   tablespoons minced garlic

3   tablespoons minced fresh ginger

2   tablespoons garam masala, or good-quality curry powder, such as Sun brand Madras-style

2½   cups thinly sliced onions

2   tablespoons rice wine or sake, if needed

2   cups grated carrots

3   cups thinly sliced Chinese (Napa) cabbage, core trimmed

3   cups bean sprouts

NOODLE SAUCE (MIXED TOGETHER)

3½   tablespoons water

1½   tablespoons rice wine or sake

1   teaspoon sugar

1   teaspoon salt, or to taste

¼   teaspoon freshly ground black pepper

2   heaping tablespoons chopped fresh cilantro leaves

FIRST Soften the rice noodles in hot water to cover for 20 minutes. Drain in a colander and set aside. Separate the lettuce leaves, press to flatten, rinse, spin dry, and arrange around the edges of a serving platter.

SECOND Heat a wok or a heavy skillet over high heat until very hot. Add the oil and heat until very hot but not smoking. Add the Curry Seasonings and the onions and stir-fry about 1½ minutes over medium-high heat. Add the 2 tablespoons of rice wine if the mixture is dry. Reduce the heat slightly, cover, and cook for about 1½ minutes, until the onions are tender.

THIRD Add the grated carrots and toss lightly for 1½ minutes over medium-high heat, adding 2 tablespoons of water if the mixture is dry. Add the Napa cabbage, cover, and continue to cook for about 2 to 3 minutes, stirring occasionally, until the cabbage is just tender. If the rice noodles have clumped together, rinse them in a colander under warm running water and drain. Add them to the pan along with the bean sprouts, Noodle Sauce, and cilantro. Carefully stir over medium-high heat until the ingredients are well mixed and the noodles are just tender, about a minute or two. Scoop the noodles onto the serving platter in the middle of the lettuce.

FOURTH To eat, spoon some of the noodle mixture onto a lettuce leaf, roll it up, tucking in the edges, and eat with your fingers. Alternatively, you may omit the lettuce packages and eat the rice noodles directly from plates.

+ *Cilantro is not only a diuretic, but also is believed to reduce cholesterol and aid digestion.*

Spicy Vegetable Sambal

SIX SERVINGS

"Sambal" is a common term used by Asian cooks to refer to a fresh or cooked relish, a curry, or a sauce. Inevitably it contains chile peppers and is quite spicy.

§ *For the health-giving properties of chile peppers, garlic, and ginger, refer to "Key to Primary Indian Spices" on page 288.*

INGREDIENTS

SPICY SAMBAL SEASONINGS

- 2   small bird's-eye chiles, ends trimmed and seeds removed*
- 1   small jalapeño chile, ends trimmed and seeds removed*
- 3   stalks lemongrass, ends trimmed to tender heart and tough outer stalks removed
- 6   cloves garlic
- 1   2-inch length fresh ginger
- 10 small shallots, peeled and ends trimmed
- 1   tablespoon ground cumin
- 1   tablespoon ground coriander

2½ tablespoons virgin olive oil

- 2   medium red onions, coarsely chopped (about 2 cups)
- 1   28-ounce can whole tomatoes, diced, with juice (about 2 cups)

1½ cups light unsweetened coconut milk

1½ tablespoons firmly packed light brown sugar

1½ pounds cauliflower, cut into 1-inch pieces and florets

- 2   cups fresh or thawed frozen peas

1½ teaspoons salt, or to taste

1 to 2 tablespoons freshly squeezed lemon juice, or to taste

*If unavailable, substitute 1½ teaspoons dried chile flakes, or to taste.

FIRST Prepare the Spicy Sambal Seasonings by dropping the ingredients in descending order down the feed tube of a food processor with the machine running or puree in a blender. Pulse several times and scrape down the sides of the bowl with a spatula so that everything is chopped evenly. If the lemongrass remains in large pieces, carefully scrape the sambal seasonings onto a cutting board and chop by hand.

SECOND Heat a heavy wok or a Dutch oven or large casserole over medium-low heat until very hot. Pour in the oil and heat until very hot but not smoking. Add the sambal seasonings and stir-fry over medium heat, stirring constantly with a wooden spoon, for 3 to 4 minutes. They should be very fragrant.

THIRD Add the chopped onion and stir, then cover and cook, stirring occasionally, for about 3 to 4 minutes, until soft and translucent. Add the tomatoes, coconut milk, and sugar, and cook, partially covered, for 5 to 7 minutes. Add the cauliflower and cook, covered, until the cauliflower is almost tender, about 18 to 20 minutes. If using fresh peas, add and cook 4 to 5 minutes, or until tender.

FOURTH Add the thawed frozen peas, if using, salt, and lemon juice and heat briefly. Taste for seasoning and scoop into a serving bowl or platter. Serve with steamed jasmine or basmati rice.

Five-Spice Scallion Soba Noodles

SIX TO EIGHT SERVINGS

I like to make this hearty and flavorful soup as a filling meal during cool weather. The soba noodles, which are made with buckwheat, add a slightly nutty flavor, but in a pinch you can substitute other noodles, such as Japanese flour-and-water udon or spaghettini.

+ *Refer to note on page 267 for the health-giving properties of tofu.*

INGREDIENTS

1	recipe Five-Spice Hoisin Tofu (page 267)
4	cups good-quality vegetable broth
2	cups water
½	cup sake or rice wine
1	tablespoon minced fresh ginger
2	tablespoons soy sauce
1½	cups scallions (about 10 scallions), mainly greens, cut finely into diagonal slices
½	pound baby spinach, rinsed and spun dry
½	pound soba noodles

FIRST Prepare the Five-Spice Tofu as directed. Let cool and cut into ¼-inch-thick slices that are about 2 inches long and ½ inch wide, making sure that the slices are still coated with the hoisin marinade.

SECOND While the tofu is baking, mix the vegetable broth, water, rice wine, minced ginger, and soy sauce together in a large pot and heat until very hot. Cook for about 10 minutes to blend flavors. Add the tofu slices and scallions and cook until the liquid comes back to a boil. Add the spinach and stir carefully. Cook briefly until the spinach leaves are slightly wilted and then turn off the heat. Taste for seasoning, adjusting if necessary.

THIRD Meanwhile bring 3 quarts of water to a boil, add the soba noodles, and stir to separate. When the water returns to a boil, reduce the heat to medium and cook for 3½ to 4 minutes, until al dente. Drain the noodles in a colander, rinse under warm water, and portion into serving bowls. Spoon some of the broth, tofu, and spinach over the noodles and serve.

Spicy Penne with Fresh Tomato Sauce and Greens

My family loves all types of noodles, Asian and Italian, so I'm always looking for new ideas. The fresh arugula tossed into the hot pasta at the last minute makes this dish special and is a great way to get my son to eat more vegetables. The sauce is particularly good during tomato season, but I use canned tomatoes when necessary.

INGREDIENTS

- 12 ripe plum tomatoes, rinsed, drained, and stems removed
- 2 tablespoons extra-virgin olive oil
- 1 tablespoon minced garlic
- ¾ to 1 teaspoon dried chile flakes
- 12 large fresh basil leaves (about ⅔ cup), rinsed, drained, and roughly chopped
- 1 teaspoon salt
- ½ teaspoon freshly ground black pepper
- 1 pound dried penne pasta
- 5 cups arugula, rinsed, spun dry, and coarsely cut into bite-size pieces
- ½ cup freshly grated Pecorino Romano cheese

FIRST Make a shallow X in the non-stem end of each tomato, put them in a bowl, and pour in boiling water to cover. Let sit 10 minutes, refresh in cold water, and peel. Cut the tomatoes in half crosswise and coarsely chop.

SECOND Heat the olive oil in a large skillet until hot. Add the garlic and chile flakes and sauté for 5 seconds, until fragrant. Add the chopped tomatoes and cook over medium-high heat until the tomatoes are beginning to thicken, about 15 to 20 minutes. Gently break up the tomatoes and stir while they are cooking. Add the basil, salt, and pepper and cook gently for a few minutes.

THIRD Meanwhile, bring 3 quarts of salted water to a boil in a large pot. Add the penne and cook about 10 to 12 minutes, until al dente. (Refer to package instructions.) Drain in a colander and add to the tomato sauce along with the arugula. Toss lightly to mix, and portion onto serving plates. Sprinkle with the freshly grated cheese and serve immediately.

+ *Tomatoes are one of the most powerful disease fighters. For their health-giving properties, refer to the "Seven Colors of Health" chart on page 199.*

Chef Suresh Vaidyanathan
Spices of Life

I met Indian master chef Suresh Vaidyanathan in 2001, while working on a unique project with Legal Sea Foods Restaurants of Boston. Roger Berkowitz, the owner, and I had developed the idea of bringing a master chef from Southern India to introduce people to the magic of Southern Indian cooking, with its emphasis on health-giving spices. At the same time, we wanted to present Dr. U. K. Krishna and his inspirational views on Ayurveda, the ancient practice of Indian medicine.

After a great deal of research, I was put in touch with Oberoi Hotels, a premier hotel group in India. They in turn recommended Chef Suresh for the project. When I asked to see the chef's résumé, Mr. Oberoi said, "Just come to India and taste his food."

Watching Chef Suresh cook, as I discovered the following day in Delhi, was a revelation. Forty or more spices were meticulously arranged in small ramekins next to the stove. Half of the pots were filled with fragrant whole spices; the other half contained freshly roasted and ground spices.

While I had already visited Kerala, the spice capital of India, and tasted some of the area's irresistible fiery specialties, nothing had prepared me for Chef Suresh's distinctive, aromatic dishes. Spices were his forte, and Chef Suresh taught me how to temper the different seasonings to bring out subtle nuances of flavor.

For each dish, he first carefully selected different combinations of whole spices and sautéed them in ghee, coconut oil, or peanut oil to bring out their full, rich flavors. Later he combined pinches of the brightly colored ground seasonings on a plate as an artist would mix dabs of paint on his palette. These were added toward the end of the cooking to create overlapping layers of flavor. It was Indian food such as I had never tasted before—vibrant, yet refined.

As he cooked, Chef Suresh told me about his unique background. His great-grandfather had been a cook for the prince of Cochin some eighty years ago, and he passed along to his daughter-in-law, Suresh's grandmother, a substantial repertory of classic recipes as well as considerable knowledge of the different health-giving properties of foods.

Although Chef Suresh began cooking professionally at the age of twenty-one, he had been grinding spices and helping his grandmother and his mother cook since he was a small child. Now, two decades later, he cooks at the Oberoi Hotel in Mumbai and conducts workshops at the Oberoi Center for Learning and Development, which is considered one of the best training schools in Asia. He is not only well versed in the food of his native Kerala, he has also traveled extensively around Southern India and become an expert in other regional styles.

"Whatever spices or foods you use," he tells his students, "before you cook with them, try to learn about how they affect the body's chemistry. Food is the most natural medicine you can put in your body. Turmeric, for instance, is one of the most basic Indian seasonings. It's also antibacterial, antiallergenic, and it's considered a potent medicine by Ayurvedic doctors when used properly: It can cure the whole person."

Here are some of Chef Suresh's recipes, followed by a guide to the major Indian spices, with information on their health-giving properties.

A CHEF SURESH DINNER MENU
(Pages 282–287)

Suresh's Chettinad Spice Powder

Suresh's Chettinad Fillets or Scallops

Suresh's Fresh Cilantro Chutney

Suresh's Grilled Seafood with Fresh Dill

Suresh's Spicy Cumin Green Beans

Suresh's Lemon Rice

Suresh's Chettinad Spice Powder

MAKES ABOUT 1¼ CUPS

Chef Suresh introduced us to this vibrant spice blend when we were creating recipes for Legal Sea Foods' "Spices of Life" project. Use it to flavor all types of seafood. (See Suresh's Chettinad Fillets or Scallops on facing page.) I also use it to season roasted and grilled vegetables such as eggplant, zucchini, sweet potatoes, and squash. It will keep for months stored in an airtight container in a cool, dry place.

INGREDIENTS

¼   cup dried red chiles (measuring about 2 to 3 inches long), ends trimmed and seeds removed

½   cup coriander seeds

2½ tablespoons fennel seeds

2½ teaspoons cumin seeds

3 to 4 whole star anise, smashed with the flat side of a knife

1   teaspoon cardamom pods (about 18), smashed with a rolling pin

½   teaspoon whole cloves

2½ teaspoons whole black peppercorns

4   cinnamon sticks, broken in half, then smashed into bits with a rolling pin

1 or 2 whole bay leaves

FIRST Heat a heavy skillet or a cast-iron pan and add the spices. Toast them over low heat, stirring frequently with a wooden spoon, for 4 to 5 minutes, until very fragrant.

SECOND Let cool slightly and carefully pour the spices into a spice grinder or a food processor and grind to a coarse powder, about 4 to 5 minutes. Transfer to an airtight container and use as directed in the recipe.

Suresh's Chettinad Fillets or Scallops

Chettinad cooking, which is Southern Indian, is renowned for its pungent flavors. Most dishes are liberally seasoned with generous amounts of cinnamon, peppercorns, cardamom, bay leaves, and green and red chiles. Chef Suresh recommended the spice powder for any firm-fleshed fish, and I discovered that it is also excellent for scallops and shrimp.

INGREDIENTS

CHETTINAD SEAFOOD RUB

1   teaspoon Chettinad Spice Powder (facing page)

1   teaspoon ground coriander

1   teaspoon ground turmeric

1½ tablespoons minced fresh ginger

1½ tablespoons minced garlic

1½ pounds firm white fish fillets (about 1 inch thick), such as sea bass, halibut, or cod, skin removed, or sea scallops, rinsed lightly and drained

2   tablespoons peanut or olive oil

3 to 4 limes, cut into wedges

FIRST Mix the ingredients for the Chettinad Seafood Rub and, using your hands, rub it all over the fish fillets or scallops to coat them. Cover and refrigerate for at least an hour.

SECOND Heat a large frying or sauté pan with a lid until very hot. Pour in the oil, swirl or brush around the pan, and heat until very hot. Arrange the fillets or scallops in the pan, cover, and cook over medium-high heat for 6 to 7 minutes per side for the fish, or 2 to 3 minutes per side for the scallops. Slide the seafood onto a platter and squeeze the lime wedges over the top. Serve with a fresh herbal chutney, if desired, and rice or chappatis.

Suresh's Fresh Cilantro Chutney

MAKES 1¼ CUPS

Americans usually associate the term "chutney" with a spicy pickle, but in Southern India, chutneys are pungent, pesto-like mixtures that are made with fresh herbs, spices, tamarind, chiles, and freshly grated coconut.

INGREDIENTS

¼ cup warm water

1 tablespoon-size piece dried tamarind

1 fresh jalapeño chile, ends trimmed, seeds removed, and cut into ½-inch pieces

½ medium onion, peeled and cut into large pieces

2 cups closely packed fresh cilantro leaves, rinsed and blotted dry

1½ cups unsweetened grated coconut

2 to 3 tablespoons whole-milk or low-fat plain yogurt

1 teaspoon salt, or to taste

1 teaspoon peanut or coconut oil

1 teaspoon black or brown mustard seeds

FIRST Pour the warm water over the tamarind and let sit for 10 minutes. Mash the mixture until smooth, and pick out and discard the seeds.

SECOND Drop the onion and chile down the feed tube of a food processor fitted with a steel blade while the motor is running, or into a blender, and chop finely. Sprinkle the cilantro into the work bowl and pulse to chop it evenly. Then let the machine run until the mixture is almost a puree.

THIRD Add the coconut to the bowl and continue processing. Slowly pour the tamarind water into the feed tube with the machine running and continue pureeing, then add the yogurt. Scrape down the sides of the bowl with a rubber scraper and process to a smooth paste. Add the salt and stir to blend.

FOURTH Heat the oil until near smoking in a heavy pot. Sprinkle in the mustard seeds and cook over medium heat, stirring constantly, until they pop. Slowly pour the oil and mustard seeds down the feed tube of the food processor while the machine is running, and mix well. Taste for seasoning, adjusting if necessary. Scrape the chutney into a bowl and serve with chappatis and/or grilled, pan-fried, or steamed seafood.

Suresh's Grilled Seafood with Fresh Dill

SIX SERVINGS

Chef Suresh's dishes have a subtle blending of fresh and dried herbs and spices that accentuates the fresh, natural flavors of foods. This marinade can be used for all types of seafood, but it is particularly good with salmon.

INGREDIENTS

MARINADE

- 1 cup shallots (about ½ pound), peeled and ends trimmed
- 3 cloves garlic, or 1 tablespoon minced garlic
- 1 cup closely packed fresh dill, rinsed and blotted dry
- 1 tablespoon peanut or virgin olive oil

SEASONINGS

- 1½ tablespoons fennel seeds
- 1¼ teaspoons dried chile flakes
- 1½ whole star anise, smashed to small bits with a rolling pin
- 1 teaspoon salt
- ½ teaspoon freshly ground black pepper

- 2 pounds firm-fleshed fish fillets (about 1 inch thick) with skin on, such as salmon, swordfish, or sea bass
- 2 tablespoons virgin olive oil

FIRST Drop the shallots and garlic down the feed tube of a food processor fitted with a steel blade, or into a blender, and chop finely. Add the fresh dill and continue to chop to a fine mince, but not a paste.

SECOND Heat the oil until hot, add Seasonings, and sauté over medium heat for a few minutes. Add this mixture to the fresh dill mixture to complete the Marinade. Place the fish in a bowl, and, using your hands, coat the fillets on both sides. Cover and refrigerate for several hours.

THIRD Heat a heavy skillet with a lid, add the oil, and heat until near smoking. Place the coated fillets in the pan skin side down, cover, and cook over high heat for 6 to 7 minutes. Carefully flip over and cook on the other side for another 6 to 7 minutes, or until just cooked. You can also broil the fish, placing it about 3 inches from the broiler and cooking it about 7 to 8 minutes per side, depending on the thickness. Slide the fish onto a serving platter and serve with Suresh's Fresh Cilantro Chutney (facing page) and rice or chappatis.

§ *Western herbalists and Ayurvedic doctors credit fresh and dried dill with having numerous health-giving effects. It is anti-inflammatory, a reliable digestive, and believed to have a calming effect on the body.*

Suresh's Spicy Cumin Green Beans

SIX SERVINGS

This dish is similar to a stir-fry, so you should prepare and line up all of the ingredients before you start cooking.

+ For other beneficial properties of cumin, refer to "Key to Primary Indian Spices" on page 288.

INGREDIENTS

SPICY SEASONINGS

2 to 3 dried red chiles, ends trimmed, or about 1 teaspoon dried chile flakes

1½-inch piece peeled fresh ginger

4 cloves garlic, peeled

2 pounds green beans, ends trimmed, cut in half crosswise

2½ tablespoons peanut or coconut oil

1½ teaspoons black or brown mustard seeds

2 teaspoons cumin seeds

2 or 3 curry leaves, rinsed, blotted dry, and shredded finely

2 cups sliced red onions (about 2 medium)

1 teaspoon salt, or to taste

FIRST Drop the Spicy Seasonings down the feed tube of a food processor fitted with a steel blade while the machine is running, and process until the ingredients are finely chopped.

SECOND Bring 3 quarts of water to a boil. Add the green beans and cook for about 8 minutes, or until the beans are just tender. Remove from the pan, refresh in cold water, and drain thoroughly.

THIRD Heat a wok or a heavy skillet, add the oil, and heat over medium-high heat until very hot. Sprinkle in the mustard seeds and cook, stirring until they pop, then add the cumin seeds and curry leaves and fry for about a minute, until fragrant.

FOURTH Add the Spicy Seasonings and sauté over medium heat for 15 seconds, until fragrant. Add the onions and sauté for several minutes, until they are soft and transparent. Turn the heat to high and add the cooked green beans and salt. Toss lightly over high heat, mixing together. Taste for seasoning and adjust if necessary. Scoop onto a serving platter and serve.

Suresh's Lemon Rice

Kerala, the state in southwestern India where Chef Suresh was born, is renowned for its vibrant spices and aromatic cooking. This dish is a fine example. It is so light and refreshing that I often serve it as a side dish with non-Indian food.

INGREDIENTS

2½ cups basmati rice

1	**tablespoon peanut or coconut oil**
1	**teaspoon black mustard seeds**
½	**teaspoon ground turmeric**
2	**curry leaves, rinsed, blotted dry, and shredded finely (optional)**

Zest and juice of 2 medium lemons

1	**teaspoon salt, or to taste**

FIRST Put the rice in a medium saucepan. Using your hands as a rake, rinse the rice in cold water. Drain and repeat several times. Pour 4¾ cups of water into the saucepan and set over medium-high heat. When the water reaches a boil, cover, turn the heat to low, and let simmer for about 17 to 19 minutes, or until the water has evaporated and craters appear in the rice. Remove from the heat, fluff the rice with a fork, and spread out on a tray to cool.

SECOND Heat a wok or a heavy skillet, add the oil, and heat until hot. Add the mustard seeds and cook, stirring over medium heat, until they begin to pop. Add the ground turmeric, curry leaves, and lemon zest and cook for about 1 minute, then add the rice and cook over medium heat, stirring so it will heat evenly. Once the rice is hot, stir in the lemon juice and salt, and heat through, tossing lightly. Taste for seasoning and adjust if necessary. Spoon into a serving bowl and serve.

Key to Primary Indian Spices and Their Healing (Ayurvedic) Properties

Ayurveda (*ayu* means life and *veda* means science in Sanskrit), the ancient medical system of India, encompasses the healing of body, mind, and spirit through diet, lifestyle, and rejuvenation. (For more information on Ayurveda, see page 292.) Food and diet can have a profound influence on maintaining good health. Ayurvedic doctors credit herbs and spices (as well as certain foods) with health-giving properties, and recent scientific research is confirming some of these beliefs. Here are some of the most prominent seasonings used in Indian cooking, with their therapeutic properties.

Note: Herbs, foods, and other natural remedies are not substitutes for professional medical care.
For a specific health problem, consult a qualified health-care giver for guidance.

BLACK PEPPER

Once green peppercorns are dried in the sun, they become black. When black peppercorns are soaked, their skins and pulp are removed and the resulting seed is the white peppercorn. Black, white, and green peppercorns are all used by Indian chefs. Black pepper is known as the king of spices, and its name in Sanskrit refers to the sun, alluding to the belief that a substantial dose of the sun's energy is contained in the grains and pods. In India, black pepper is often added to tea as a stimulant, and peppercorns are sucked to soothe a sore throat.

key benefits:

- Aids digestion

- Improves the appetite

- Prevents disease, since it is antibacterial

CARDAMOM

Secondary to black pepper, cardamom, which is often called the queen of spices, is one of the most important Indian spices. It has been prized since ancient times and was chewed by the Moghul emperors of India as a breath freshener, a tradition that still exists today.

key benefits:

- Considered a key digestive and is used to treat stomach disorders

- Helps to prevent vomiting, since it has antispasmodic properties

- Refreshes the breath and soothes the throat

CHILE PEPPERS

Although chile peppers were introduced to India only four hundred years ago by the Portuguese, it is difficult to imagine Indian cooking without them. Like black pepper, chiles are warming to the body. They are used in Ayurvedic medicine to promote digestion and to soothe a sore throat. When ground with coriander seeds and ginger, chiles soothe abdominal pain and nausea.

key benefits:

- Contain vitamin A and more vitamin C than citrus fruits

- Soothe abdominal pain, nausea, and throat irritation

CUMIN

Recognized as one of the kings of Indian spices, cumin is used in the regional cookery and medicine of every part of India, from Kashmir to Gujarat to Bengal. The spice appears in street snacks and banquets alike, and is blended into drinks to act as a cooling protection against indigestion or waterborne stomach infections. Most of the digestive properties of cumin lie in the toasted seeds. (According to T. V. Sairam, author of Home Remedies, cumin seeds are actually the fruit of the plant.) Cumin is hot in nature and is believed to purify blood, stimulate digestive juices, and reduce nausea, particularly in pregnant women.

key benefits:

- Excellent for colds and fevers when infused in hot water

- Easily digested and effective in relieving indigestion, gas, and flatulence

- Purifies the blood and protects against stomach infections

CINNAMON

Cinnamon, along with cardamom and bay leaf, is part of the Ayurvedic trio of aromatics used to heal the body and disguise the taste of medicines. When steeped in warm water to make cinnamon tea, it harmonizes the flow of circulation, aids digestion, and helps the stomach to discharge gas. It reduces nausea and congestion and leaves an appealing flavor in the mouth.

key benefits:

- Strengthens the heart, stimulates the kidneys, and aids circulation

- Cinnamon tea soothes colds and nervous tension, and stimulates digestion

- Cinnamon oil is used as a liniment to soothe headaches, rheumatic pains, body aches, and toothaches

CLOVES

One of the earliest texts on Ayurveda describes cloves as "the flowers of the heavens." The Portuguese, Dutch, and French all fought to control the trade of these little "flowers" throughout the sixteenth and seventeenth centuries. Cloves are the unopened flower buds of the clove tree, which are picked and dried in the sun. The word "clove" is derived from the French *clou,* meaning nail. In Sanskrit, cloves are known as *lavanga.* Cloves are a cure for halitosis. Through their scent and digestive action, they are also reputed to combat acidity in the stomach and purify blood.

key benefits:

- Act as a stimulant and are aromatic

- Their antiseptic action helps numb the digestive system and reduce gastric pain

- Relieve colic and expel gas

CORIANDER

Coriander, the first known spice in India, was mentioned more than three thousand years ago in ancient Sanskrit texts. Its leaves, seeds, and roots are used in Indian cooking and medicine, making coriander the most popular culinary plant in India. Cooling in nature, coriander is believed to balance the body. Fresh coriander juice can be administered internally or externally for allergies, skin rashes, or inflammation. The seeds, when crushed, roasted, and infused in warm water, are diuretic, and increase the flow of urine.

key benefits:

- diuretic
- may reduce cholesterol and improve eyesight
- aid digestion

DILL

Dill seeds have been cultivated for more than two thousand years. Indian dill, *Anethum sava,* is much like the common variety, *Anethum graveolens.* Both have similar culinary properties, but Indian dill also plays a specific role in medicine. Dill seeds are often eaten after a meal, since they enhance the secretion of digestive juices, cleanse the mouth, and reduce flatulence. A hot infusion of dill seed and honey soothes colds and flu, and stimulates menstrual flow and breast milk.

key benefits:

- An infusion of seeds and water relieves colic and hiccups
- Seeds soothe the stomach by enhancing the secretion of digestive juices
- Relieves colds and flu

290

FENUGREEK SEED

Although first imported from eastern Europe, fenugreek seeds are a prominent part of Indian food, culture, and medicine. This strong-scented herb grows in abundance in the north. The seeds, which are rich in iron, are excellent for combating anemia in pre- and postpartum mothers. When a child is born in India, it is customary to give the mother foods flavored with fenugreek seeds for forty days after the birth. Fenugreek seeds also play a major role at weddings, funerals, festivals, and religious ceremonies.

key benefits:

- Enhances the performance of insulin, so it is good for diabetics
- Soothes persistent coughs
- Relieves flatulence and aids digestion
- Both fenugreek seeds and leaves are cooling to the body

FENNEL SEED

Fennel has been known to Indian herbalists for centuries, and is still part of every Indian household's medicine chest. There are several varieties of fennel in India, all known as *saunf.* Like cumin seeds, fennel seeds are in fact the fruit of the plant. The seeds are infused in water and given to infants to relieve wheezing, asthma, and colic, and to adults to reduce fevers and indigestion. Fennel seeds are also eaten after meals to aid digestion and freshen the breath.

key benefits:

- Provide an excellent remedy for stomach and intestinal disorders
- Reduce heat in the body
- Combat diseases of the chest, spleen, and kidney

GARLIC

Garlic, or the "bulb of life," as it was known to ancient Indian physicians, has been celebrated for its medicinal properties for centuries. All parts of the plant are eaten: Pungency is found in the bulb, bitterness is in the leaves, salinity at the crown, astringency in the stem, and sweetness in the seeds. Garlic is added to the majority of Indian curries, since it lends a good taste to meat and fish. It also helps to digest them. Some feel it is an aphrodisiac and they avoid it.

key benefits:

- Traditionally used to treat asthma, deafness, and congestion
- Lowers cholesterol and blood pressure, and relieves rheumatism
- Clears eye infections when rubbed on the area, since it is antibacterial
- Powerful detoxifier, rejuvenator, and cleanser for the blood

GINGER

This flavorful rhizome has been used for centuries in Indian cuisine and medicine. Ayurvedic texts credit it as a "universal great medicine." Although ginger is widely used by both Indian and Chinese physicians, it originated on Indian soil and was introduced to China just three hundred years ago. Besides having a hot, vibrant flavor, ginger is an excellent digestive and aphrodisiac. It cures nausea and is good for rheumatism. Ayurvedic doctors suggest eating slices of ginger sprinkled with salt before meals to aid digestion. Chewing on a piece of fresh ginger relieves a sore throat and hoarseness.

key benefits:

- Ginger tea warms the body and soothes fevers, motion sickness, and nausea
- Chewing fresh ginger cleanses the throat and tongue
- Combats cardiac disorders, since it has anticoagulant and anticholesterol properties
- Relieves rheumatic pain

MACE AND NUTMEG

The nutmeg tree is a wide evergreen native to the Spice Islands of Indonesia. However, it has been used in India as a spice and medicinally since as early as 700 B.C. Mace and nutmeg are two different spices from the same fruit. Nutmeg is the dried seed and mace the dried aril, or "cage," that surrounds the seed. Nutmeg is more aromatic, sweeter, and more delicate than mace, and it is believed to impart strength and enhance sexual prowess.

key benefits:

- Nutmeg relieves diarrhea and colic

- Ground mace has been used as a remedy for rheumatism

MUSTARD

Mustard plants are easily identified in India, because their blossoms create a carpet of gold throughout the countryside. The seeds of the plant are used medicinally and in the kitchen. There are three types of mustard seed—white, brown, and black—and all are believed to share the same properties. When taken daily in food, mustard seeds will increase the appetite by stimulating the production of gastric juices. Mustard seeds also relieve headaches and muscle tension; they calm the mind and sharpen intelligence. Beware of mustard's potency—this sharp, slightly bitter spice can be deceptively hot when consumed in large doses.

key benefits:

- Mustard seeds increase appetite by stimulating production of gastric juices

- Calms the mind and sharpens intelligence

- Purifies blood and increases circulation

- Mustard oil relives arthritic pain

SAFFRON

It's not surprising that saffron has been said to be "worth its weight in gold." It takes 750,000 crocus flowers to produce just one pound of saffron strands. This valuable spice has been revered for centuries, since Arab traders brought saffron from central Asia into Persia, Arabia, Greece, the Roman Empire, India, Burma, and China. Today India and Spain are the major producers. Ayurvedic doctors use saffron to treat all types of ailments, including fevers, melancholia, and uterine problems.

key benefits:

- Antibacterial and useful in treating digestive disorders

- A remedy for headaches when applied to the temples

- Effective in the treatment of liver, urinary, and uterine dysfunction

- Aphrodisiac

SALT

Kala namak, or rock salt, is the salt most commonly used in Indian cuisine. It is produced from the fertile quarries of the Gangetic Plain in central India. Ayurvedic doctors believe rock salt and sea salt are the most beneficial forms of salt because, unlike ordinary salt, they don't increase the sodium content of blood and are preferable for patients with high blood pressure. Salt activates the flavors of food, thereby enhancing the taste. It is also a rejuvenator, aids digestion, and improves eyesight.

key benefits:

- Cure for flatulence and heartburn

- Aids digestion

- Improves eyesight

- Helps to lower high blood pressure

STAR ANISE

Star anise has been used in Chinese and Ayurvedic medicine and cooking for centuries. Both cultures use it as a breath freshener and digestive. It's soothing to the stomach and is often used in cough medicines. Star anise is usually used together with ginger and clove to treat nausea and vomiting.

key benefits:

- Aids digestion

- Freshens the breath

- The oil is believed to relieve rheumatism

TURMERIC

Turmeric is an herbaceous perennial that flourishes throughout India. Turmeric spice comes from the underground rhizome that is boiled, drained, dried in the sun, then ground into a powder. India is the largest producer and consumer of turmeric in the world: The spice is the heart and soul of curries, it's indispensable in Hindu rituals, it's an important ingredient in cosmetics, and it's essential in Ayurvedic medicine. Ancient Indian sages claimed that "all poisons can be removed from the human body if treated with a paste of turmeric." India is tropical and subtropical in some parts, making it susceptible to germs, viruses, and bacteria. Since turmeric is antibacterial, antiallergenic, and a preservative, a sprinkling protects the body from tropical germs.

key benefits:

- Cools down the digestive, circulatory, and reproductive systems

- Arrests cholesterol problems and helps to control diabetes

- Purifies the blood and eliminates toxins

- As an antiseptic and aromatic, a washing with a paste of turmeric and lentil flour will cleanse and disinfect without removing the skin's natural oils

Dr. U. K. Krishna
Ayurvedic Tips for Happy
and Healthy Living

Dr. Upadhyaya Karinje Krishna's charmingly boyish face glows—especially when he is talking about his life's passion: explaining the virtues of Ayurveda, the Indian holistic system of medicine. "Ayurveda, which is a Sanskrit word meaning 'science of life,' evolved in India five thousand, even possibly seven thousand, years ago," he says. "What makes Ayurveda especially unique is that it is the only health science which relates to lifestyle and spirituality."

Ayurveda seeks to establish harmony between the body, mind, and spirit through diet, regimen, and a variety of rejuvenating therapies such as massage, yoga, meditation, herbs, and detoxification programs. Ayurveda not only helps to maintain balance in one's physical and mental health, it embraces spirituality, since the mind and spirit are considered to be inseparable.

Although I had read about Ayurveda years ago and knew its similarities to Traditional Chinese Medicine, I was formally introduced to the basic principles and practices in 2000 when I visited the Indus Valley Ayurvedic Centre (IVAC) in Mysore, India. The center, which is located on a twenty-five-acre farm in southern central India, has been in operation only since 1999, yet it has become one of the most innovative Ayurvedic centers in India, offering traditional rejuvenation therapies and treatments for chronic ailments. Dr. Krishna—or Dr. U.K., as he prefers to be called—is the chief consultant to IVAC, and he helped to establish the center. He is also one of the leading international authorities on Ayurveda, and he has lectured all over the world.

Dr. U.K. explained to me that one of the most basic principles of Ayurveda is that everything in the universe is interconnected and is composed of five elements: fire, air, earth, water, and ether (space). The human body is composed of these elements too, but it is influenced by three bio-energies, which are known as doshas. The three doshas are: Vata, which corresponds to air and ether; Pitta, which corresponds to fire and water; and Kapha, which corresponds to water and earth. The doshas govern all physiological and chemical activities in the body.

Each person has the characteristics of all three doshas, but one or two may be dominant. Like the concept of yin and yang in Traditional Chinese Medicine, balance or equilibrium between the three energies in the body constitutes good health. An imbalance leads to a loss of energy and various ailments. (For tips on determining what your dosha or constitution might be, see page 294.)

According to Dr. U.K., food is one of the primary means by which good health may be promoted and maintained: It nurtures the body and balances the constitution. Herbs and spices, in particular, are credited with having specific health-giving properties. (For more details on a number of herbs and spices, refer to "Key to Primary Indian Spices" on page 288.)

Food is also believed to have certain characteristics: It may be hot or cold, light or heavy, oily or dry, slow or sharp, stable or mobile, soft or hard, slimy or rough, gross or subtle, cloudy or clear. These qualities affect how easily the body digests a particular food. According to Ayurveda, the heating or cooling effects of the food are particularly important to maintaining balance in the body: People with a Pitta constitution should eat cooling foods, Kapha types should eat heating foods, and Vata individuals should eat some of each (see the "General Eating Guide to Balance Your Dosha," page 295).

Every food or herb also has one of six specific tastes—sweet, sour, salty, pungent, bitter, and astringent—and has a direct effect on the doshas in the body. For instance, foods with a sweet flavor increase Kapha, thereby calming Vata and Pitta. Sour foods decrease or calm Vata and increase Pitta and Kapha. In general, you should eat foods that complement or balance your dosha. In many cases, herbs, spices, and cooking methods can affect and balance a particular food so that it will not have a harmful effect on the system. Spices and herbs, in particular, are used to alter the qualities of foods to make them more digestible and to reduce negative effects.

According to Ayurvedic beliefs, a balanced meal should feature foods that incorporate the six tastes, and the general makeup of dishes should be a staple food such as a complex carbohydrate, a protein dish, and one or more vegetables. Ultimately, according to Dr. U.K., all food and every meal should nurture as well as provide pleasure.

DR. U.K.'S TIPS FOR HEALTHY AND HAPPY LIVING

■ GETTING UP EARLY in the morning is a long-term investment for energetic living. It helps us to be in a positive mood and enhances longevity and youthfulness. Establishing a regular sleeping and waking pattern has a rejuvenating effect.

■ Doing SUITABLE EXERCISE for an appropriate amount of time is recommended, but it should not be overdone. Regular exercise prevents disease and increases immunity.

■ CONTEMPLATION in the form of meditation, prayer, or just sitting quietly in a peaceful, natural setting will help to quiet and energize the mind and produce a positive effect on activities and thoughts for the entire day.

■ Eating a meal in a settled atmosphere and ENJOYING YOUR FOOD not only nourishes the body but is instrumental in preventing disease.

■ Eating only when you are hungry and NOT OVEREATING are good habits to adopt. (You should eat until your stomach is about two-thirds full.) Leaving space in your stomach promotes good health and longevity.

■ A BRIEF REST after lunch and a LIGHT WALK after dinner help to improve digestion and use the body's energy efficiently.

The Three Doshas: Which Type Are You?

According to Ayurveda, all functions within a living body are controlled by the three bio-energies, or doshas: Vata (air and ether), Pitta (fire and water), and Kapha (water and earth). Each person's individual constitution, or prakruti, is determined at birth according to hereditary factors, diet, lifestyle, and emotions of the parents. It rarely changes in a lifetime. A few individuals are born with a balanced prakruti, where all three doshas are equal, but most people have one or two doshas prominent.

The main aim of Ayurveda is to help to maintain equilibrium among the three doshas. When the doshas are in harmony, the body is able to fight disease and sustain good health. Balance and optimum health can be achieved and maintained with a proper diet and lifestyle, but it is helpful to know your constitution. According to Dr. U. K. Krishna, diagnosing the prakruti of each individual is not a simple task. Ideally, an Ayurvedic doctor should be consulted to do so. There are, however, some features that determine whether you are a Vata, a Pitta, or a Kapha.

DOMINANT FEATURES OF EACH CONSTITUTION

VATA

- Walks, talks, and eats quickly

- Has dryness in different parts of the body, including skin, scalp, and hair

- Is creative, imaginative, and quick to learn

- Has an irregular appetite and a tendency to be constipated

- Finds falling asleep difficult and/or has disturbed or shallow sleep

- Is restless, loves to travel

- Is sensitive to cold

- Has a tendency to be anxious and depressed

PITTA

- Has a thin, delicate skin with a fair complexion and freckles (easily sunburns)

- Has a tendency to develop acne

- Has a voracious appetite, but doesn't gain weight, and is often thirsty

- Suffers from loose bowels

- Loses one's temper easily and is a perfectionist who can be very critical

- Has a high body temperature and easily perspires

- Dislikes hot weather

KAPHA

- Walks, talks, and eats slowly

- Has thick, oily hair and skin

- Has a calm and steady nature and can be lethargic

- Is conservative and patient

- Possesses great stamina

- Loves to sleep

- Gains weight easily and has difficulty taking it off

- Dislikes cold and damp

General Eating Guide to Balance Your Dosha

The following eating tips are advised for each constitution, but generally moderation is advised, with an even balance of spicy and nonspicy dishes. Specific needs vary for each individual. For more information, refer to *Ayurvedic Cooking for Self-Healing*, by Usha Lad and Dr. Vasant Lad, and *The Ayurvedic Cookbook*, by Amadea Morningstar with Urmila Desai.

SUGGESTED FOODS OF EACH CONSTITUTION

VATA

- Garlic is an elixir to Vata types.

- Seafood such as salmon, sardines, and shrimp is advisable, as well as chicken and lamb.

- Spices such as black pepper, ginger, and mustard are suggested, as well as asafetida, an herb used frequently in Ayurvedic cooking.

- Warm milk or yogurt that is not too sour is recommended.

PITTA

- Ghee is considered a nectar of life for Pitta individuals, and healthy fats like butter and olive oil should be consumed according to one's capacity to digest and assimilate them.

- Warm milk is recommended, as well as sweet ripe fruits, green leafy vegetables, barley, rice, wheat, and mung beans.

- Spices such as clove, cinnamon, coriander, and fennel seeds are also suggested.

KAPHA

- The diet should include more vegetables than meat and dairy products. Apples and honey are recommended. Honey is believed to maintain balance of the bio-energies, but it should not be heated.

- Steamed or lightly cooked vegetables are preferable to those in raw form.

- Foods that enhance heat energy in the body are suggested, such as black and red pepper, ginger, cumin, turmeric, mustard, nutmeg, garlic, fenugreek, and ajwain, an Ayurvedic herb.

- Grains such as buckwheat, millet, rye, and tapioca are advised, as well as legumes such as yellow lentils and mung beans.

satisfying staples: noodles, rice, and other grains

I used to be afraid of staple dishes. Like many Americans, I thought that in order to maintain a svelte figure, I could eat rice and noodles only sparingly, if at all. Then I went to live in Asia, and for the first time, while living with my surrogate Chinese family, I was introduced to the *fan-cai* idea of eating, which is fundamental to the Asian diet.

The concept is that staples, composed primarily of whole grains, form the bulk of your diet, with generous servings of vegetables, some seafood, and occasionally tastes of meat that "flavor" or garnish the *fan* (rice). In my new home, we ate much the same way as every Asian family: All the food (*cai*) was placed informally on a lazy Susan in the middle of the table, and each person was given a bowl of rice or grains. You were expected to take *a little bit* of the dishes in the middle and mainly eat the grains.

It was not easy for me to change my eating patterns. At first, like most Westerners, I ate primarily from the center of the table, with a little rice on the side. I soon found out, to my embarrassment, that my Chinese brothers and sisters had pegged me as the "big pig" in Chinese. So I began to emulate their way of eating, and after a while I realized that not only was I more satisfied at the end of the meal (so I was less inclined to snack between meals or crave sweets), but I had more energy and felt more in balance.

Later I studied Traditional Chinese Medicine and Ayurveda, traditional Indian medicine. In India, a typical meal also consists of a healthy quantity of grains, with a selection of legumes, vegetables, occasional meat, and flavorings. And I learned that not only are rice, millet, sorghum, and wheat nourishing, but they are believed to increase strength and vitality. Furthermore, they

Chapter opener: Crisp-Fried Noodles with Barbecued Pork and Broccoli Rabe

help the body relax and the mind focus, and they are essential to an overall balanced diet or regimen.

While there has been some controversy among contemporary nutritionists, most agree that complex carbohydrates, in the form of starches such as whole grains, legumes, and certain vegetables, are necessary in providing fiber and protein, which converts to energy. And a groundbreaking study that began in the 1980s proved that the Asian diet, with its *fan-cai* principle, is very effective in preventing disease and promoting longevity (see page 328).

Today, I find it quite simple to integrate this idea into my family meal planning. I usually start by choosing the vegetables and seafood or meat, then decide which staple dish of rice, noodles, or bread is appropriate. I also like to use rice, noodles, couscous, and quinoa with different vegetables, meats, seafood, or leftovers to make easy dishes that have become family favorites.

Staple dishes, as you'll see from the following recipes, are versatile, satisfying, and wonderfully appealing. Many constitute a meal by themselves. From a simple rice pilaf to a stir-fried noodle to a fragrant couscous, they are foods that energize the body and calm the spirit.

Basic White Rice

MAKES 6 CUPS COOKED RICE, OR SIX SERVINGS

There's nothing more basic or delicious than fragrant white rice. I prefer the fluffy long-grain varieties such as basmati and jasmine, which are sold in Asian markets. The cooking time varies depending on the rice, so test the rice for doneness and cook until *just* tender. It will continue cooking even after being removed from the heat.

✣ Chinese doctors believe that rice strengthens the spleen and pancreas and is soothing to the stomach. It also increases the body's qi, or energy.

§ Ayurvedic doctors credit rice as sweet and cooling to the body and easy to digest. Basmati rice is considered the most beneficial for the body.

✣ § Rice porridge, or congee, is prescribed by Asian doctors for fevers and digestive disorders.

INGREDIENTS

2 cups long-grain rice (for smaller and larger quantities, see chart, page 302)

3¼ cups water

FIRST Put the rice in a bowl and, using your fingers as a rake, rinse the rice under cold running water to remove some of the talc. Drain the rice in a strainer.

SECOND Put the rice and water in a heavy 2-quart saucepan with a lid. Heat, uncovered, to the boiling point. Reduce the heat to low, cover, and simmer for about 12 to 15 minutes, or until the water has evaporated and craters appear on the surface. Remove from the heat and fluff lightly with a fork to separate the grains. Serve or, if using for fried rice, spread the rice out in a thin layer on a tray. Let cool completely, cover with plastic wrap, and chill in the refrigerator overnight. *To steam the rice:* Fill a wok or a pot with water for steaming and heat until boiling. Spread the rice in a steamer tray lined with damp cheesecloth or parchment paper. Place the steamer over boiling water, cover, and steam 35 to 40 minutes, or until tender. Fluff the rice with a fork and serve or spread out and chill on a tray as directed above. (Rice can also be steamed in a microwave with very good results, but a microwave rice cooker is essential for this. Cook according to the manufacturer's instructions.)

Boiled Long-Grain Brown Rice

SIX SERVINGS

Brown rice used to be available only at health food stores. These days it is sold in most supermarkets, and different varieties such as brown basmati or short-grain brown rice are offered. I prefer brown basmati for its fragrant flavor and drier texture. However, if you are pressed for time, short-grain brown rice may cook in just 30 to 35 minutes and require slightly less water.

INGREDIENTS

2½ cups long-grain brown rice (preferably brown basmati)

4¼ cups water

FIRST Put the rice in a pot and, using your fingers as a rake, rinse the rice under cold running water. Drain the rice in a strainer.

SECOND Put the rice and water in a heavy saucepan with a lid. Bring to a boil, cover, and reduce the heat to low. Simmer for 40 to 50 minutes, until the rice is just tender. Remove from the heat and fluff lightly with a fork to separate the grains. If the rice is wet or there is still unabsorbed water, drain the rice in a strainer, put back into the pot, and cover. Serve hot or warm. (If using in a pilaf or fried rice dish, spread out in a thin layer to cool.)

+ *Brown rice is rich in fiber, vitamin B, potassium, and magnesium. It may help reduce the risk of colon cancer.*

Selected Grains and Their Preparation

The following cooking times are for selected grains other than white rice. The cooking time and amount of water varies with different manufacturers and whether the grain is processed. Make certain to check the label for suggested water amount and cooking time.

GRAIN VARIETY	WATER	SUGGESTED COOKING TIME
1 cup long-grain brown rice	1¾ cups	45 to 50 minutes (See page 301)
1 cup cracked kasha	2 cups	Toast, then boil for 15 minutes
1 cup bulgur* (medium grind)	1½ cups	15 minutes
1 cup cracked wheat[†]	2½ cups	Cover in boiling water, let stand 15 minutes
1 cup quinoa	1½ cups	15 minutes
1 cup wheat berries[‡]	2–3 cups	1 to 2 hours

A Note about Brown and White Rice

Rice is white if the grains have been hulled or the outer bran has been removed. Experts agree that brown rice is nutritionally superior to white rice, even if the white rice has been "enriched," which only restores some of the vitamins and none of the fiber.

"The starchy part of the grain of white rice basically supplies the body with energy," says Dr. Ed Blonz, author of *Power Nutrition.* "It doesn't really give you the variety of nutrients such as thiamin, riboflavin (B_2), niacin (B_6), protein, minerals, and fiber that are present in brown rice." I like brown basmati rice, and there are some wonderful, different multigrain blends, but usually I tend to eat white long-grain rice, such as basmati and jasmine. I make up the difference in vitamins and fiber by eating a variety of vegetables and fruits.

* Traditional Middle Eastern bulgur is sold at ethnic markets. It is usually available in three types of grind—coarse, medium, and fine.
[†] Cracked wheat is more thoroughly milled than bulgur and is now sold in supermarkets. It should not be confused with bulgur. For more information and a recipe, see page 156.
[‡] Wheat berries (hard and soft) are sold in natural food stores and Middle Eastern markets. The cooking time will vary according to the variety.

Simple Asian Fried Rice with Fresh Herbs

SIX SERVINGS

This lovely vegetable fried rice is excellent served as a side staple with a stir-fried, steamed, or grilled meat or seafood. Depending on your tastes, you may vary the herb, replacing cilantro with fresh dill, basil, or mint. Add cooked meat or seafood to make a light meal.

INGREDIENTS

2   tablespoons olive or canola oil

2   large eggs, lightly beaten

2   cups minced scallions, greens and white part

2   cups cooked fresh or defrosted frozen peas (or a 10-ounce package)

5   cups cooked long-grain rice, chilled, and fluffed with a fork

SAUCE (MIXED TOGETHER)

2   tablespoons rice wine or sake

2   tablespoons chicken broth

1   tablespoon soy sauce

1   teaspoon salt

1   teaspoon toasted sesame oil

¼   teaspoon freshly ground black pepper

¼ cup chopped fresh cilantro or parsley leaves

FIRST Heat a wok or a skillet, add the oil, and heat until hot. Add the eggs and stir-fry over high heat for about 30 seconds to scramble. Add the minced scallions and stir-fry for about 1 minute.

SECOND Add the peas and toss lightly to heat through, then add the rice, breaking it up with the spatula. Cook about 2 to 3 minutes, until heated through. Add the Sauce and toss lightly to coat. Sprinkle in the fresh herbs. Spoon the rice into a serving dish and serve.

Sweet Pepper Rice Pilaf

SIX SERVINGS

I have rediscovered the pleasure of a good rice pilaf. It's an extremely easy, versatile dish (side or entrée), to which all kinds of vegetables—such as onions, different-colored peppers, snap peas, and broccoli—can be added.

INGREDIENTS

1½ tablespoons virgin olive oil

2 tablespoons minced fresh ginger

1½ tablespoons minced garlic

10 scallions, ends trimmed, greens and white part separated and minced

1 medium red bell pepper, cored, seeded, ends trimmed, and cut into ¼-inch dice

1 medium orange bell pepper, cored, seeded, ends trimmed, and cut into ¼-inch dice

¼ cup rice wine or sake

2 cups basmati or regular long-grain rice, rinsed once and drained

3 cups reduced-sodium chicken broth or water

1½ tablespoons soy sauce

1 teaspoon salt

FIRST Heat a heavy saucepan with a lid, add the oil, and heat until hot. Add the ginger, garlic, and white part of the scallions (reserving the greens), and stir-fry over medium heat until fragrant, about 10 seconds.

SECOND Add the diced peppers and the rice wine and toss lightly for about 1 minute. Add the rice and stir about 1½ minutes, until the tips begin to become transparent.

THIRD Add the chicken broth or water, soy sauce, and salt, stir, and bring the mixture to a boil. Reduce the heat to low, cover, and cook for 8 to 10 minutes, or until the rice has absorbed all the liquid. Add the scallion greens, stir with a fork to fluff the rice, and remove from the heat. Cover and let sit another 5 minutes. Serve hot.

Middle Eastern Herbal Rice

SIX SERVINGS

This dish was inspired by a recipe from Claudia Roden's *The New Book of Middle Eastern Food*. The rice is fragrant and delicious. I think it goes especially well with grilled, steamed, or roasted meats and seafood. It's also a terrific base for the Five-Treasure Seafood Rice Salad (page 140). You may vary the herb quantities according to taste.

✳ § *Dill enhances the secretion of digestive juices and eases flatulence and colic. See "Dr. Jim Duke's Herbal Farmacy" on page 158 for other health-giving properties.*

INGREDIENTS

2   cups basmati or jasmine rice

3½ cups water

HERBAL SEASONINGS

1½ cups minced scallion greens

1¼ cups chopped fresh dill

½   cup chopped fresh flat-leaf or curly parsley leaves

2   tablespoons fruity olive oil

2   tablespoons unsalted butter

1½ teaspoons salt, or to taste

FIRST Put the rice in a bowl and, using your fingers as a rake, rinse the rice under cold running water to remove some of the talc. Drain the rice in a strainer.

SECOND Put the rice and water in a heavy 3-quart saucepan or pot with a lid. Heat uncovered until boiling. Reduce the heat to low, cover, and simmer for about 10 minutes, or until the water has evaporated and craters appear on the surface.

THIRD Remove from the heat and add the Herbal Seasonings. Fluff the cooked rice lightly with a fork to separate the grains and mix the seasonings evenly with the rice. Cover and let stand for 10 minutes. Serve warm, at room temperature, or chilled.

Fluffy Lemon Quinoa

Small, pearly quinoa grains have a slightly nutty flavor and are an excellent source of vegetable protein. Quinoa can be purchased at health food stores and some supermarkets. Check the label instructions: In their natural form, quinoa grains have an outer coating and require repeated rinsing in water. With some brands, the outer coating has been removed.

INGREDIENTS

2	cups quinoa
2¾	cups good-quality reduced-sodium chicken broth
½	teaspoon salt
3	tablespoons freshly squeezed lemon juice
½	cup chopped fresh parsley leaves

FIRST Rinse the quinoa in a bowl, using your hand as a rake, with two changes of water. Drain in a colander.

SECOND Put the quinoa with the chicken broth and salt in a medium saucepan with a lid. Bring the chicken broth to a boil, reduce the heat to low, cover, and cook for about 15 minutes. The quinoa should be tender to the bite. Remove from the heat, uncover, and fluff with a fork. Let cool slightly and then stir in the lemon juice and parsley. Taste for seasoning, adjusting if necessary. Serve warm or at room temperature as a staple dish instead of rice or couscous.

Five-Spice Chicken Pilaf

SIX SERVINGS

Five-spice powder, which usually includes star anise, cinnamon, licorice root, fennel, and black or Sichuan pepper, enhances the sweetness of the pumpkin or squash and lends extra flavor to the chicken. This dish is a light meal by itself or could be served with an additional green vegetable.

INGREDIENTS

¾   pound boneless, skinless chicken breasts, cut into ¼-inch dice, or leftover cooked chicken or pork

MARINADE (MIXED TOGETHER)

½   tablespoon soy sauce

½   tablespoon rice wine or sake

3   tablespoons virgin olive oil

1   medium onion, peeled and chopped finely

1½ tablespoons minced fresh ginger

1   tablespoon minced garlic

1½ teaspoons five-spice powder*

2   cups basmati rice or regular long-grain rice (rinsed as directed on page 301)

1½ pounds pumpkin or butternut squash flesh, cut into ½-inch dice

SAUCE (MIXED TOGETHER)

3   cups good-quality reduced-sodium chicken broth, or Easiest Chicken Broth (page 79)

1½ tablespoons soy sauce

1   tablespoon rice wine or sake

1½ teaspoons salt, or to taste

½   teaspoon freshly ground black pepper

1   cup minced scallion greens

*If unavailable, substitute a mixture of ½ to ¾ teaspoon ground allspice and ½ teaspoon ground ginger.

FIRST Place the diced chicken in a bowl. Add the Marinade and toss lightly to coat.

SECOND Heat a heavy saucepan or casserole with a lid, add a tablespoon of the oil, and heat until very hot, about 15 seconds. Add the chicken and toss lightly over high heat for about 2 to 3 minutes, or until the chicken becomes opaque and is cooked. Remove with a slotted spoon and set aside.

THIRD Reheat the pan, pour in the remaining oil, and heat until hot, about 10 seconds. Add the onion and sauté over medium heat for 2 to 2½ minutes, then add the ginger, garlic, and five-spice powder, and continue frying until the onion is soft.

FOURTH Add the rice and stir for about 1½ minutes, until the tips of the grains begin to become transparent. Add the pumpkin or squash, cooked chicken, and Sauce. Bring to a boil, reduce the heat, cover, and let simmer about 15 to 17 minutes, or until the rice is cooked and the pumpkin or squash is tender. Add the scallion greens, carefully fluff the rice with a fork, and remove from the heat. Taste for seasoning, adding salt if necessary, and serve warm.

+ *The spices found in five-spice powder, such as cinnamon, fennel, star anise, and licorice root, all aid digestion.*

Spicy Garlic Soba with Mushrooms and Greens

SIX TO EIGHT SERVINGS

Nutty Japanese soba, or buckwheat, noodles are extremely versatile. They can be served cold or hot in soups and stir-fried dishes. Here, soba noodles are mixed with wild mushrooms, Chinese garlic chives, and bok choy. Serve this as a light lunch or dinner, or as a vegetable or staple side dish.

INGREDIENTS

- ½ pound shiitake mushrooms, rinsed and drained
- ½ pound cremini mushrooms, minced and drained
- 1 pound bok choy or baby Chinese cabbage, stem ends trimmed
- ½ pound soba noodles
- 2½ tablespoons canola or virgin olive oil

- 3½ cups garlic chives cut into 1-inch lengths (if not available, use shredded leeks with 3 tablespoons chopped garlic)
- 1 teaspoon dried chile flakes (optional)
- 5 tablespoons Chinese rice wine or sake
- 5½ tablespoons light soy sauce, or to taste

FIRST Remove and discard the stems from the shiitake mushrooms. Trim the cremini stem ends. Cut the mushroom caps into thin slices.

SECOND Cut the bok choy on the diagonal into ½-inch sections, separating the leafy parts from the stalk sections.

THIRD Bring 3 quarts of water to a boil in a large pot. Add the stalk sections of bok choy and cook for about 2 minutes, then add the leafy parts and cook for 1 minute, until just tender. Remove with a slotted spoon and refresh under cold running water in a strainer. Drain thoroughly. Bring the water to a boil again and add the soba noodles. Once the water returns to a boil, reduce the heat slightly and cook for 3½ minutes, until al dente. Drain in a colander and rinse the noodles under warm running water. Drain again.

FOURTH Heat a large wok or a skillet until very hot. Add the oil and heat until hot, about 10 seconds. Add the garlic chives and dried chile flakes, if using, and stir-fry until fragrant, about 10 seconds. Add the sliced mushrooms and stir-fry over medium-low heat. Add the rice wine or sake, cover, and cook for 3 minutes, or until the mushrooms are tender. Uncover and turn the heat to high. Add the bok choy and soy sauce, and toss lightly over high heat to heat through. If the soba noodles are sticking together in clumps, rinse in a colander under cold running water. Drain thoroughly. Add the noodles and toss lightly to mix and heat through. Scoop out onto a serving platter and serve immediately.

*+ For hundreds of years, the Japanese have credited **soba** noodles, made of buckwheat and wheat flour, with cleansing and energizing the body.*

Stir-Fried Ramen Noodles with Vegetables

SIX SERVINGS

Ramen are thin Japanese noodles made of wheat flour, eggs, and water. Most Westerners know them as instant soup noodles. Since fresh ramen are not widely available, I often substitute dried Chinese egg noodles or angel hair pasta.

INGREDIENTS

- ¾ pound fine dried Japanese ramen, Chinese egg noodles, or angel hair pasta
- ½ small head Chinese (Napa) cabbage (about ¾ pound)
- 2 tablespoons virgin olive oil
- 2 tablespoons minced fresh ginger
- 2 tablespoons minced garlic
- 1 teaspoon dried chile flakes, or to taste
- 2 medium red onions, peeled and cut into thin julienne slices (about 2½ cups)
- 2 carrots, peeled, ends trimmed, and grated
- 2 tablespoons rice wine or sake

NOODLE SAUCE (MIXED TOGETHER)

- 5 tablespoons soy sauce
- 2 tablespoons mirin (or 2 tablespoons rice wine or sake plus 1½ tablespoons sugar)
- 1½ tablespoons Worcestershire sauce
- 3 tablespoons soy sauce

- 2 tablespoons toasted sesame seeds

FIRST Bring 3 quarts of water to a boil in a large pot. Drop the noodles into the water and stir to prevent them from sticking together. Bring the water again to a boil and cook 4½ to 5 minutes, or until the noodles are just cooked. (Since the cooking time varies with the type of noodle, refer to the package for the recommended time.) Drain the noodles in a colander and rinse under warm running water. Drain again and set aside.

SECOND Cut the cabbage leaves from the stem. Trim the leafy tip ends and discard. Rinse the leaves thoroughly and drain. Cut them into julienne strips about ¼ inch wide, separating the stem sections from the leafy sections.

THIRD Heat a wok or a heavy skillet, pour in the oil, and heat over medium-high heat until hot. Add the ginger, garlic, chile flakes, and onions, and stir-fry for about a minute. Cover and cook for several minutes, until the onions are soft. Add the cabbage stem shreds, carrots, and rice wine. Stir-fry lightly, cover, and cook for about 1½ minutes, until almost tender. Add the leafy cabbage shreds, toss, cover, and cook for a minute or two. Pour in the Noodle Sauce, bring to a boil, and add the noodles and the sesame seeds. Toss lightly to coat the noodles and vegetables and spoon onto a serving platter. Serve immediately.

Saucy Chinese Noodles

SIX SERVINGS

This dish is an adapted version of a Northern Chinese classic. I usually substitute fresh or dried pasta from the supermarket for Chinese noodles, since the quality is better and there are no artificial ingredients used. You may vary the vegetables, using bean sprouts, shredded cucumber, or peppers instead of the lettuce.

INGREDIENTS

1   pound boneless, skinless chicken breasts

MARINADE

1   tablespoon soy sauce

1   tablespoon rice wine or sake

1   teaspoon toasted sesame oil

2   teaspoons cornstarch

½   pound round Chinese egg noodles, or spaghettini

1   teaspoon toasted sesame oil

2½ tablespoons olive or canola oil

3   cups grated carrots

3   cups leafy or Boston lettuce, rinsed, drained, and cut into thin julienne shreds

1   cup minced scallion greens

3   tablespoons minced scallions, white part only

1   tablespoon minced fresh ginger

1   tablespoon minced garlic

SAUCE (MIXED TOGETHER)

¾   cup hoisin sauce or sweet bean sauce

3   tablespoons water

3   tablespoons rice wine or sake

2   tablespoons soy sauce

2   tablespoons sugar

FIRST Put the chicken breasts flat on a cutting board. Holding the blade of your knife horizontal to the cutting board, cut the chicken into thin slices about ¼ inch thick, then cut into thin matchstick-size shreds about 1 inch long. Put the shreds in a bowl, add the Marinade ingredients, and toss the chicken lightly to coat.

SECOND Heat 4 quarts water in a large pot until boiling. Add the noodles and swirl in the water. Cook until just tender, about 7 to 8 minutes. Drain in a colander and rinse under cold running water. Drain again. Add the sesame oil and toss lightly to coat. Arrange the noodles in a deep serving platter.

THIRD Heat a wok or a skillet until hot, pour in 1½ tablespoons of the oil, and heat until very hot. Add the chicken and stir-fry over high heat for about 3 to 4 minutes, until the meat changes color and is cooked. Scoop it into a colander and drain. Arrange the carrots, lettuce, and chicken over the noodles in separate concentric circles. Sprinkle the minced scallion greens on top.

FOURTH Reheat the pan until hot, add the remaining oil, and heat until hot. Toss in the minced scallion, ginger, and garlic, and stir-fry until fragrant, about 10 seconds. Add the Sauce and bring to a boil over high heat, stirring. Cook the sauce until thickened, and pour it evenly over the noodles. Toss the noodles lightly to mix the ingredients, and serve at room temperature or chilled.

Toasted Sesame Noodles with Scallions and Ginger

SIX TO EIGHT SERVINGS

This is a wonderful noodle side dish for grilled meats and seafood. Alternatively, you could increase the dressing, add some assorted shredded vegetables, and serve it as a light lunch or dinner. For those who like spicy food, serve with a dollop of chile sauce on the side.

INGREDIENTS

¾ pound thin egg noodles
1½ tablespoons olive oil
3 tablespoons minced fresh ginger
½ cup minced scallions, white part only
3 cups ¼-inch lengths scallion greens
3 tablespoons rice wine or sake
4 cups bean sprouts, rinsed and drained

TOASTED SESAME DRESSING (MIXED TOGETHER UNTIL SUGAR DISSOLVES)

7 tablespoons soy sauce
3½ tablespoons toasted sesame oil
1 to 1½ tablespoons sugar
¼ teaspoon freshly ground black pepper
2 tablespoons Japanese clear rice vinegar

3 tablespoons sesame seeds, toasted until golden in a dry pan

FIRST Heat 4 quarts of water in a large pot until boiling. Add the noodles and swirl in the water. Cook until nearly tender, about 8 to 9 minutes. Drain in a colander and rinse under cold running water to remove the starch. Drain again thoroughly in a colander. (It is considered bad luck, but you may clip the noodles in half to make them easier to stir-fry.)

SECOND Heat a wok or a heavy skillet over high heat. Add the oil and heat until very hot, about 15 seconds. Add the ginger and minced scallion white parts, and stir-fry until fragrant, about 20 seconds. Add the scallion greens, rice wine, and bean sprouts and toss lightly for a minute.

THIRD Add the Toasted Sesame Dressing and the cooked noodles and toss lightly over high heat until the noodles are heated through. Add the toasted sesame seeds, reserving some for the top. Toss lightly to coat and spoon onto a serving platter. Garnish with the reserved sesame seeds. Serve warm or at room temperature.

Barbecued Pork

This simple barbecued pork requires little time or effort. Double the amount so you have plenty to use in the following noodle recipe, or serve it with a vegetable and cooked rice as a satisfying meal.

INGREDIENTS

1½ pounds center-cut pork loin, pork tenderloin, or pork steak

BARBECUE SAUCE

½	cup hoisin sauce
2	tablespoons soy sauce
1½	tablespoons ketchup
1	tablespoon minced garlic
3	tablespoons water

Preheat the oven to 350 degrees. Trim any fat or gristle from the pork with a sharp knife or a cleaver. Mix the Barbecue Sauce ingredients in a bowl. Add the pork and toss to coat. Place the pork on a baking sheet lined with aluminum foil, and bake for 35 to 45 minutes, until cooked through. Let cool. Cut the pork into slices about ¼ inch thick and 1½ inches long.

Crisp-Fried Noodles with Barbecued Pork and Broccoli Rabe

SIX TO EIGHT SERVINGS

Golden-fried noodles are very popular in my family. You can vary the topping by using different cooked meats and vegetables. If I'm making barbecued pork, I double the recipe and make this dish later in the week. Traditionally the noodles are pan-fried, but this broiling method is much easier.

INGREDIENTS

1   recipe Barbecued Pork (page 317)*

1   pound broccoli rabe, or Chinese, purple, or Western broccoli

¾   pound thin Chinese egg noodles, or angel hair or vermicelli

1   teaspoon toasted sesame oil mixed with 1 teaspoon virgin olive oil

2   tablespoons virgin olive oil

2   tablespoons minced garlic

1½ tablespoons minced fresh ginger

1½ cups ½-inch lengths scallion greens

SAUCE (MIXED TOGETHER)

1½ cups good-quality reduced-sodium chicken broth

6   tablespoons oyster sauce

1½ tablespoons rice wine or sake

1   teaspoon soy sauce

1   teaspoon toasted sesame oil

1½ tablespoons cornstarch

*You may also purchase barbecued pork loin at an Asian deli or use leftover roasted pork loin.

FIRST Prepare the Barbecued Pork as directed in the recipe.

SECOND Trim the stem ends and wilted leafy ends of the broccoli rabe and discard. If using Western broccoli, with a sharp paring knife cut away the stem ends and peel away the tough outer skin and separate the florets. Cut the broccoli stems on the diagonal into 1½-inch sections.

THIRD Bring 3 quarts of water to a boil, drop in the broccoli, partially cook for 2 minutes, or until just tender, remove with a slotted strainer, and refresh in cold water. Drain and set aside. Bring the water back to a boil, add the noodles, stir, and cook 5 to 6 minutes, until nearly tender. Drain in a colander, rinse lightly to remove the starch, and drain again thoroughly in a colander. Put in a bowl and toss lightly with the mixed toasted sesame and olive oils. Spread the noodles out on a large baking sheet.

FOURTH Heat the broiler until red-hot. Place the noodles 3 inches under the broiler and cook about 10 minutes on each side, until golden brown, flipping them over once. Turn off the broiler and keep the noodles warm in the oven.

FIFTH Heat a wok or large skillet, add the 2 tablespoons oil, and heat until very hot, about 15 seconds. Add the garlic, ginger, and scallion greens and stir-fry about 30 seconds, until very fragrant. Add the Sauce and cook over medium heat until it thickens. Add the barbecued pork and cooked broccoli and toss gently in the sauce. Place the browned noodles on a deep platter or in a large pasta bowl and spoon the pork, broccoli, and sauce on top. Serve immediately.

+ *As a result of recent research, **broccoli** is regarded as a superfood. The National Cancer Institute has named it one of the key vegetables that may prevent numerous cancers, including those of the lung, stomach, breast, prostate, and colon. For further information, see the "Seven Colors of Health" chart on page 199.*

Vietnamese Rainbow Salad

Rice stick or cellophane noodles make a wonderful textural foil for this entrée salad or cold starter course. They absorb the flavors of the fresh and pungent Vietnamese dressing. You may, of course, substitute other vegetables and use cooked scallops, chicken, pork, or beef instead of shrimp.

✣ *Fresh cilantro (coriander) adds flavor and is believed to benefit the lungs and spleen. For further information, see "Key to Primary Indian Spices" on page 288.*

INGREDIENTS

2 ounces rice stick or cellophane noodles, softened in hot water for 20 minutes and drained

1 teaspoon virgin olive oil

2 large eggs, lightly beaten with ½ teaspoon salt and 2 tablespoons water

2½ cups grated carrots

2½ cups English seedless or Kirby cucumbers grated or cut into thin julienne shreds

2½ cups bean sprouts, rinsed and drained

FRESH VIETNAMESE HERBAL DRESSING

1¼ teaspoons dried chile flakes

Juice of 4 to 5 limes or 2½ lemons (about ⅔ cup)

⅓ cup fish sauce, or more to taste

⅓ cup sugar

1½ tablespoons minced garlic

⅓ cup coarsely chopped fresh cilantro leaves

⅓ cup coarsely chopped fresh basil leaves

3 tablespoons chopped dry-roasted peanuts (optional)

FIRST Bring 2 quarts of water to the boil in a large pot. Add the softened noodles and swirl in the boiling water. Cook for 10 seconds, or until just tender. Drain thoroughly in a colander and rinse under cold running water. Clip the noodles, if desired, into 3-inch lengths and arrange on a deep serving platter with a slight depression in the center.

SECOND Dip a paper towel in the oil and wipe the inside of a 9- or 10-inch nonstick or well-seasoned frying pan. Heat over medium-high heat until hot (a little water sprinkled on it should evaporate immediately). Pour half the egg mixture into the pan and tilt to form a thin circular pancake. Cook briefly until set, about 10 seconds. Flip over, using a spatula, and cook briefly on the other side, about 10 seconds. Remove from the pan and let cool. Repeat the process for the remaining egg mixture. Let cool, cut the pancakes in half, then cut into julienne shreds.

THIRD Arrange the carrots, cucumbers, bean sprouts, and egg shreds in separate concentric circles over the noodles.

FOURTH Soak the chile flakes in the lime juice for 2 to 3 minutes in a medium bowl. Add the remaining Dressing ingredients, and stir to dissolve the sugar. Pour into a serving bowl.

FIFTH Sprinkle the chopped cilantro, basil, and peanuts, if using on top of the vegetables. Spoon the dressing over the salad, or serve on the side at room temperature or chilled.

Kung Pao Scallops with Snap Peas over Lo Mein Noodles

I like to use flat egg noodles such as fettuccine or linguine for Chinese "lo mein" noodle dishes, since they absorb the sauce well and can be purchased easily at supermarkets. You can substitute shrimp or shredded chicken meat for the scallops for a delicious variation.

INGREDIENTS

1 pound sea scallops, rinsed lightly and drained

GINGER MARINADE (MIXED TOGETHER)

3 tablespoons rice wine or sake

1 tablespoon minced fresh ginger

½ teaspoon toasted sesame oil

½ pound flat egg noodles, such as fettuccine or linguine

3 tablespoons virgin olive oil

1 medium red onion, peeled and cut into thin julienne slices

2½ tablespoons minced garlic

1½ teaspoons hot chile paste

1½ cups thinly sliced water chestnuts, blanched briefly in boiling water, refreshed in cold water, drained, and patted dry

2 tablespoons rice wine or sake

KUNG PAO SAUCE (MIXED TOGETHER)

1½ cups good-quality reduced-sodium chicken broth or Easiest Chicken Broth (page 79)

5 tablespoons soy sauce

2 tablespoons sugar

3 tablespoons Chinese black vinegar or Worcestershire sauce

1 teaspoon toasted sesame oil

1 teaspoon salt

1 tablespoon cornstarch

½ pound snow peas or snap peas, ends snapped and veiny strings removed, blanched briefly in boiling water, refreshed in cold water, and drained

FIRST Holding the knife horizontal with the cutting board, cut the scallops in half through the thickness. Place in a bowl, add the Ginger Marinade, toss lightly to coat, and let marinate for 15 minutes.

SECOND Bring 3 quarts of water to a boil, drop in the noodles, and cook about 2 to 3 minutes for fresh noodles or 9 to 11 minutes for dried, until nearly tender. (Since the cooking time varies with the type of noodle, refer to the package for the recommended time.) Drain in a colander, rinse lightly to remove the starch, and drain again thoroughly. Drain the scallops.

THIRD Heat a wok or a large skillet, add 1½ tablespoons of the oil, and heat until very hot but not smoking. Add the scallops and toss lightly for 3 to 5 minutes, until they change color and are cooked. Remove with a slotted spoon or a strainer and drain. Wipe out the pan.

FOURTH Reheat the pan, add the remaining 1½ tablespoons oil, and heat until hot, about 15 seconds. Add the onion, garlic, and chile paste and stir-fry over medium heat for about 3 minutes, until the onion is soft. Add the water chestnuts and the 2 tablespoons of rice wine. Turn up the heat to high and stir-fry until heated through. Add the Kung Pao Sauce and cook until thickened, stirring constantly to prevent lumps, about 2 to 3 minutes. Add the snow or snap peas, cooked scallops, and noodles and toss lightly to coat with the sauce. Scoop onto a serving platter and serve immediately.

Garlic Chicken with Fennel over Couscous

SIX TO EIGHT SERVINGS

This dish is equally good for a family dinner or for entertaining guests. The couscous cooks in minutes, and the chicken and fennel bake in the oven. Throw it all together at the last minute, or make it in advance and serve it at room temperature or reheated.

INGREDIENTS

1½ pounds free-range or organic boneless chicken leg and/or thigh meat, trimmed of fat*

CHICKEN MARINADE

1½ tablespoons minced garlic

3 tablespoons soy sauce

2 tablespoons rice wine or sake

3 large fennel bulbs (about 1½ pounds with stalks), rinsed

2 tablespoons virgin olive oil

2½ tablespoons minced fresh ginger

1½ tablespoons balsamic vinegar

2½ teaspoons salt

¼ teaspoon freshly ground black pepper

2 cups quick-cooking couscous

4 cups boiling water, or amount indicated on the couscous package

1 tablespoon fruity virgin olive oil

1 cup toasted sliced almonds

3 tablespoons chopped flat-leaf parsley

*Free-range and organic chickens usually have more flavor and less fat.

FIRST Preheat the oven to 375 degrees. Place the chicken in a bowl, add the Chicken Marinade, toss lightly to coat, cover with plastic wrap, and set aside for 30 minutes or refrigerate overnight. Arrange the chicken pieces in one layer, skin side up, on a baking sheet that has been lined with aluminum foil. Bake the chicken, turning once, for about 30 minutes, until the meat is tender and the skin is crisp. Set aside to cool slightly.

SECOND While the chicken is marinating, trim the fennel, leaving ⅛ inch of the root base to hold it together. Cut each fennel bulb lengthwise in half, then cut into slices about ¼ inch thick and 2 inches long. Put the fennel slices in a bowl, add the olive oil, minced ginger, balsamic vinegar, 1 teaspoon of the salt, and pepper and toss lightly to coat. Arrange the fennel slices in one layer on a baking sheet that has been lined with aluminum foil. Bake 30 to 40 minutes, turning fennel once or twice to make sure it is evenly cooked. The edges should be brown and the inside should be tender. Remove from the oven. Preheat the broiler and broil the fennel slices for about 2 minutes, until golden brown.

THIRD Pour the couscous into a large round serving bowl or spread out in a gratin pan. Pour the boiling water on top and let sit for 5 minutes (or cook according to the package instructions). Fluff lightly with a fork, while adding the olive oil, the remaining 1½ teaspoons salt, and the toasted almonds.

FOURTH Arrange the fennel slices on top of the flavored couscous and pour any juice on top. Cut the chicken through the skin into thin matchstick-size shreds and sprinkle on top of the fennel. Skim away any fat from the cooked chicken juice and pour over the chicken. Before serving, sprinkle the chopped parsley on top. Serve warm or at room temperature. You may also reheat in a 350-degree oven for 10 minutes, or in a microwave oven.

Lemon Couscous with Fresh Parsley

SIX SERVINGS

I often serve couscous as a side staple with grilled meat, seafood, or chicken and a green vegetable or even a stir-fry. It's also a terrific base for a main-dish salad. Directions and water amounts vary for quick-cooking couscous, so check the package and revise accordingly.

INGREDIENTS

1½ medium lemons

6 cups water, or amount indicated on the couscous package

3 cups quick-cooking couscous

1 tablespoon fruity virgin olive oil

1½ teaspoons salt, or to taste

¼ teaspoon freshly ground pepper, or to taste

1 cup minced fresh parsley leaves

FIRST Using a vegetable peeler, remove the lemon peel in strips. Bring 2 cups of water to a boil. Add the lemon peel and cook for a minute to remove the bitterness. Drain, and blot dry. Mince finely. Squeeze the juice from the 1½ lemons and set aside.

SECOND Bring the 6 cups of water to a boil in a large pot or casserole with a lid. Add the couscous and cook for a minute, stirring with a spoon or a fork. (Or follow the cooking instructions on the package.) Cover and remove from the heat. Let sit for 10 minutes. Fluff the couscous lightly with a fork to separate the grains.

THIRD Add the olive oil, lemon peel and juice, salt, and pepper, and stir with a fork to mix. Let the couscous sit for 5 to 10 minutes, then add the parsley and fluff with a fork. Taste for seasoning, adding more salt if necessary, and serve warm or at room temperature.

Opposite: Italian parsley leaves

✛ *Recent studies have shown that people who regularly eat citrus fruits have a reduced risk of developing cancer and cataracts. For further information on the health-giving properties of lemons, see the "orange/yellow" section of the "Seven Colors of Health" chart on page 199.*

✳ *Lemon juice destroys bad bacteria in the intestines and mouth. It sweetens the breath and alleviates flatulence and indigestion.*

T. Colin Campbell and Lessons from China

T. Colin Campbell, Professor Emeritus of Nutritional Biochemistry at Cornell University, is a pioneer in the field of diet and lifestyle research. In the 1950s Campbell began to study the effects that nutrition has on long-term health, long before anyone was drawing a serious link between diet and disease. His new book, *The China Study: Startling Implications for Diet, Weight Loss and Long-Term Health,* documents this project.

In 1983 Campbell, along with three other researchers from Oxford University, the Chinese Academy of Preventive Medicine, and the Chinese Cancer Institute in Beijing, began one of the largest and most comprehensive epidemiological studies ever undertaken. They gathered data on 6,500 Chinese individuals in sixty-five counties across rural China to assess lifestyle practices and their effect on disease.

Even then, Campbell suspected that the Asian *fan-cai* method of eating, with its emphasis on vegetables, fruits, and grains, was the reason for China's low rates of certain types of cancer and chronic disease. For years researchers had noted that heart disease, diabetes, and cancers of the breast, colon, and prostate are less prevalent in China and Japan.

The initial findings, which were released in 1990, were noteworthy at the time and are still relevant. They showed:

■ While the rural Chinese consume 20 percent more calories than Americans, they are 25 percent thinner (their rigorous lifestyle helps). Seventy percent of calories in the Chinese diet come from complex carbohydrates and only 15 percent come from fat.

■ In the rural Chinese diet, 89 percent of protein comes from plant sources, whereas in the West, it is only 30 percent—at best. Seventy percent or more of protein in the Western diet comes from animal foods such as meat and dairy.

■ Although Chinese women get half as much calcium in their diets as Americans, osteoporosis is fairly uncommon.

Furthermore, comparisons between regional diets in China showed that higher consumption of fruits, vegetables, and grains, and less animal protein, resulted in a lower incidence of breast cancer and heart disease. Perhaps most importantly, the study showed that as China has been changing from a rural, agrarian society and adopting Western lifestyle practices (less exercise, adding more meat to the diet, and eating fast food), cancer, diabetes, and heart disease have all shown a marked increase. "The China study has shown that consumption of even small amounts of animal foods can be problematic," says Campbell, "and consuming a lot of protein, especially animal protein, is definitely linked to chronic disease."

Campbell has always been outspoken, particularly regarding his differences with the USDA and its dietary guidelines. In 1982 he was a member of the National Academy of Sciences panel on diet, nutrition, and cancer. "As far as my input was concerned, I always promoted complex carbohydrates. The problem is that commercial entities and media distorted the earlier recommendations, so that there was no distinction between refined and complex carbohydrates, which makes a big difference."

Campbell, in his seventies, is tangible proof of his beliefs: He begins each day by running four to six miles. He and his wife have been practicing vegans (except for a little salmon) since 1991. Officially he has retired, but he has an active life: He still teaches, continues to work on the China study, and is writing a book on his life experiences in the world of diet and disease, as well as working with colleagues to develop a think-tank program where experts and the public can explore some of the more contentious issues in nutrition and health.

"The China study's lessons are far-reaching," says Campbell. "The study not only emphasizes that nutrition should be considered the most important medical science, when it is often relegated to last place. It also shows that nutrition, when properly understood and practiced, has an overwhelming ability to control otherwise difficult circumstances such as bad genes, exposure to environmental chemicals, and chronic infection with microorganisms."

light and sumptuous sweets

I have always had a weakness for sweets, especially when I was younger. My first culinary venture, in the sixth grade, was to make chocolate chip cookies, and I earned the money for my first ticket to Asia by baking desserts and pastries in a bakery and then in restaurants. Back then I couldn't get enough. Like many Americans, I was addicted.

Once I moved to Asia and ate less sugar, my cravings disappeared. My diet became more balanced, and I was introduced to the custom of eating fruit at the end of meals. It's light, refreshing, and an ideal palate cleanser. In addition to their nutritional benefits, fruits help to cleanse the body and counterbalance the effect of rich or heavy foods. Spices also aid digestion, and counterbalance the cooling effects of the fruit. Indian doctors believe that fruits balance the constitution, or dosha. They suggest that fruit should be eaten alone or at the beginning of a meal, rather than at the end.

But there are times when one craves a little more than fresh fruit. In this chapter I offer recipes for some of my favorite sweets. Many I cherish because my mother baked them for me when I was a child. I particularly appreciate old-fashioned, seasonal favorites like Mom's Apple Crisp and Gingery Peach-a-Berry Cobbler. They are simple recipes and can be varied with all different types of fruits. (When selecting them, ideally organic varieties are preferable.) There's coffee cake, cookies, and muffins, all of which I like to bake when I have time and then freeze so that I have them on hand for special occasions, or as a treat on an otherwise ordinary day.

I still appreciate a great sweet dish, but I'm more apt to enjoy it with tea in the mid or late afternoon, when the ritual can be relaxed, yet energizing.

I've also cut back on my intake. As I've grown older, I've realized the importance of moderation and balance in my regimen.

Many of these sweet dishes are timeless. They have been handed down from generation to generation, from one friend to another. I hope that they give you as much pleasure as they have given my family and me.

Mango Lassi

Lassis are a popular yogurt drink in India. The sweet variety is made with different fresh fruit purees, and the savory drinks may be flavored with different spices. Lassis provide a refreshing complement to spicy Indian dishes, as they cool the body.

INGREDIENTS

- 1 pound ripe mango flesh (about 2 mangoes), skin and pit removed
- 9 ounces whole-milk plain yogurt
- ¾ cup milk
- 3 tablespoons sugar
- 1 tablespoon freshly squeezed lemon juice

FIRST Cut the mango into ½-inch pieces and chop or blend until smooth in a food processor fitted with a steel blade or a blender. If there are any large fibrous pieces, remove them.

SECOND Pour the yogurt into the processor work bowl or into the blender with the mango and blend until smooth, about 1½ minutes. Pour in the milk, sugar, and lemon juice and blend for another minute. Taste for seasoning, adjusting if necessary. Pour into glasses and serve. You can also add crushed ice to make a cold drink.

Spiced Pears in Red Wine

SIX SERVINGS

Many Asian meals end with the serving of fruit. This dish is particularly good after a meal, since it is satisfying and therapeutic: The cinnamon, star anise, and ginger all aid the digestive process.

INGREDIENTS

POACHING MIXTURE

- 1 bottle red wine (such as French or American merlot)
- 6 cups water
- 1½ cups sugar
- Peel of 1 orange
- 2 sticks cinnamon
- 2 whole star anise

- 6 slightly underripe Bosc pears
- 2 lemons, cut in half
- 2 tablespoons chopped candied ginger for garnish (optional)

FIRST Mix the ingredients of the Poaching Mixture in a large nonreactive pot. Bring to a boil, stirring until the sugar dissolves. Reduce the heat and simmer uncovered for 10 minutes.

SECOND Peel the pears, leaving the stems on. Rub the surface of the pears with the cut lemons to prevent them from turning brown. Lower the pears into the poaching liquid and squeeze the juice from the lemons into the pot. Bring the liquid to a boil again, then reduce the heat to low, and simmer uncovered until the pears are tender, about 40 minutes. Test by piercing the pears with a knife. Using a slotted spoon, transfer the pears to a bowl, reserving the poaching liquid.

THIRD Strain out the orange peel, cinnamon sticks, and star anise and discard. Pour 3 cups of the poaching liquid into a heavy saucepan and bring to a boil. Reduce the heat to medium and cook for about 30 minutes, until the liquid is reduced to a syrup. Pour over the pears. Serve warm, or chilled, for at least 3 hours, with a little of the syrup. Sprinkle with the candied ginger, if desired. The pears can be poached 1 day ahead and refrigerated.

❊ The Chinese believe that pears eliminate heat from the lungs and relieve dryness.

❊ Cinnamon, along with cardamom and bay leaf, is part of the Ayurvedic trio of aromatics used to heal the body and disguise the taste of medicines. For more information on the therapeutic properties of cinnamon, refer to "Key to Primary Indian Spices" on page 288.

Roasted Winter Fruit with Ginger and Port Wine

SIX SERVINGS

This dish is so simple, but the combined flavors of apricot, ginger, and port are a wonderful topping for the slow-roasted pears. Serve them warm or cold. They are also lovely paired with Mrs. Shaw's Molasses Spice Cookies (page 349).

§ *Refer to "Key to Primary Indian Spices" on page 288 for the therapeutic properties of ginger.*

INGREDIENTS

- 1 **cup dried apricots**
- 1 **cup boiling water**
- 6 **slightly underripe Bosc pears, peeled and cut in half lengthwise**
- 1 **lemon, cut in half**
- 1 **tablespoon unsalted butter**
- 3 **tablespoons candied ginger**
- 1 **cup good-quality port wine**
- 2½ **tablespoons sugar**

FIRST Preheat the oven to 375 degrees. Put the apricots in a small bowl, pour the boiling water on top, and soak for 10 minutes. Rub the surface of the pears with the cut lemon to prevent them from turning brown.

SECOND Spread the butter on the bottom of a 14-x-10-inch gratin pan or other baking dish and arrange the pears, cut side up, in the pan. Drain the apricots, saving the juice, and chop them, along with the candied ginger, coarsely. Mix with the port wine, reserved juice from the apricots, and sugar, and fill the cavity of each pear half with some of the mixture. Pour the remaining mixture all over the pears.

THIRD Roast the pears, uncovered, on the middle shelf of the oven until tender, about 40 to 45 minutes, basting occasionally. Arrange the pears in a shallow bowl and serve warm or at room temperature, drizzled with the pan juices.

Mom's Apple Crisp

SIX SERVINGS

This remains one of my favorite desserts. You can substitute most seasonal fruits, including pears, peaches, and rhubarb. I often mix blueberries with peaches, cranberries with apples, and rhubarb with strawberries. My son adores it warm with vanilla ice cream.

INGREDIENTS

TOPPING

- **1 cup unbleached all-purpose flour**
- **½ cup sugar**
- **½ cup lightly packed light brown sugar**
- **1 teaspoon cinnamon**
- **½ teaspoon salt**
- **½ cup (1 stick) cold unsalted butter, cut into tablespoon-size or ½-inch pieces**

1½ tablespoons unsalted butter for the pan

FRUIT FILLING

- **10 large Cortland or McIntosh apples (about 3 pounds)**
- **1 lemon, cut in half**
- **1 teaspoon ground cinnamon**
- **2 tablespoons sugar (if the apples are very tart)**

FIRST Preheat the oven to 375 degrees. Put the flour, white and brown sugars, cinnamon, and salt in a food processor fitted with a steel blade. Add the butter pieces and pulse until the mixture resembles cornmeal. Set aside. Alternatively, you may make the topping in a bowl, using a pastry blender or a knife, cutting the cold butter into the dry ingredients.

SECOND Generously butter an 8- or 9-inch-square baking dish (preferably ceramic or glass) or a 10-inch pie dish with high sides. Peel and core the apples and rub with the cut lemon. Cut the apples into ½- to ¾-inch pieces and toss lightly with the cinnamon and sugar in a bowl. Pour the apples into the prepared pan. Spoon the topping over the apples, sprinkling it evenly.

THIRD Bake about 40 to 45 minutes, until the crumb topping is golden but with a few spots of light brown, and the apples are tender when tested with a knife. Let cool slightly before serving warm, or serve at room temperature. To reheat, bake uncovered in a preheated 300-degree oven for 10 to 15 minutes, until hot.

+ **Apples** *contain a form of soluble fiber called pectin, which helps to lower cholesterol. Apples also strengthen the immune system and may prevent heart disease and cancer.*

Gingery Peach-a-Berry Cobbler

SIX SERVINGS

Essentially a cobbler is a fruit dessert baked with a crust, which may be made from a biscuit dough or a bread dough. In this recipe, you drop spoonfuls of dough over the fruit and it all blends together in the oven, creating a lovely cobbler topping. You can use different fruits or pair two together, as in this recipe.

INGREDIENTS

- 1 pint or 2 cups fresh blueberries, rinsed and drained
- 6 peaches, peeled, pitted, and cut into ½-inch slices (about 5 to 6 cups)
- ⅓ cup light brown sugar
- 1½ tablespoons cornstarch
- 1½ tablespoons freshly squeezed lemon juice
- ½ teaspoon ground cinnamon
- 3 tablespoons chopped candied ginger

TOPPING

- 1¾ cups unbleached all-purpose flour
- ½ cup sugar
- 2 teaspoons baking powder
- ½ teaspoon salt
- 8 tablespoons cold unsalted butter, cut into tablespoon-size pieces
- ¾ cup whole milk
- 1½ teaspoons vanilla extract
- 2 tablespoons sugar mixed with ¼ teaspoon ground cinnamon

FIRST Preheat the oven to 375 degrees. Put the blueberries and peaches in a heavy medium saucepan. Add the brown sugar, cornstarch, lemon juice, cinnamon, and candied ginger and mix together. Heat and stir until the mixture thickens, about 5 minutes. Pour into a 12 × 10 × 2-inch baking dish or other shallow 2½-quart baking dish (no deeper than 2 inches).

SECOND While the fruit cooks, mix together the flour, sugar, baking powder, and salt in a large bowl. Pinch or cut in the butter with your fingertips, a pastry blender, or a knife until the mixture resembles cornmeal. Pour in the milk and vanilla, and stir until a dough forms. Put the dough onto the hot fruit mixture in small separate mounds and sprinkle the top with the cinnamon sugar. Place the baking dish on a cookie sheet to catch drips. Bake the cobbler in the middle of the oven about 30 minutes, until the top is golden. Remove from the oven, cool slightly, and serve warm.

+ *Peaches* are an excellent source of vitamin C and provide the body with ample amounts of beta-carotene and fiber.

+ *Blueberries* have been shown to contain more antioxidants than any other fruit or vegetable. They also appear to contain potent anti-inflammatory agents. Both properties protect and nurture the brain as it ages.

Lemon Sponge Roll with Lemon Filling

TEN TO TWELVE SERVINGS

Some people crave chocolate after a meal. Personally, I love the flavor of lemon. This ethereal rolled sponge cake, with its tart lemon filling, is so refreshing and satisfying. You can buy a good-quality lemon curd or make it yourself using the recipe on page 342.

INGREDIENTS

1   recipe Lemon Curd (page 342), or 2 cups good-quality store-bought

1   cup all-purpose flour

¾   teaspoon salt

2   tablespoons unsalted butter for the pan

1   tablespoon flour for dusting the pan

6   large eggs, separated, at room temperature

1   cup sugar

2   tablespoons freshly grated lemon zest

1   teaspoon vanilla extract

¼   teaspoon cream of tartar

¼   cup confectioners' sugar

FIRST Preheat the oven to 375 degrees. If making Lemon Curd, prepare as directed and let cool. Sift together the flour and ½ teaspoon salt.

SECOND Line a 15 × 10-inch jelly-roll pan with parchment or wax paper, leaving a 2-inch overhang on each of the short sides. Butter the parchment or wax paper and dust with a little flour. Shake out the excess.

THIRD Beat the egg yolks, sugar, lemon zest, and vanilla extract for 3 to 4 minutes in a mixing bowl with an electric mixer until thick, foamy, and lemon-colored.

FOURTH In another bowl, beat the egg whites with ¼ teaspoon salt briefly, then add the cream of tartar and continue beating until the egg whites are stiff. Sift the flour and the salt again, into the beaten egg yolks, and fold them in gently but thoroughly. Add the stiff egg whites and fold into the batter gently but thoroughly. Spread the batter evenly in the pan with a spatula and bake the cake for 15 minutes, until it is puffed and golden.

FIFTH While the cake is baking, dust the surface of a tea towel lightly with some of the confectioners' sugar. Remove the cake from the oven and let it sit for a few minutes. Invert it onto the lightly sugared kitchen towel. Carefully peel away the parchment or wax paper and, starting with a long side, roll the cake up jelly-roll fashion in the towel. Let cool completely, then unroll it, removing the towel, and spread the lemon curd evenly over the inside of the cake (unsugared side). Reroll the cake and slide it onto a serving platter. Sprinkle the top with a little confectioners' sugar. Cut into slices and serve.

+ ***Lemons** are an excellent source of vitamin C. They are also a great source of bioflavonoids, which act as antioxidants and help fight disease. For other health-giving benefits, refer to the "Seven Colors of Health" chart on page 199.*

Asian doctors believe that lemons are antiseptic and increase the production of fluids in the body.

Lemon Curd

This lemony curd can be used as a filling for cakes or spread on cookies, biscuits, or toast. It will keep, tightly covered, in a jar for months in the refrigerator.

INGREDIENTS

- **3 large eggs**
- **9 tablespoons sugar**
- **10 tablespoons freshly squeezed lemon juice (about 3 lemons)**
- **8 tablespoons unsalted butter, cut into tablespoon-size pieces**
- **1 heaping tablespoon grated lemon peel**

FIRST Whisk the eggs and sugar lightly in the top of a double boiler or in a heavy saucepan. Add the lemon juice, butter, and lemon peel. Set the pan over simmering water. (Do not allow the bottom of the pan to touch the water.) Whisk the mixture until it thickens to a pudding consistency, about 4 to 6 minutes. Let cool slightly, then pour into a bowl and let cool completely.

SECOND Press a buttered square of plastic wrap or parchment paper directly onto the surface of the curd and chill until cold. Serve on scones, biscuits, or use as directed in the Lemon Sponge Roll on page 340.

Chocolate Brownie Pudding

EIGHT TO TEN SERVINGS

This dish was my sister Susan's favorite dessert as a child, but our whole family loved it as well. My sister and I used to peer through the oven window and watch the batter as it baked, magically separating into a layer of cake with a rich chocolate sauce underneath.

INGREDIENTS

1   cup all-purpose flour

⅔   cup unsweetened cocoa powder

¾   teaspoon baking powder

¾   teaspoon salt

2   large eggs

1   cup sugar

6   tablespoons (¾ stick) unsalted butter, melted

½   cup milk

1½   teaspoons vanilla extract

¾   cup firmly packed light brown sugar

1⅓   cups boiling water

FIRST Preheat the oven to 350 degrees. Sift together the flour, ⅓ cup of the cocoa powder, the baking powder, and the salt. With a hand-held electric mixer or by machine, whisk together the eggs, sugar, butter, milk, and vanilla in another bowl and beat until smooth. Add the flour mixture and stir until the batter is just mixed together.

SECOND Spread the batter evenly in an ungreased 8-inch-square baking pan. Mix together the remaining ⅓ cup cocoa powder, the brown sugar, and the boiling water and pour over the batter. Bake in the middle of the preheated oven for 35 to 40 minutes, or until a cake tester or a toothpick inserted in the center comes out clean. Serve warm with vanilla ice cream or slightly sweetened whipped cream.

+ *Much has been written lately about the therapeutic effects of* **chocolate.** *A major ingredient of the cocoa bean is theobromine, which appears to release "feel good" endorphins in the brain. For some, it acts as a natural antidepressant. Chocolate and cocoa also contain flavonoids, which promote a healthy heart, and antioxidants, which strengthen the immune system.*

Pumpkin-Applesauce Muffins

MAKES 21 MUFFINS

Although these muffins are delicious year-round, to me they are synonymous with fall, when apples and pumpkins are in season. To save time, I usually use a good store-bought applesauce and canned pumpkin puree. This recipe makes quite a few muffins, so I freeze them or make two loaves of tea bread instead.

INGREDIENTS

1½ tablespoons melted butter or cooking spray

DRY INGREDIENTS

3⅓ cups all-purpose flour

2   teaspoons baking soda

½   teaspoon baking powder

2   teaspoons ground cinnamon

½   teaspoon ground cloves

½   teaspoon freshly grated nutmeg

1   teaspoon salt

½   cup unsalted butter, softened

2   cups sugar

4   large eggs

1   cup applesauce

1   cup canned pumpkin puree

1   teaspoon vanilla extract

⅔   cup apple juice, cider, or orange juice

1½ cups raisins

FIRST Preheat the oven to 375 degrees and grease 12 (or however many you happen to have) ½-cup muffin cups. Sift together the Dry Ingredients.

SECOND With an electric mixer beat the butter and sugar for about 2 to 3 minutes. Add the eggs, applesauce, pumpkin, and vanilla and beat lightly. Alternately add some of the dry ingredients and pour in some of the apple juice or cider, beating until smooth. Fold in the raisins.

THIRD Spoon the batter into the greased muffin tins, filling each cup two-thirds full. Bake in the middle of the oven for 20 to 25 minutes, or until puffed and a cake tester or a toothpick comes out clean. Cool for several minutes in the pan, then turn out onto a rack. Serve the muffins warm or at room temperature.

You can also use this batter to make tea bread by baking in two 9 × 5 × 3-inch loaf pans for about 55 to 60 minutes. Cool, remove from the pans, cut into slices, and serve. The muffins and bread freeze beautifully.

Cinnamon Streusel Sour Cream Coffee Cake

TEN TO TWELVE SERVINGS

My Aunt Pauline used to bake this traditional Jewish cake for special occasions. It is commonly served at the meal following Yom Kippur and on Shavuot and the Sabbath. My son adores it, so I bake it for special breakfasts and tea. You can add 1¼ cups of apple or pear slices or blueberries to the middle with the streusel for extra flavor.

INGREDIENTS

2 tablespoons butter for greasing the cake pan

STREUSEL TOPPING

¼ cup light brown sugar

¼ cup sugar

½ cup all-purpose flour

1 teaspoon ground cinnamon

¼ cup cold unsalted butter, cut into tablespoon-size pieces

2 cups all-purpose flour

1 teaspoon baking powder

½ teaspoon baking soda

1 teaspoon salt

½ cup unsalted butter, at room temperature

1 cup sugar

2 large eggs

1 cup sour cream or whole-milk plain yogurt

1½ teaspoons vanilla extract

½ cup milk

FIRST Preheat the oven to 350 degrees. Butter a 9-inch Bundt or tube pan or a 9-inch spring-form pan.

SECOND To make the Streusel Topping, mix together the brown and white sugars, flour, and cinnamon. Cut in the butter with a knife or a pastry blender until the mixture resembles coarse crumbs. Set aside.

THIRD Sift or mix together the flour, baking powder, baking soda, and salt. Using a hand-held electric mixer or by machine, beat the ½ cup butter and the sugar in another bowl until light and fluffy, about 3 minutes. Break in the eggs and beat lightly for another minute. Add the sour cream, vanilla extract, and milk and beat until smooth. Stir in the flour mixture and beat evenly.

FOURTH Pour a little less than half of the batter into the Bundt pan and smooth the top. Sprinkle in half of the streusel. Add the remaining batter, covering the streusel, and sprinkle the top with the remaining streusel.

FIFTH Bake the cake on the middle shelf of the oven for about 45 to 50 minutes, until a cake tester or a knife comes out clean. Set on a rack and let cool in the pan for about 10 minutes. Invert onto a dinner plate and serve warm or at room temperature.

Mrs. Shaw's Molasses Spice Cookies

Ann Shaw, my friend Julie's mom, is a talented home baker. Sometimes I dream of her layer cakes, cookies, and pies. Her spice cookies are excellent by themselves, or you can serve them with poached or roasted pears (pages 335 and 336). They freeze beautifully, so you can make a batch and keep them on hand for tea or special occasions.

INGREDIENTS

DRY INGREDIENTS

- 2 cups all-purpose flour
- 2 teaspoons baking soda
- Heaping 1 teaspoon cinnamon
- Heaping ½ teaspoon ground ginger
- ½ teaspoon ground cloves
- ¼ teaspoon salt

- ½ cup corn oil
- 1 cup sugar
- ¼ cup molasses
- 1 large egg, lightly beaten
- 1½ tablespoons melted butter or cooking spray for greasing cookie sheets
- 1 cup crystallized (coarse) sugar*

FIRST Preheat the oven to 350 degrees. Sift together the Dry Ingredients.

SECOND Mix the corn oil with the sugar in a mixing bowl, beating until light and fluffy. Stir in the molasses and the egg. Add the dry ingredients in several batches and mix thoroughly. Gather up the dough, wrap in plastic, and chill in the refrigerator for 2 hours, or in the freezer for 30 minutes.

THIRD Roll heaping teaspoons of the dough into balls. Dip one side of each ball into the crystallized sugar and arrange the balls, sugared side up, about 3 inches apart on greased cookie sheets. Bake the cookies in batches in the middle of the oven for 8 to 10 minutes, or until they are puffed and cracked on top. Slide the cookies with a spatula to a cooling rack and let them cool.

*Crystallized sugar is sold at gourmet specialty stores and many supermarkets, or may be mail-ordered from King Arthur Flour (www.bakerscatalogue.com) as "sparkling white sugar." If unavailable, use granulated sugar.

Dr. Jeffrey Blumberg: Tea and Its Therapeutic Effects

Tea has long been hailed as a soothing beverage that nurtures the soul as well as the body. The ancient Chinese credited tea with clearing the mind and vision, quenching thirst, aiding digestion, and cleansing the body of toxins. Over the past twenty-five years, a number of studies have substantiated tea's role as a for-midable source of antioxidants and as having a preventive effect on a number of forms of cancer and heart disease. (Antioxidants prevent or delay oxidative damage in the body's cells and tissues, which contributes to disease.)

Dr. Jeffrey Blumberg, of the Jean Mayer USDA Human Nutrition Research Center on Aging at Tufts University in Boston, has been researching the antioxi-dant effects on older adults for more than a decade and is encouraged by the mounting body of evidence. "More research is needed, but tea, both green and black, appears to provide real health benefits. We've moved into human studies in both healthy and diseased people and research has shifted from East to West, so we're now getting data from studies here in the U.S., the Netherlands, and the United Kingdom, as well as Japan and China."

Scientists know that tea contains flavonoids and catechins, which are both antioxidants with potential health benefits such as being antibacterial, anticarcinogenic, anti-inflammatory, antiviral, and antithrombotic (they prevent blood clots).

Consuming 30 to 32 ounces of tea daily (roughly the equivalent of two and a half cans of soda) may also lower cholesterol levels by 10 percent and decrease the risk of DNA damage caused by smoking. Other research has shown the following:

- Two cups of tea provide as much flavonoid phytochemicals as a serving of fruits or vegetables. (Flavonoids have extensive biological properties that promote health.)

- In addition to having protective effects against several forms of cancer (including oral, stomach, lung, and colorectal), tea may also play a ben-eficial role in preventing dental cavities and osteoporosis.

- Regular tea consumption is associated with a reduction in the risk of heart disease and strokes.

■ Consuming tea may also prime human T cells, which are part of the body's natural immune system, for resisting microbial infections as well as tumors.

The highest concentrations of flavonoids are found in brewed hot tea and lower amounts in iced and ready-to-drink tea. Decaffeinating reduces the catechin content of black tea by 10 to 20 percent. Despite some early controversy, research seems to indicate that the addition of milk to tea does not interfere with catechin absorption.

"The bottom line," says Dr. Blumberg, "is that tea is showing a very promising role in health promotion, disease prevention, and playing an adjunctive role in the actual treatment of disease."

In addition to its physiological benefits, there's nothing quite like the soothing, meditative ritual involved in making and drinking a nice "cuppa" tea.

foods that fight common ailments

For thousands of years, doctors and herbalists have promoted the therapeutic effects of certain foods, and today scientists are corroborating many of these beliefs, but research is still ongoing. A balanced regimen with an emphasis on fruits and vegetables is highly recommended to maintain general good health.

It is believed that a number of common ailments can be prevented by eating certain foods. Similarly, some foods may help to relieve the symptoms of a condition. Consult the following list for specific ailments and note the recipes in the book that relate to these foods.

Note: Herbs, foods, and other natural remedies are not substitutes for professional medical care. For specific health problems, consult a qualified healthcare provider for guidance.

AGING Aging is a natural process, which is affected by genetics, nutritional history, and life experiences. There are a number of FOODS THAT FORTIFY THE BODY AND HELP TO RETARD THE AGING PROCESS. Among them are soy products, oily fish, nuts, whole grains (brown rice, pasta), and fruits high in vitamin C, such as oranges and lemons.

ANEMIA There are several forms of anemia, and a visit to a physician will determine which type you may have, but the most common is iron deficiency. This is usually caused by a lack of iron and CAN BE PREVENTED BY CONSUMING FOODS THAT ARE RICH IN IRON. Red meats are often recommended, as well as apples, apricots, asparagus, bananas, broccoli, leafy greens, and garlic and onions, which aid in the absorption of iron into the body.

ARTHRITIS Millions suffer from arthritis, both osteoarthritis, a degenerative joint disease, and rheumatoid arthritis, an inflammatory, autoimmune disorder. Both create an inflammation of one or more joints, which causes swelling, stiffness, pain, and limited mobility. DIET AND EXERCISE CAN RELIEVE ARTHRITIS AND SOMETIMES REVERSE IT. Eat foods like asparagus, eggs, garlic, whole grains, fresh vegetables, and nonacidic fruits like apples, pineapples, and cherries.

BRONCHITIS Bronchitis is an inflammation or obstruction in the bronchial tubes that causes a buildup of mucus, coughing, fever, and pain. SYMPTOMS CAN BE RELIEVED BY DRINKING FLUIDS such as pure water, herbal teas, and soups, and consuming garlic, onions, root and green vegetables, whole grains, avocados, and oily fish. Avoid mucus-producing foods such as dairy products, as well as processed foods and sugar.

CANCER Malignant tumors or growths in the body due to the multiplication of damaged cells are referred to as cancer. The cause is unknown, but genetics, lifestyle, environmental factors, and poor diet are all contributing factors. A DIET RICH IN FRUITS AND VEGETABLES, which contain precious phytonutrients, CAN HELP TO PREVENT CANCER, especially cruciferous vegetables such as broccoli, cabbage, and cauliflower, as well as soybeans, onions, garlic, leeks, tomatoes, shiitake mushrooms, carrots, citrus fruits, berries, and cantaloupes. Green and black tea contain catechins, which also help to prevent cancer.

CATARACTS A cloudy area in the lens of the eye is known as a cataract. Although cataracts are painless, they cause blurred vision and blindness if left untreated. A DIET RICH IN ANTIOXIDANTS, CAROTENOIDS, AND VITAMIN C can aid in their prevention, in particular cabbage, carrots, apricots, yellow peppers, citrus, berries, and leafy green vegetables.

CHOLESTEROL (HIGH) Cholesterol is naturally present in foods and in the bloodstream. When the balance between the two is upset, fatty deposits build up on artery walls and reduce blood flow around the heart and the brain. MAINTAINING A HEALTHY WEIGHT AND CUTTING DOWN ON FOODS HIGH IN FAT and cholesterol will help restore the balance. Include in your diet the following CHOLESTEROL-LOWERING FOODS: oily fish, oat bran, brown rice, apples, garlic, green vegetables, soybeans, and olive oil.

COLDS The common cold is an infection of the upper respiratory tract. STRENGTHENING THE IMMUNE SYSTEM through diet will protect the body from the 200-plus viruses that can cause a cold. Eating FOODS SUCH AS ORANGES, GRAPE-FRUITS, whole grains, legumes, garlic, oily fish such as mackerel, salmon, and sardines, and protein from chicken and lean meats will protect the respiratory tract. Chinese doctors believe that there are two main types of colds: The "hot wind type" is accompanied by a fever, chills, a sore throat, and a yellowish tongue. YIN FOODS such as peppermint and chrysanthemum tea, chilled tofu, and Chinese (Napa) cabbage are recommended. The "cold wind type" is accompanied by fever, chills without perspiration, runny nose, and a whitish tongue. YANG FOODS such as ginger-and-brown-sugar tea or scallion-ginger tea are recommended. Drink hot tea and then wrap the body in blankets to perspire.

COLD SORES Cold sores are caused by herpes simplex, a virus related to the virus that causes genital herpes. The virus lies dormant in the body (predominantly around the mouth) until triggered by fever, cold, stress, or infections. A STRONG IMMUNE SYSTEM WILL PROTECT THE BODY from the virus and prevent blistering. Eat oranges, grapefruits, apples, grapes, onions, peppers, yogurt, fish, and chicken.

CONSTIPATION Constipation is the condition that results from trying to pass hard, dry stools through the large intestine. Stools can be softened by INCREASING THE AMOUNT OF FIBER: eat prunes, figs, apples, and green leafy vegetables, and drink fresh fruit juices and plenty of liquids. Chinese doctors recommend honey tea, papaya, bananas with toasted black sesame seeds, and Chinese (Napa) cabbage juice.

DIABETES Diabetes is present in the body when glucose builds up in the bloodstream instead of being taken away and used by cells. This causes hyperglycemia, an abnormally high level of glucose in the blood. TYPE 1 DIABETES IS AN AUTOIMMUNE DISEASE in which the body destroys insulin-producing cells in the pancreas. With type 2 diabetes, which is the most common, either the body does not produce enough insulin or the cells ignore the insulin. TYPE 2 CAN BE TRIGGERED BY OBESITY and is becoming prevalent among children. Those who have diabetes should eat regular meals and increase their intake of soluble fiber with plenty of raw fruits and vegetables, legumes, and root vegetables. Recent research has shown that a phytonutrient found in onions, bananas, tomatoes, honey, garlic, and Jerusalem artichokes will benefit the body by increasing glucose tolerance.

FLU Influenza, otherwise known as the flu, is a highly contagious viral infection in the upper respiratory tract accompanied by a high fever, headache, congestion, and bodily aches and pains. Although a loss of appetite occurs, IT IS IMPORTANT TO STRENGTHEN THE BODY. Drink fresh fruit and vegetable juices, clear broths, and chicken and turkey soup. Avoid dairy products. Chinese doctors recommend cooked daikon radish with rice congee or porridge, peppermint–licorice root tea, and soybeans cooked with coriander.

HEARTBURN Heartburn is a burning sensation or pain that occurs when large amounts of stomach acids back up past the stomach valve and into the esophagus. CHANGE YOUR EATING HABITS: Eat smaller, more frequent meals and chew your food well. Eat more raw vegetables. Certain foods, such as lean meats, fish, and poultry, can improve the valve function at the top of the stomach. Whole grain cereals and breads as well as fruits will prevent constipation, which releases pressure on the stomach and in turn eases heartburn.

HYPERTENSION The heart pumps blood through arteries and presses blood against the walls of blood vessels. Hypertension occurs when this pressure is too high. To prevent and treat hypertension, INCREASE YOUR INTAKE OF FRUITS AND VEGETABLES, especially apples, asparagus, celery, broccoli, cabbage, eggplant, garlic, green leafy vegetables, pears, squash, and sweet potatoes. Chinese doctors recommend celery juice with Chinese dates, wood ears, mung beans, fuzzy melon, kelp, and bitter gourd.

IMMUNE SYSTEM Our bodies are made up of a number of defenses that fight bacteria, viruses, and irritants that invade the body. These defenses are known as the immune system. A weakened immune system results in an inability to fight disease or repair the body. A HEALTHY DIET has a profound effect on strengthening a weakened immune system. EAT PLENTY OF FRESH FRUITS AND VEGETABLES, especially broccoli, garlic, sweet potatoes, carrots, citrus fruits, soybeans, and nuts.

INSOMNIA Insomnia is the inability to fall or stay asleep at night. It is often attributed to psychological or emotional problems, such as depression, anxiety, stress, or grief. CAREFUL CHOICE OF FOODS AND THE TIME THEY ARE EATEN is very important when treating insomnia. For the evening meal or before bed, eat foods like bananas, dates, figs, milk, tuna, turkey, and yogurt, which contain tryptophan and thereby promote sleep. Also, bread, pasta, potatoes, and rice are rich in carbohydrates, which soothe the body and prepare it for sleep.

MENOPAUSAL (AND PERIMENOPAUSAL) SYMPTOMS Menopause is the natural stage in a woman's life when she stops ovulating and menstruation ceases. The side effects may include mood swings, headaches, hot flashes, low sex drive, anxiety, and night sweats. Perimenopause is the period when a woman's body is preparing for menopause, which brings on similar side effects. PROPER DIET AND EXERCISE can minimize and sometimes eliminate the side effects. Foods to focus on are oily fish like salmon, tuna, and sardines; flaxseed; soy products, which are rich in phytoestrogens; cruciferous vegetables such as brussels sprouts, broccoli, and cabbage; garlic, ginger, and other pungent seasonings.

MENSTRUAL SYMPTOMS Menstrual symptoms affect many women 7 to 10 days before menstruation. The symptoms vary tremendously, from bloating to acne, anxiety, backache, tender breasts, and mood swings. Because they vary, treating menstrual symptoms is difficult. However, a DIET rich in soybeans, alfalfa, flaxseeds, broccoli, oranges, grapefruits, berries, beets, green vegetables, and sardines CAN HELP EASE DISCOMFORT.

NAUSEA Nausea, the sensation of feeling sick to your stomach, can be caused by motion sickness, pregnancy, overeating or excessive drinking, migraines, or anxiety. CERTAIN FOODS WILL EASE NAUSEA by settling the stomach and strengthening the body, including vegetable broths without spice, rice, porridge, dry toast, ginger, and fennel.

OSTEOPOROSIS Osteoporosis is a disease in which the density of the bones decreases and they are more likely to break. Both men and women may develop osteoporosis, but women are especially vulnerable after menopause as a result of decreased estrogen levels. Although it is a progressive disease, it CAN BE SLOWED DOWN BY A DIET RICH in easily digestible CALCIUM and VITAMIN D. Eat calcium-rich vegetables like kale and broccoli, soybeans and tofu and other legumes, flaxseeds, oily fish, eggs, and yogurt. A weight-lifting program should be part of your exercise routine.

ULCERS (PEPTIC) Ulcers occur when the balance between digestive juices and the protective lining of the gastrointestinal tract is disturbed, leaving an open wound. Stress, which increases stomach acids, is often the cause. Certain FOODS HELP TO HEAL ULCERS AND PROTECT AGAINST FURTHER DAMAGE, including dark leafy vegetables, carrots, chile peppers, oily fish, avocados, and nuts.

for further study

"nutrition and health: state of the science and clinical applications"

Dr. Andrew Weil, a leading pioneer in the field of integrative medicine, has organized an annual conference titled "Nutrition and Health: State of the Science and Clinical Applications" under the auspices of the University of Arizona, College of Medicine, and the Richard and Hinda Rosenthal Center for Complementary and Alternative Medicine at Columbia University. For three days, participants gather for seminars, panel discussions, and demonstrations that provide an overview and practical summary of the latest information in the newly emerging field of nutritional medicine.

Weil believes that physicians are notoriously undereducated in nutrition and are unprepared to advise patients about designing diets for optimal health or using food as a primary role in disease intervention. This conference brings together many of America's leading experts to explore the social, political, and behavioral aspects of diet and health.

While some speakers, such as Dr. David Heber, director of the UCLA Center for Human Nutrition, have presented cutting-edge research on the protective phytonutrients in fruits and vegetables, *New York Times* writer Michael Pollan has explored the question "Organic Food: Is It Any Better?" Leaders from the fields of scientific research in food and medicine, clinicians, chefs, and well-respected authors all engage in current related dialogue. Periodic tastings and meals are provided, allowing an opportunity to sample some of the delicious and healthy ways today's chefs are preparing food. The program is revised annually. For further information, consult www.integrativemedicine.arizona.edu or contact the Program in Integrative Medicine, c/o Office of Continuing Medical Education, P.O. Box 245121, Tucson, Arizona 85724-5121, (520) 626-7832 or (800) 777-7552.

"food as medicine: integrating nutrition into clinical practice and medical education"

Dr. Susan Lord of the Center for Mind-Body Medicine at Georgetown Medical School has organized the most comprehensive training program in clinical nutrition geared toward physicians, medical school faculty, and other health professionals. This intense seven-day program presents a wide-range of information including such key topics as:

- The science supporting nutritional intervention for illness
- The relationship between diet and chronic disease
- How to assess a patient's nutritional status
- How to help deal with the psychological and emotional aspects of helping people change their diets
- How to individualize dietary recommendations
- The latest scientific data on controversial issues in nutrition
- Common questions asked by patients.

Special sessions also are offered in children's nutrition and how educators can integrate nutrition into the curriculum of their respective medical schools and residency programs. Attendees have praised the program, calling it the best training program for clinicians and medical school faculty who want to integrate nutrition into their practices and school curriculums.

The program is offered biannually and revised with each session. For further information consult www.cmbm.org or contact the Center for Mind-Body Medicine, 5225 Connecticut Avenue, Suite 414, Washington, D.C. 20015, (202) 966-7338.

mail-order and web sources

These days, almost all of the Asian and specialty ingredients, plus herbs and spices, used in the recipes are available at supermarkets, but if you don't find them there, you can order from the sources below.

ETHNIC GROCER
695 Lunt Avenue
Elk Grove Village, IL 60007
Tel.: (847) 640-9570
www.EthnicGrocer.com
Web site: wide selection of international (including Asian) condiments and ingredients

FUNGI PERFECTI LLC
P.O. Box 7634
Olympia, WA 98507
Tel.: (800) 780-9126 (toll-free)
Fax: (360) 426-9377
www.fungi.com
Web site and catalogue: extensive selection of medicinal and gourmet mushrooms, starter kits, books, and mushroom gifts

IN PURSUIT OF TEA
224 Roebling Street
Brooklyn, NY 11211
Tel.: (866) 878-3832 (toll-free)
Fax: (718) 388-3988
www.inpursuitoftea.com

Web site: unusual selection of very fine teas with pertinent health, history, and usage information

INDIAN HARVEST SPECIALTIFOODS, INC.
P.O. Box 428
Bemidji, MN 56619
Tel.: (800) 294-2433 (toll-free)
Fax: (800) 752-8588 (toll-free)
www.indianharvest.com
Web site and catalogue: specialty rice, grains, and beans

KALUSTYAN'S
123 Lexington Avenue
New York, NY 10016
Tel.: (212) 685-3451
Fax: (212) 683-8458
www.kalustyans.com
Web site: extensive rice, legume, spice, and condiment selection

KING ARTHUR FLOUR / THE BAKER'S CATALOGUE
P.O. Box 876
Norwich, VT 05055
Tel.: (800) 827-6836 (toll-free)
Fax: (800) 343-3002 (toll-free)
www.bakerscatalogue.com
Web site and catalogue: ever-widening

selection of baking ingredients, including different flours, sugars, flavorings, etc., as well as whole grains, bakeware, books, and appliances

LOTUS FOODS, INC.
921 Richmond Street
El Cerrito, CA 94530
Tel.: (510) 525-3137
Fax: (510) 525-4226
www.WorldPantry.com
Web site and catalogue: exotic and specialty grains, including rice

PENZEYS SPICES
P.O. Box 924
Brookfield, WI 53008
Tel.: (800) 741-7787 (toll-free)
Fax: (262) 785-7678
www.penzeys.com
Web site and catalogue: extensive selection of whole and ground spices and herbs

THE SPICE HOUSE
1941 Central Street
Evanston, IL 60201
Tel.: (847) 328-3711
Fax: (847) 328-3631
www.thespicehouse.com
Web site and catalogue: Large inventory of spices, spice mills, and various other accessories.

UWAJIMAYA
600 5th Avenue South
Seattle, WA 98104
Tel.: (206) 624-6248
www.uwajimaya.com
Web site and catalogue: wide selection of Asian condiments and ingredients

VANNS SPICES LTD.
6105 Oakleaf Avenue
Baltimore, MD 21215
Tel.: (800) 583-1693 (toll-free)
Fax: (800) 358-1617 (toll-free)
www.vannsspices.com
Web site: extensive selection of whole and ground herbs, spices and spice mixtures, assorted grains, and flavorings

ZINGERMAN'S
422 Detroit Street
Ann Arbor, MI 48104
Tel.: (888) 636-8162 (toll-free)
Fax: (734) 477-6988
www.zingermans.com
Web site and catalogue: extensive selection of oils, vinegars, and gourmet products

bibliography

Balch, Phyllis A., and James F. Balch, M.D. *Prescription for Nutritional Healing: A Practical A-to-Z Reference to Drug-Free Remedies Using Vitamins, Minerals, Herbs and Food Supplements.* 3rd ed. New York: Avery, 2000.

Bharadwaj, Monisha. *The Indian Kitchen: A Book of Essential Ingredients with Over 200 Easy and Authentic Recipes.* London: Kyle Cathie, 1999.

Braimbridge, Sophie. *Simply Italian.* Sydney: Murdoch Books, 2002.

Chevallier, Andrew. *The Encyclopedia of Medicinal Plants.* London: Dorling Kindersley, 1996.

Colton, Katharine. *The Sensible Sourcebook! Smart Guide to Healing Foods.* New York: Cader, 1999.

Duke, James A. *The Green Pharmacy: New Discoveries in Herbal Remedies for Common Diseases and Conditions from the World's Foremost Authority on Healing Herbs.* Emmaus, PA: Rodale, 1997.

———. *Dr. Duke's Essential Herbs: 13 Vital Herbs You Need to Disease-Proof Your Body, Boost Your Energy, Lengthen Your Life.* Emmaus, PA: Rodale, 1999.

———. *The Green Pharmacy Anti-Aging Prescriptions: Herbs, Foods, and Natural Formulas to Keep You Young.* With Michael Castleman. Emmaus, PA: Rodale, 2001.

———. *The Green Pharmacy Herbal Handbook: Your Comprehensive Reference to the Best Herbs for Healing.* Emmaus, PA: Rodale, 2000.

Frawley, Dr. David. *Ayurvedic Healing: A Comprehensive Guide.* 2nd rev. ed. Twin Lakes, WI: Lotus Press, 2001.

Gillie, Oliver. *Food for Life: Preventing Cancer Through Healthy Diet.* London: Hodder and Stoughton, 1998.

Godagama, Dr. Shantha. *The Handbook of Ayurveda.* Berkeley, CA: North Atlantic Books, 2004.

Gray, Rose, and Ruth Rogers. *River Cafe Cook Book Easy.* London: Ebury Press, 2003.

Hartvig, Kirsten. *Eat for Immunity: The Practical Guide to Strengthening the Body's Defence Systems.* London: Duncan Baird, 2002.

Hay, Donna. *Flavors.* New York: Morrow, 2003.

———. *New Food Fast.* New York: Morrow, 2003.

Heber, David, and Susan Bowerman. *What Color Is Your Diet?* New York: Regan Books, 2002.

Jingfeng, Cai. *Nature's Way to Healthy Eating: Dietotherapy in Traditional Chinese Medicine.* Singapore: Asiapac Publications, 1991.

Johari, Harish. *Ayurvedic Healing Cuisine: 200 Vegetarian Recipes for Health,*

Balance, and Longevity. Rochester, VT: Healing Arts Press, 2000.

———. *The Healing Cuisine: India's Art of Ayurvedic Cooking.* Rochester, VT: Healing Arts Press, 1994.

Joseph, James A., Ph.D., Daniel A. Nadeau, M.D., and Anne Underwood. *The Color Code: A Revolutionary Eating Plan for Optimum Health.* New York: Hyperion, 2002.

Kaimal, Maya. *Savoring the Spice Coast of India: Fresh Flavors from Kerala.* New York: HarperCollins, 2000.

Kalra, J. Inder Singh, and Pradeep Das Gupta. *Prashad: Cooking with Indian Masters.* Albert House Press, 2001.

Lad, Usha, and Dr. Vasant Lad. *Ayurvedic Cooking for Self-Healing.* 2nd ed. Albuquerque, NM: Ayurvedic Press, 1997.

Leung, Albert Y. *Chinese Healing Foods and Herbs.* Glen Rock, NJ: AYSL Corporation, 1984.

Mabey, Richard, ed. *The Complete New Herbal.* With Michael McIntyre, Pamela Michael, Gail Duff, and John Stevens. London: Penguin Books, 1991.

McCaleb, Robert S., Evelyn Leigh, and Krista Morien. *The Encyclopedia of Popular Herbs: Your Complete Guide to the Leading Medicinal Plants.* Roseville, CA: Prima Lifestyles, 2000.

Morningstar, Amadea. *The Ayurvedic Cookbook.* With Urmila Desai. Twin Lakes, WI: Lotus Press, 1990.

Mozian, Laurie Deutsch. *Foods That Fight Disease: A Simple Guide to Using and Understanding Phytonutrients to Protect and Enhance Your Health.* New York: Avery, 2000.

Muying, Zhao. *Chinese Diet Therapy.* Beijing: China Esperanto Press, 1996.

Ni, Maoshing. *The Tao of Nutrition.* 2nd ed. With Cathy McNease. Santa Monica, CA: SevenStar Communications, 1993.

Norman, Jill. *Herbs and Spices: The Cook's Reference.* London: Dorling Kindersley, 2002.

Ody, Penelope. *The Complete Medicinal Herbal.* London: Dorling Kindersley, 1993.

Patnaik, Naveen. *The Garden of Life: An Introduction to the Healing Plants of India.* New York: Doubleday, 1993.

Pitchford, Paul. *Healing with Whole Foods: Asian Traditions and Modern Nutrition.* 3rd ed. Berkeley, CA: North Atlantic Books, 2002.

Polunin, Miriam. *The Knopf Canada Book of Healing Foods.* Toronto: Knopf Canada, 1997.

Sahni, Julie. *Classic Indian Cooking.* New York: Morrow, 1980.

Sairam, T. V. *Home Remedies: Handbook of Herbal Cures for Common Ailments.* Vols. 1 and 3. New Delhi: Penguin Books, 1998, 2000.

Simonds, Nina. *Asian Wraps: Deliciously Easy Hand-Held Bundles to Stuff, Wrap, and Relish.* New York: Morrow Cookbooks, 2000.

———. *A Spoonful of Ginger: Irresistible, Health-Giving Recipes from Asian Kitchens.* New York: Knopf, 1999.

Sreedharan, Das. *The New Tastes of India: Over 100 Vibrant Vegetarian Recipes from Southern India.* London: Headline Book Publishing, 2001.

Svoboda, Robert E. *Ayurveda: Life, Health and Longevity.* Albuquerque, NM: Ayurvedic Press, 2004.

Ursell, Amanda. *The Complete Guide to Healing Foods: Nutritional Healing for Body and Mind.* London: Dorling Kindersley, 2000.

Vaughan, J. G., and P. A. Judd. *The Oxford Book of Health Foods.* Oxford: Oxford University Press, 2003.

Verma, Dr. Vinod. *Eating Right the Natural Way: Ayurvedic Recipes for a Healthy Life.* New Delhi: Penguin Books, 2001.

Watson, Ronald R., ed. *Vegetables, Fruits, and Herbs in Health Promotion.* Boca Raton, FL: CRC Press, 2000.

Weil, Andrew, M.D. *Eating Well for Optimum Health: The Essential Guide to Food, Diet, and Nutrition.* New York: Knopf, 2000.

Weil, Andrew, M.D., and Rosie Daley. *The Healthy Kitchen: Recipes for a Better Body, Life, and Spirit.* New York: Knopf, 2002.

Werle, Loukie, and Jill Cox. *Ingredients.* Cologne: JB Fairfax Press, 1998.

Wickramasinghe, Priya, and Carol Selva Rajah. *The Food of India.* Vancouver, B.C.: Whitecap Books, 2002.

Wildman, Robert E. C., ed. *Handbook of Nutraceuticals and Functional Foods.* Boca Raton, FL: CRC Press, 2001.

Wildwood, Chrissie. *The Encyclopedia of Healing Plants: A Complete Guide to Aromatherapy, Flower Essences and Herbal Remedies.* London: Judy Piatkus Publishers, 1998.

Willett, Walter C., M.D. *Eat, Drink, and Be Healthy: The Harvard Medical School Guide to Healthy Eating.* New York: Simon & Schuster, 2001.

index

a note about the author

At the age of nineteen Nina Simonds traveled to Taiwan, where she studied for three and a half years under the direction of Chinese master chefs and became fluent in Mandarin Chinese. Simonds also apprenticed and studied for a year at La Varenne, École de Cuisine, in Paris, and received a Grande Diplome in classic French cuisine. For the past thirty years, she has taught classes in cooking schools across the United States and Europe and traveled annually throughout Southeast Asia. She and her family lived recently for two years in London.

Simonds is a member of the Nutrition Roundtable at Harvard University's School of Public Health. She hosted a food/health/lifestyle special, *A Spoonful of Ginger: Food as Medicine,* for Public Television, which received a James Beard Award.

Simonds is an Asian correspondent for *Gourmet* magazine and a regular contributor to the *Sunday New York Times* travel section. Her articles have appeared in the *Los Angeles Times,* the *Washington Post, Health,* and *Cooking Light,* among others. Her books have received numerous awards; *A Spoonful of Ginger* won both an IACP Cookbook Award and the James Beard Foundation Book Award for health. Her children's book *Moonbeams, Dumplings & Dragon Boats: A Treasury of Chinese Holiday Tales, Activities & Recipes* was given a Parents' Choice Award and a Chapman Award for Best Classroom Read-Aloud. She lives in Salem, Massachusetts.

a note on the type

This book was set in Thesis, a typeface created by the Dutch designer Lucas de Groot (born 1963) and released in 1994 by the FontFabrik foundry in Berlin. Originally known as Parenthesis, the Thesis family of fonts is unusual because it includes a serif font, a sans serif font, and a "mixed" font, which all strive to harmonize the traditionally disparate styles. Thesis attempts to provide a complete solution to text and display type design, in spite of its idiosyncratic character mapping.

Composition and color separations by North Market Street Graphics, Lancaster, Pennsylvania
Printing and binding by Tien Wah Press, Singapore

Designed by mgmt., Brooklyn, New York